EAGLES IN THE SKY

AN AIRMANS PRAYER

My God, this night I have to fly,
And ere I leave the ground,
I come with reverence to Thy throne,
Where perfect peace is found.

I thank thee for the life I've had,
for home and all its love,
I thank thee for the faith I have,
That cometh from above.

Come with me now into the air,
Be with me as I fly,
Guide thee each move that I make,
Way up there - in the sky.

Be with me at the target lord,
When danger's at its height,
Be with me as I drop my load,
And on the homeward flight.

And should it be my time to die,
Be with me to the end,
Help me to die a Christians death,
On thee God, I depend.

Then as I leave this mortal frame,
From human ties set free,
Receive my soul, O God of love,
I humbly come to THEE

Lieutenant E B H Impey
XI Squadron, SAAF
5,9,1918 - 16/17,8,1944

EAGLES
IN THE SKY

THE RAF AT 75 – A CELEBRATION

EDITED BY
**Alan
Carlaw**

ILLUSTRATED BY
**Dugald
Cameron**

FOREWORD BY
AIR CHIEF MARSHAL **SIR MICHAEL GRAYDON,**
CHIEF OF THE AIR STAFF

MAINSTREAM
PUBLISHING

EDINBURGH AND LONDON

This book is dedicated to the
men and women of the Royal Air Force:
past, present and future

First published in Great Britain in 1993 by
MAINSTREAM PUBLISHING COMPANY (EDINBURGH) LTD
7 Albany Street
Edinburgh EH1 3UG

ISBN 1 85158 518 4

A catalogue record for this book is available from the British Library

Design by James Hutcheson

Typeset by The Midlands Book Typesetting Company, Loughborough
Originated and printed in Hong Kong, produced by Mandarin Offset

This book was compiled during a period of great change
in the Royal Air Force and its contents reflect the
anticipated formation on 1 April 1993.

CONTENTS

Acknowledgements	6
Contributors	7
Foreword *Chief of the Air Staff, Air Chief Marshal Sir Michael Graydon KCB CBE RAF*	9
Royal Air Force Command and Group Badges	10
Introduction *Alan Carlaw*	11
The Origins of the Royal Air Force *Philip Jarrett*	15
The Dawn of the Royal Air Force *Philip Jarrett*	19
Between the Wars *Philip Jarrett*	25
The Early War Years and the Battle of Britain *Air Vice-Marshal Sandy Johnstone CB DFC AE DL RAF (Retd)*	35
Operation Chastise – The Dams Raid *Dr John Sweetman*	43
The Flying Units of the Royal Air Force in 1993	49
The Far East Air Force in the 1960s *Squadron Leader David Binnie AFC RAF (Retd)*	113
Operation Corporate – The Falklands Campaign *Air Vice-Marshal Peter Squire DFC AFC RAF*	123
Enter Pavespike – Buccaneering in the Gulf *Squadron Leader Norman Browne DFC RAF*	135
The Gulf Conflict – Some Personal Reflections *Air Vice-Marshal Ian Macfadyen CB OBE FRAeS RAF*	139
Humanitarian Aspects of the Service 1. Help from the Hercules *Squadron Leader George C. Martin RAF*	145
2. RAF Search and Rescue *Flight Lieutenant Chris Haward RAF*	149
Selected Bibliography	155
Order of Battle 1993	156

ACKNOWLEDGEMENTS

We would like to thank all the authors for their contributions and photographs. We would also like to acknowledge the following for their help in the preparation of this book: Air Vice-Marshal A.J.C. Bagnall OBE RAF, Squadron Leader David A. Hunter RAF, Flight Lieutenant Ian M. Pride MBE RAF, Ian G. Stott, Richard L. Ward, Roger Lindsay, Jimmy Hamilton, G. Stuart Leslie, John D.R. Rawlings, James Scott, Ian G. McIntosh, the Ministry of Defence, the Department of Public Relations (RAF), Graham Day of the Air Historical Branch, the Squadrons and other Flying Units of the RAF, the Community Relations Officers of the RAF and the Air Cadet Central Gliding School.

Squadron Prints enjoy a particularly close relationship with the Royal Air Force and are greatly indebted to the facilities afforded in the preparation of the artwork and for the many friendships formed over the years.

Alan B. Carlaw,
Dugald Cameron,
Glasgow, October 1992

CONTRIBUTORS

Philip Jarrett

After a short period with Beaumont Aviation Literature, Philip Jarrett became a library assistant at the Royal Aeronautical Society in 1965, and began writing short articles on aviation history in 1967. In 1971 he became Assistant Editor on the Society's newspaper, *Aerospace*, and in 1973 he accepted the post of Assistant Editor on the newly launched magazine *Aeroplane Monthly*. After seven years in that position he moved within the company to take up the post of Chief Sub-Editor of *Flight International*, later becoming Production Editor. In November 1989 he left *Flight* to work as a freelance writer, editor, sub-editor, reviewer and consultant, specialising in aviation history. Apart from a short period with Patrick Stephens Ltd, he has continued freelancing. Philip has written widely on British aviation, and his book *Another Icarus*, on the life and work of the pioneer Percy Sinclair Pilcher, was published by the Smithsonian Institution in 1987.

Air Vice-Marshal Sandy Johnstone
CB DFC AE DL RAF (Retd)

Sandy Johnstone joined the Auxiliary Air Force in 1934. With No. 602 (City of Glasgow) Squadron he saw action in the first raid of WWII (over the Firth of Forth) and later accounted for the first enemy aircraft brought down by a Spitfire at night. He commanded No. 602 Squadron throughout the Battle of Britain and was credited with eight aircraft destroyed and four probably destroyed for which he was awarded the DFC. Later in the War he commanded the Spitfire wing during the Siege of Malta and was involved in the D-Day operations. He was the air attache to Dublin between 1946 and 1948 and the Station Commander at Ballykelly (Coastal Command) in 1951. Between 1952 and 1953 he was the Officer Commanding, Air Sea Warfare Development unit at St Mawgan and from 1953 to 1955, the Senior Air Staff Officer with No. 12 Group Fighter Command. In 1956 he was seconded to the Malayan Government to form the Royal Malayan Air Force. He returned to this country, serving as Officer Commanding at Middleton-St-George and Director of Personnel at the Air Ministry, but in 1964 he was once again in the Far East as Air Commander Commonwealth Air Forces during the period of confrontation between Malaysia and Indonesia. Following a period as Air Officer Scotland and Northern Ireland and Air Commander North Atlantic (NATO), he retired from the RAF as Air Vice-Marshal in September 1968.

Dr John Sweetman

Dr John Sweetman was educated at Brasenose College, Oxford, where he read History, and King's College, London, where he gained a Ph.D. He subsequently joined the War Studies Department at the Royal Military Academy, Sandhurst, where he is currently Head of Defence and International Affairs. In addition to numerous articles on military subjects in British and American journals, his publications include: *Schweinfurt – Disaster in the Skies*, *Ploesti – Oil Strike* and *The Dambusters Raid*.

Squadron Leader David Binnie
AFC RAF (Retd)

David Binnie joined the RAF in 1964. In 1966 his first tour took him to Singapore where he flew Javelin MK9s on No. 60 Squadron. When the Squadron disbanded in 1968 he was posted to Central Flying School where he qualified as a flying instructor. He joined RAF Valley to instruct on the Gnat T1 and became a member of the Standards Squadron. He was the Station low-level Aerobatic Pilot for two years. In 1971 he was selected for the Red Arrows and was a member of the Synchronised Pair for three years, the last two as leader. He was awarded the AFC in 1975. He then converted to the Harrier and was posted to RAF Germany, first with No. 3 (F) Squadron and later with No. 4 (AC) Squadron as Flight Commander. In 1983 he graduated from Staff College at RAF Bracknell before a posting to MOD (Operations Requirements) in the Harrier office. In 1987 he joined the world of civil aviation flying Boeing 737s with Britannia Airways and, since 1991, flying Boeing 747s worldwide with Virgin Atlantic Airways.

Air Vice-Marshal Peter Squire
DFC AFC RAF

Peter Squire was commissioned into the RAF in 1966 and posted to No. 20 Squadron in Singapore in March 1968. There he flew Hunters and the Single Engine Pioneer as an airborne Forward Air Controller. Following a tour as a flying instructor at RAF Valley he was promoted to Squadron Leader in 1973. In 1975 he converted to the Harrier and took up an appointment as Flight Commander on No. 3 (F) Squadron in Germany. Returning to the UK in 1978, he was posted to Headquarters Strike Command as a member of the UK Air Forces Taceval Team. He attended the Royal Naval Staff College in 1980 and in March 1981 took command of No. 1 (F) Squadron, again flying Harriers. A second tour at High Wycombe followed in 1983, firstly as leader of the newly-formed Command Briefing and Presentation Team and then as PSO to the Air Officer Commanding-in-Chief. Promoted to Group Captain in 1985, he was posted to command the Tri-National Tornado Training Establishment at RAF Cottesmore.

On completion of this tour he moved to the MOD to serve within Air Plans. In 1989 he transferred to the Air Staff as Director Air Offensive and in 1991 he returned to High Wycombe where, at the time of writing, he is Senior Air Staff Officer Headquarters Strike Command and Deputy Chief of Staff Operations United Kingdom Air Forces.

Squadron Leader Norman Browne
DFC RAF

Norman Browne joined the Royal Air Force in March 1967 and first saw squadron service on Sea Vixens with No. 893 Naval Air Squadron on HMS *Hermes* from July 1969, later serving on No. 899 NAS on HMS *Eagle*. He transferred to Yeovilton in 1971 for conversion to Phantoms with No. 767 NAS, and then to No. 43 Squadron at Leuchars in September 1971. In September 1976 he moved to No. 19 Squadron at Wildenrath and was the navigator in the Alcock and Brown anniversary flight in 1979. He converted to Buccaneers with No. 237 OCU at Lossiemouth in September 1979 and joined No. 16 Squadron at Laarbruch in February 1980. Having returned to the staff of No. 237 OCU in November 1984, he joined No. 208 Squadron at Lossiemouth in October 1986, after which he returned once more to No. 237 OCU in February 1989. After promotion to Squadron Leader he joined No. 12 Squadron at Lossiemouth as Officer Commanding 'A' flight. While at Leuchars he flew in the Phantom aerobatic display aircraft for three years. He served in the joint Phantom Force in the Cyprus war in 1974 and flew in Operation Pulsator in Beirut in 1983. In 1991 he was involved in Operation Desert Storm and was awarded the DFC for his contribution to the success of the Buccaneer operations. In 1976 he was awarded the Air Officer Commanding-in-Chief's Commendation and twice received the Queen's Commendation for Valuable Service in the Air (1979 and 1983).

Air Vice-Marshal Ian Macfadyen
CB OBE FRAeS RAF

Ian Macfadyen joined the RAF in 1960. He was commissioned as a pilot in 1963 and flew Lightnings and Phantoms in the UK and Germany. As a Flight Lieutenant he was ADC to the Air Officer Commanding-in-Chief Strike Command between 1968 and 1970. He also spent a tour at Cranwell as a flying instructor where for two years he was a member of the Poachers aerobatic team. After attending the 1973 course at the RAF Staff College he joined No. 111 Squadron. While serving as a Flight Commander on No. 43 Squadron in 1976 he was the Phantom solo aerobatic pilot. Between 1980 and 1983 he commanded No. 29 Squadron, a tour on which he saw service in the Falkland Islands both during and after the conflict. His staff appointments have included the Personal Staff Officer to the Commander of the Second Allied Tactical Air Force and Commander-in-Chief RAF Germany, and Deputy Director in the Ministry of Defence on Operational Requirements. He commanded RAF Leuchars from 1985 to 1987 and attended the 1988 RCDS course. In late 1988 he took up a post in the Central Staffs Concept Division at the MOD until, in November 1990, he was appointed Chief of Staff at HQ British Forces in Riyadh. After the Gulf War he succeeded Sir Peter de la Billière as Commander of British Forces in the Middle East. He took up his present post as Assistant Chief of the Defence Staff Operational Requirements for Air Systems in September 1991.

Squadron Leader George C. Martin RAF

George Martin joined the RAF as an apprentice in 1978 and was commissioned in 1982. After 18 months of professional engineering training at RAF Cranwell, he served as a Junior Engineering Officer at RAF Shawbury between 1984 and 1985, working on Gazelle helicopters. A further period of training was followed by two years as a specialist weapons officer at RAF Leuchars in support of the F4 Phantoms of Nos. 43 and 111 Squadrons. In October 1987 he went to Hong Kong as the Officer Commanding Wessex Servicing Flight at RAF Sek Kong. On his return to this country in March 1990 he served as weapons trials officer at Boscombe Down specialising in aircraft flare and gun systems and bomb fusing. At present he is the Officer Commanding Aircraft Engineering Squadron at RAF Lyneham, responsible for second-line servicing of a fleet of 61 Hercules aircraft. He was the Deputy Project Officer for the 25th Anniversary celebrations of the Hercules in RAF service.

Flight Lieutenant Chris Haward RAF

Flight Lieutenant Chris Haward joined the Royal Air Force in 1964 and qualified as a helicopter pilot in 1966. After a short tour with No. 72 Squadron flying Wessex 2s, he served in an exchange post with No. 848 Naval Air Squadron flying Wessex 5s from HMS *Albion*. On returning to RAF service, he became a qualified helicopter instructor and after a spell teaching *ab initio* pilots on the Sioux at RAF Tern Hill, he became the Training Officer on 28 (AC) Squadron which operated the Wessex 2 from RAF Kai Tak in Hong Kong. Since then Flight Lieutenant Haward has flown a variety of helicopters in the flight trials role for the Radar Research Squadron at RAE Bedford. A tour with RAF Handling Squadron at Boscombe Down involved three years behind a desk with responsibility for a number of helicopter 'Pilots Notes' before returning to the RAE. Types of aircraft flown on this tour included Wessex (Mk 1, 2 and 5), Puma, Gazelle and Sea King (Mk 1, 2 and 4). In 1986 he started his present job as a Unit Test Pilot with Search and Rescue Wing at RAF St Mawgan where the task is the flight testing of SAR Sea King Mk 3s and Wessex Mk 2s after second-line servicing with the SAR Engineering Squadron.

FOREWORD

It is entirely appropriate that this book, a celebration in prints compiled from the paintings of Dugald Cameron, should be published to mark the 75th Anniversary of the Royal Air Force. Squadron Prints have become essential items of squadron memorabilia, found upon the walls of crew rooms and messes worldwide, as well as in the homes of countless past and present members of the Service.

I first met Alan Carlaw, the other half of this remarkable team, in the 1970s when I was commanding a squadron whose fund was not in the healthiest condition! He made me an offer I couldn't refuse. I am delighted, therefore, to commend this book to you, not just as a roll-call of Royal Air Force squadrons operational at the time of our 75th Anniversary, but as a record of those squadrons' formation, achievements and disbandments, as the Royal Air Force has evolved and adapted over three-quarters of a century. Moreover, the contributions from a wide cross-section of people give even more life to the superb illustrations within these pages. They record, in a very personal way, the milestones, the successes and the difficulties encountered from the earliest days of aviation. But, most importantly, they highlight the courage and professionalism of those who have served in the Royal Air Force. The exploits of the squadrons recorded here are, of course, a mirror for the exploits of squadrons now disbanded, and I am sure that many who read this book will cast their mind back to famous squadrons whose standards now reside in St Clement Danes or the Royal Air Force College Cranwell. Above all, this book is a tribute to the men, women and the aircraft who have made the Royal Air Force what it is today.

I extend my appreciation to Dugald Cameron and to Alan Carlaw for all their support both to our Service and to the RAF Benevolent Fund which will benefit from the sale of every copy.

Air Chief Marshal Sir Michael Graydon, Chief of the Air Staff,
November 1992

ROYAL AIR FORCE
COMMAND AND GROUP BADGES

Introduction

ALAN CARLAW

Since its formation on 1 April 1918 the Royal Air Force has seen many changes. It has adapted to meet the needs of the times, growing and contracting as required. From its earliest days it has been involved in the pioneering aspects of aviation and this was most vividly seen by the world during the Gulf War in 1991 when many new weapons, systems and equipment were deployed. It is also a caring force participating in humanitarian operations worldwide. The Royal Air Force of today is smaller but certainly more mobile than in the past and its composition has had to change to reflect these alterations.

Control of the Royal Air Force stems from the Ministry of Defence (Air), through the Air Force Board to Strike and Support Commands. The front-line squadrons, flying units, and training schools are indeed the essence of the Force and it is these that we aim to highlight within these pages. This is not to diminish in any way the work and roles of all the other equally important parts of the Service without whom the flying side could not function. In this we include the Royal Air Force Regiment, the Royal Auxiliary Air Force, the RAF Volunteer Reserve and the Air Cadets organisation. The RAF Regiment operates the Rapier Airfield Defence squadrons, together with light-armoured and field squadrons for ground defence. It also administers the Defence Fire Service. Although the flying squadrons of the Royal Auxiliary Air Force were disbanded in 1957 the force today supports three Maritime Headquarters units, an Air Movements squadron and an Aeromedical Evacuation squadron plus eight RAuxAF Regiment squadrons. The RAF Volunteer Reserve embraces all the people involved in the Air Training Corps squadrons but also staffs four flights in the intelligence, photographic interpretation, interrogation and public relations fields.

Strike Command, with Headquarters at High Wycombe, was formed on 30 April 1968 by the merging of Fighter and Bomber Commands. It later absorbed Coastal and Air Support Commands and now controls the United Kingdom's front-line aircraft worldwide. Its assets include fighters, strike/attack, transport, refuelling and maritime aircraft and helicopters. It is an essential part of the NATO organisation and although most of the Command's resources are committed to Allied Command Europe a proportion, notably maritime forces, are committed to the Supreme Allied Commander Atlantic (SACLANT). Strike Command is divided into five Groups. No. 1 Group, with Headquarters at Upavon, is responsible for strike/attack operations and support of the Army in the field. It controls Harrier, Jaguar and Tornado aircraft together with Puma, Chinook and Wessex helicopters.

No. 2 Group, with Headquarters at Rhinedahlen, is responsible for the operations in Germany and controls Harrier and Tornado aircraft and Puma and Chinook helicopters. No. 11 Group, with Headquarters at Bentley Priory, is responsible for air defence and controls Tornado F3 and Sentry AEW aircraft. No. 18 Group, with Headquarters co-located with the Royal Navy at the Fleet Headquarters at Northwood, is responsible for maritime search and rescue and ancillary operations and controls Buccaneer, Nimrod, Canberra and Hawk aircraft and Wessex and Sea King helicopters. No. 38 Group, with Headquarters at High Wycombe, is responsible for transport and refuelling operations and controls VC10, Tristar, Victor, Hercules, Andover, BAe 125 and BAe 146 aircraft and Gazelle and Wessex helicopters. Strike Command is also responsible for overseas operations in Cyprus (Wessex helicopters), Hong Kong (Wessex helicopters), Belize (Harriers and Puma helicopters) and the Falkland Islands (Tornado F3 and Hercules C1K aircraft and Chinook and Sea King helicopters). Additionally it covers the Tornado F3 Operational Evaluation Unit, the Strike/Attack Operational Evaluation Unit and the Institute of Aviation Medicine.

Royal Air Force Support Command, with Headquarters at Brampton, was formed in June 1977 by the merging of Training and Air Support Commands. It is responsible for all training in flying and ground branches and trades, communications, storage and supply, medical services and many administrative services. It controls Chipmunk, Bulldog, Tucano, Jet Provost, Hawk, Dominie and Jetstream aircraft and Gazelle and Wessex helicopters. It is also responsible for the Red Arrows. The Air Training Corps (ATC) exists to encourage an interest in aviation and the RAF for young people from the age of 13. The Air Officer Commanding Air Cadets is also Commandant of the ATC and Director of Reserve Forces and is responsible for some 36,000 young people in 928 squadrons formed into 40 wings throughout the UK; a further 9,000 cadets are to be found in schools within the RAF sections of the Combined Cadet Force. All cadets have the opportunity to gain gliding experience at one of the 28 Volunteer Gliding Schools and fly from one of the 13 Air Experience Flights in the UK.

The RAF Regiment was established on 1 February 1942 as a Corps within the Royal Air Force. It exists to provide ground and short range air defence for RAF installations and to train all RAF combatant personnel so that they can contribute to the defence of their unit. It maintains Short Range Air Defence squadrons equipped with the Rapier system, together with field squadrons for airfield ground defence. There are Rapier detachments in Belize and the Falkland Islands and there is also a field squadron assigned to internal security duties within the United Kingdom. In addition, there are six Royal Auxiliary Air Force Regiment field squadrons. The RAF Regiment also mans the Queen's Colour squadron which undertakes ceremonial duties for the Royal Air Force in peacetime and has a war role as a field squadron.

The Women's Royal Air Force shares the same date of birth as the RAF – 1 April 1918 – but it disbanded in 1920 and did not reform until 1939 when 48 RAF companies of the ATC transferred to form the Women's Auxiliary Air Force (WAAF). During the war the Service expanded to cover 22 officer branches in 75 trades. It was decided to retain women in the RAF on a permanent basis after the war so on 1 February 1949 the WRAF was reformed. A number of advances have been made in conditions of service and areas of employment. Women officers are now recruited into all branches except the RAF Regiment and may fly all types of aircraft including fast jets. The WRAF is an integral part of the RAF; however, the title is retained to differentiate between male and female personnel.

The Royal Air Force Nursing Service was formed on 1 June 1918 and was granted its present title in June 1923 when HM King George V gave the Royal Assent for the Service to be known as Princess Mary's Royal Air Force Nursing Service (PMRAFNS). Her Royal Highness Princess Mary, later the Princess Royal, became its first Air Chief Commandant. During the war the Service was enlarged to provide nursing sisters in hospitals abroad, on troop ships and on casualty evacuation flights. Today the PMRAFNS is fully integrated in the Royal Air Force and members of PMRAFNS serve at RAF Hospitals and Medical Centres at home and overseas. The PMRAFNS also deploys specialist Aeromedical Evacuation and Mobile Renal Dialysis teams to aid both Service and civilian personnel around the world.

This, then, is the present structure of the RAF and its constituent elements. Squadron Prints has been privileged to have been associated with the Service and has formed a close relationship with it extending over 15 years. It has the greatest pleasure in producing this book through which it salutes the RAF's past, celebrates its present and looks forward with confidence to its future.

In the Beginning – Montrose, Upper Dysart Farm, February 1913 with BE 2 No. 218 in the foreground and No. 205 in the temporary canvas shed. Overflying is Maurice Farman S 7 No. 266 allocated to the all Farman 'C' Flight of 2 Squadron for training NCO pilots. It crashed on 5 May 1913 near Aberdeen – neither pilot nor observer being injured. The Indian Army Sheds, modified for aircraft use, were erected during 1913 at Broomfield and are still in existence. (For a more detailed account of early aviation at Montrose see page 160)

The Origins of the
Royal Air Force
PHILIP JARRETT

B ritish military aeronautics had its origins in the age of the balloon. The potential of that device as a means of reconnaissance was realised in 1794, at the Battle of Fleurus, when the French republican army used a captive observation balloon to gain a decisive tactical advantage. However, it was not until 1878 that the military authorities in Britain began to experiment with them at Woolwich Arsenal and a Balloon Equipment Store was established. Within a year the Army had a fleet of five 'thoroughly sound and reliable' balloons under the management of a few trained officers and men from the Royal Engineers.

In 1880 and 1882 balloon sections took part successfully in the Army manoeuvres at Aldershot, and in 1893 the Balloon Equipment Store was moved to the School of Military Engineering at Chatham. A small balloon factory, depot and school of instruction was set up and, under the guidance of Major Templer, several balloons of three basic sizes were made during the following year. An expedition to Bechuanaland in the autumn of 1884 took with it a detachment of three balloons and a staff of 15 NCOs and men under Major Elsdale and Captain F.C. Trollope. The following year another small detachment of nine men under Major Templer used balloons on active service with the Sudan Expeditionary Force.

Although it had been shown that aeronautics had practical military applications, it was subsequently left to Majors Elsdale and Templer to make the best of such resources as were available, and it was only by virtue of their efforts and the successful operation of a balloon detachment during the 1889 manoeuvres that, in May 1890, a Balloon Section was established as a unit of the Royal Engineers. The factory and school moved to South Farnborough, while the depot remained at Chatham. Two years later the depot and factory were moved to Aldershot and the Army's School of Ballooning was established.

With the outbreak of war in South Africa in 1899, No. 2 Balloon Section was sent out and served throughout the siege of Ladysmith, reporting Boer positions and directing fire during the Battle of Lombard's Kop. It was followed in December by No. 1 Section, which proved its worth at the Battle of Magersfontein by enabling the howitzer batteries to range on concealed enemy positions, and early in 1900 No. 3 Section joined the Tenth Division at Kimberley. In spite of prejudice and operational difficulties and shortcomings, the balloon units proved their worth and were treated with due respect by the Boers.

After the war, the Balloon School continued its experimental work with a variety of spherical and elongated balloons, dirigibles and kites, and personnel underwent training during manoeuvres and divisional field-days in the techniques of ballooning, kiting, and observation. Important experiments were also conducted with wireless telegraphy, and by 1908 signals could be received and transmitted over good distances.

Meanwhile, following the first successful powered flights made by the Wright brothers in 1903, the aeroplane was gradually evolving into a practical vehicle. The military potential of such a machine had long been appreciated. As early as 1897 Captain B.F.S. Baden-Powell of the Scots Guards, speaking at a lecture given by gliding pioneer Percy Pilcher, had said: 'If we can only get a machine which will travel about in the air, and be able to go a good many miles through the air at a considerable height up, a great deal could be done, not only in the way of observation of the enemy, but also in the way of attacking fortifications and positions from above.' His vision was capped by that of Major-General Lord Frankfort de Montmorency, who added: 'Two people can play at that game, so that if we had our machine in the air, probably the enemy would have their machine also, and it would probably come to the two machines trying to get at each other.'

By 1911 aeroplanes had achieved sufficient reliability and usefulness to be worth consideration for Army duties. Indeed, in September 1910 a Bristol Boxkite flown by Captain Bertram Dickson RFA, and a Farman biplane piloted by Lieutenant L.D.L. Gibbs had taken part in the Army manoeuvres, albeit unofficially, and had gained the interest of General Sir John French. Although there were still many sceptics in the military, progress had to be acknowledged, and in October 1910 the purchase of a military-type Farman and a Paulhan biplane by the War Office was announced. This was followed on 28 February 1911 by a special Army Order for the formation of the Air Battalion of the Royal Engineers, for systematic training in the use of aeroplanes for military purposes. The battalion, comprising a headquarters at South Farnborough, No. 1 (Airship) Company, also at South Farnborough, and No. 2 (Aeroplane) Company at Larkhill on Salisbury Plain, became operational on 1 April 1911. At the time, the only officer in the War Office who had learned to fly was Captain F.H. Sykes, a general staff officer in the Directorate of Military Operations, and in addition to his normal duties he visited France, Germany and Italy, gathering information and producing reports on progress abroad.

The Air Battalion was created with the object of forming a body of expert airmen, organised so as to facilitate the formation of units ready to take to the field with troops, and capable of expansion by reserve formations. The machines available to meet both naval and military requirements amounted to two small airships and fewer than 12 aeroplanes, and it quickly became apparent that the newly created battalion was inadequate to meet the demands which might be placed upon it in a war, especially in view of developments abroad.

Consequently, on 18 November 1911 the Prime Minister, the Rt. Hon. Herbert Asquith, requested that the Committee of Imperial Defence 'consider the future development of air navigation for naval and military purposes', and a standing sub-committee chaired by the Under-Secretary of State for War, Colonel the Rt. Hon. J.E.B. Seeley, was set up to this end. In its ensuing report, completed by 27 February 1912, the Committee recommended the creation of a British air service designated the Royal Flying Corps and divided into a Military Wing, a Naval Wing, and a Central Flying School. The Government's formal adoption of the Committee's proposals was announced in a Command Paper published on 12 April 1912, and the Royal Flying Corps (RFC) was constituted by Royal Warrant the following day. Exactly a month later the Air Battalion and its reserve were assimilated into the RFC.

The Central Flying School was established near Upavon on Salisbury Plain, and opened on 19 June. The first course began on 17 August and was completed at the end of December, both Wings depending almost entirely on the School for pilot training.

In May, No. 1 (Airship) Company of the Air Battalion became No. 1 Airship and Kite Squadron, remaining at Farnborough until 1 January 1914, when all airship work was transferred to the Navy and the Squadron was reorganised as No. 1 Squadron RFC. No. 2 Company of the Air Battalion, stationed at Larkhill, became No. 3 Squadron RFC, and had 18 aeroplanes on charge by September 1912. The third unit to be formed was No. 2 Squadron, which began life at Farnborough and moved by air and road to Montrose in February 1913.

In September of that year six of No. 2 Squadron's aircraft took part in the Irish Command manoeuvres, all six pilots crossing the Irish Sea in both directions. On 22 November 1913 Captain C.A.H. Longcroft made a non-stop flight from Montrose to Farnborough via Portsmouth, some 445 miles, for which he was awarded the Britannia Challenge Trophy for the year's most meritorious flight. His aircraft was a BE2 biplane designed and built at the Royal Aircraft Factory, Farnborough.

In September 1912 No. 4 Squadron was formed and then moved to Netheravon to join No. 3 Squadron. A detached flight of the latter unit formed the nucleus of No. 5 Squadron, formed in July 1913, and personnel from the first four squadrons formed No. 6 Squadron, which came into being in January 1914. No. 7 Squadron began to form in May 1914.

As well as participating in the 1912 and 1913 Army Manoeuvres, the Military Wing undertook experimental flying, conducting trials to develop wireless telegraphy, aerial photography, bomb-dropping, aerial gunnery, night flying and the direction of artillery fire.

In June 1914 the entire strength of the Military Wing was gathered at Netheravon in a 'concentration camp' to put the work and training of the Wing to the test and resolve the numerous problems of military aircraft operations. The camp broke on 2 July and the squadrons returned to their respective stations to prepare for that year's manoeuvres, but the outbreak of war intervened.

The Navy had been experimenting with aircraft for some years before the Naval Wing was formed, its first essay being the Vickers-built Naval Airship No. 1, the *Mayfly*, which was completed in 1911. It proved to be aptly named, as it was destined never to fly. Meanwhile Mr F.K. McClean offered the use of two Short biplanes to train naval officers in flying, and four officers began the first course, at the Royal Aero Club's flying ground at Eastchurch, Kent, on 2 March 1911, with technical training at the nearby works of Short Brothers. In October the Admiralty purchased the aeroplanes and established its own flying school at Eastchurch.

Simultaneously, another naval officer, Commander O. Schwann, had purchased an Avro biplane with which he undertook experiments with float undercarriages at

Cavendish dock. The aircraft became the first twin-float seaplane to fly in Britain. From 1911 the Naval Wing also carried out a great deal of experimental work on the duties its aircraft would have to perform. This included bomb and torpedo dropping, the fitting of machine-guns and wireless, and operations from water and ships. The first take-off from a British warship was made by Lieutenant Commander C.R. Samson in a Short S38 on 10 January 1912. Meanwhile a chain of air stations was established along the country's east and south coasts.

Such was the growth of the Naval Wing that, in the middle of 1914, it was reorganised and renamed the Royal Naval Air Service (RNAS) from 1 July. Its aircraft played a conspicuous part in the review of the Fleet at Spithead by the King from 18 to 22 July.

The Dawn of the Royal Air Force

PHILIP JARRETT

The mobilisation of the RFC started on 3 August 1914, the day before Britain declared war on Germany. On 13 August Nos. 2 and 3 Squadrons flew from Dover to France to join the Expeditionary Force, and the two Eastchurch-based flights of No. 4 Squadron flew there direct on the same day. No. 5 Squadron followed two days later. A total of 64 aeroplanes went on the 13th, all of them two-seaters – Avros, BE2s, BE8s, Blèriots and Henri Farmans. In France the RFC were under the command of General Sir David Henderson.

The first flights against the enemy were made from Maubeuge aerodrome, the first reconnaissance occurring on 19 August. Valuable work was performed during the retreat from Mons that month, and the British Army was saved from defeat by information on the enemy's movements provided by RFC pilots and observers.

On 15 September, during the Battle of the Aisne, the first aerial photographs were taken of enemy positions. Wireless telegraphy was also used to signal enemy movements, and on 27 September a Headquarters Wireless Section was formed, later to become No. 9 Squadron.

Through the first Battle of Ypres, which began on 19 October, the principal role of the RFC was still reconnaissance. On 7 October eight aeroplanes of No. 6 Squadron boosted the RFC's strength in the field, but even so the demands of artillery co-operation kept the force at full stretch. Enemy aircraft were attacked whenever they were encountered.

On 29 November reorganisation took place and wings were created: Nos. 2 and 3 Squadrons were grouped to form the 1st Wing under Lieutenant Colonel H.M. Trenchard, and Nos. 5 and 6 Squadrons formed the 2nd Wing under Lieutenant Colonel C.J. Burke. No. 4 Squadron remained at RFC headquarters at St Omer, along with the wireless unit and the advanced base of the Aircraft Park.

Great Britain had been left almost defenceless against air raids, and towards the end of December German aeroplanes launched attacks on Dover. Gradually the strength of the RFC at home was increased, and by the beginning of 1915 there were three wings in Britain. Several new squadrons had been formed and were in training.

Coastal defence against air attacks and hostile vessels was the allotted task of the RNAS, using landplanes, seaplanes and airships. Four cross-channel steamers and the Cunarder *Campania* were equipped as seaplane carriers for work in open stretches of sea, especially in the anti-submarine role.

On 3 September the Admiralty took over the air defence of Britain, the primary concern of the RNAS being to counter the threat of Zeppelin raids.

Moreover, a base was established at Dunkirk for offensive operations against the enemy's airship sheds. The first British air raid into enemy territory took place on 22 September, when one aeroplane succeeded in dropping bombs on sheds at Dusseldorf, but caused little damage. Greater success came in later raids which disrupted German airship operations.

Two of the Dunkirk RNAS squadrons were later moved to Belgium, where they performed valuable work in co-operation with Belgian forces until they returned to Dunkirk at the beginning of November.

The principal developments of 1915 centred on improvements to wireless and camera equipment, which greatly enhanced the RFC's ability to help the Army. A light and compact wireless was evolved, and the box-type camera was introduced. Bombing became more organised, and by the end of the year virtually every British aeroplane was armed with a machine-gun. One spur to the latter development was the appearance in the autumn of the Fokker monoplane fitted with a machine-gun synchronised to fire through the arc of the revolving propeller. The new opponent caused alarm and heavy losses, and led to changes in air tactics as the RFC sought to regain air superiority. Artillery co-operation was enhanced in January 1915 by the development of the 'clock code' which greatly improved aiming. Throughout the Battle of Neuve Chapelle in March, the second Battle of Ypres in April and May, and the Allied offensive at Aubers Ridge and Festubert in May and June, RFC aircraft gave valuable service to the Army.

On 19 August Colonel H.M. Trenchard took command of the RFC in France. By this time the number of squadrons with the Expeditionary Force had grown from four to 11, but Trenchard pushed for more. The 1st Wing played a conspicuous part in the Battle of Loos in September, with special bombing operations by the 2nd and 3rd Wings.

Other theatres of operation were German South-West Africa, Egypt, and Mesopotamia, where the RNAS also played a part.

At the end of 1915 the War Office was able to relieve the Navy of responsibility for the air defence of Great Britain. The RNAS offensive against submarines was stepped up, and airship patrols of the Dover Straits and Irish Sea were instigated. The squadron at Dunkirk caused such heavy damage in attacks on airships and their Belgian base that the sheds had to be abandoned. The RNAS also operated against the Turkish forces in the Dardanelles and during the Gallipoli landings.

To cope with the continued expansion of the RFC, in January 1916 each army was allotted two wings grouped as a brigade. The Fokker monoplane was still dominant, making long reconnaissance flights by lone aircraft impossible, and it became necessary to provide reconnaissance machines with an escort. By the spring the menace was on the wane with the advent of pusher fighters such as the de Havilland DH2, and in May the first Allied aircraft with interrupter gear, the Sopwith1½ Strutter, came into service. By the time of the Somme offensive, in July 1916, squadron strength had been increased from 12 to 18 aircraft, and the RFC had 27 squadrons in the field. Britain's superior fighting aircraft and the offensive policy of fighting the air war far over the enemy's lines gave it the edge, though Germany's new fighter units (*Jagdstaffeln*) and the new Halberstadt and Albatros fighters posed greater opposition and caused heavier casualties.

Great advances were made in artillery co-operation, and nearly 18,000 bombs were dropped on enemy targets between 1 July and 17 November, usually by formations of bombers under escort.

Middle East operations had become so extensive by mid-1916 that all of the RFC units in the Egyptian, Salonikan, Mesopotamian and East African theatres were combined under one command.

At home, a Home Defence Wing was formed to counter raids by German airships and bombers.

The evacuation of Gallipoli in January 1916 and the transfer of home defence to the RFC released large numbers of RNAS personnel and aircraft, enabling the offensive against enemy bases in Belgium to be intensified and allowing long-distance bombing raids into Germany to be initiated. In the Eastern Mediterranean the RNAS was considerably reorganised and undertook many bombing raids on strategic targets. Towards the end of October a squadron of 18 aeroplanes was drawn from the Dunkirk wings to serve with the RFC on the Somme as No. 8 (Naval) Squadron.

When 1917 opened the Germans were again enjoying superiority in aircraft, but in March and April the DH4 bomber and the Bristol F2B and SE5 fighters began to appear on the Western Front. In addition, three more RNAS squadrons arrived. The Battle of Arras, the Flanders offensive, and the fighting in Cambrai towards the end of the year kept the RFC heavily committed, and units also accompanied British Forces to the Italian Front at the end of October.

Intensive air activity, comprising reconnaissance, artillery co-operation flights, offensive patrols and bombing raids preceded the Battle of Arras. On 3 May the RFC carried out the first low-level strafing attacks on enemy ground forces, but at this time the threat posed by the German air service, with its newly-established fighter 'circuses', was at its greatest. On the Flanders Front during the battle of Messines, which began on 7 June, intensive low-flying attacks continually harassed the enemy.

In England, the Home Defence squadrons were adapted to deal with the new threat posed by enemy bombers attacking by both day and night. Night-fighting techniques were developed and practised from September onwards. The RFC establishment at home was greatly expanded in 1917, and pilot training was greatly improved.

For the RNAS, the year saw the successful deployment of flying boats against the submarine menace, and the use of shipborne fighters to attack Zeppelins. In April No. 7 Squadron began to re-equip with Handley Page bombers, and was soon restricted to night-bombing missions against targets in Belgium and Germany.

On 18 January 1918 Major-General J.M. Salmond took command of the RFC in France, and General Trenchard returned to England to become Chief of the Air Staff at the newly created Air Ministry.

In France, air activity increased as the German offensive on the Somme approached in March. The RFC and RNAS sustained their attacks on enemy ground forces in support of the hard-pressed infantry, and the offensive was stemmed. Strafing by night was developed, using parachute flares to illuminate targets.

During the most critical period of fighting, on 1 April 1918, the Royal Air

The Dawn of the RAF – Bristol F 2B Fighter, C4810 'N', of No. 22 Squadron which flew the first sorties at dawn on 1 April 1918 – the birthday of the Royal Air Force. They were operating from Vert Galand airfield on the Western Front. The Bristol F 2B was designed by Frank Barnwell from Stirling. The Barnwell brothers were among the first Scottish aviation pioneers. C4810 was a presentation machine named 'Gold Coast No. II' delivered to No. 20 Squadron and subsequently transferred to No. 22 Squadron. It was written off on 22 April 1918

Zeppelin Encounter – Air action involving Lieutenant S.D. Culley in a Beardmore-built Sopwith Camel 2F-1, N6812, which on 11 August 1918 shot down Zeppelin L53 off Heligoland Bight. With the amalgamation of the RFC and RNAS on 1 April 1918 the RAF was formed and naval aviation came under RAF control from that date. This was an unhappy situation which continued for the next 20 years before the Navy regained control of its Air Arm

Force came into being. Although the RFC had been created as a combined military and naval force, the demands of war had forced the two branches of the service to compete for equipment. In 1916 the Air Board had been formed to co-ordinate the needs and the work of the RFC and RNAS, but it lacked power. As a result of the Bailhache Committee of Inquiry into the administration of the air services, the Air Board became a ministry in February 1917, but there was still public dissatisfaction with the administration. In the middle of August 1917 General J.C. Smuts advocated the institution of an Air Ministry and the amalgamation of the air services. His proposals were accepted by the Government, and in November a Bill sanctioning the formation of the Air Force was passed by Parliament and given Royal Assent.

It is interesting to note that while Viscount Trenchard is rightly known as the 'Father of the Royal Air Force', he was initially a somewhat reluctant parent. It was two notable Glaswegians, General Sir David Henderson (an engineering graduate of the University of Glasgow) and William Weir (later Sir William and First Viscount Weir of Eastwood) who played a significant role in bringing about the new independent Royal Air Force. Trenchard is recorded as paying tribute to the vision of Henderson, the Royal Flying Corps' first commander in France in 1914, and it was Weir who as Air Minister prevailed upon Trenchard to take command of the new Independent Air Force and eventually the Royal Air Force.

Early on the morning of 1 April the pilots and observers of the newly-created air arm were barely aware of the change of identity. The men flying the Bristol Fighters of No. 22 Squadron from Vert Galand were more concerned with containing the hordes of German infantry. That day saw 23 enemy aircraft and two observation balloons shot down, and by the end of the first week in April the offensive was coming to a halt.

Extract from flying log of Major W. Sholto-Douglas MC, Officer Commanding No. 43 Squadron based at Falleninch, Stirling and dated 28 April 1916. Noteworthy are the flights from Montrose, Troon and Turnhouse

Between the Wars
PHILIP JARRETT

When the Armistice was signed on 11 November 1918, the strength of the RAF stood at more than 200 squadrons with 22,647 aircraft. These included 3,300 on first-line strength and 103 airships. More than half of the 27,333 officers were trained pilots, and there were 263,837 other ranks. There were 133 squadrons and 15 flights in overseas theatres (99 in France), 55 home operational squadrons, plus 56 Training Depot Stations, each usually comprising three squadrons, and 19 training squadrons.

Demobilisation brought a rapid reduction in this massive force, so that by the end of October 1919 only one squadron remained with the Army of the Rhine. The reduction in personnel was equally drastic. By March 1919 the RAF was reduced to 5,300 officers and 54,000 men, and by December the totals had fallen to 4,000 and 31,500 respectively. Likewise, the Air Estimates had been cut from a wartime figure of £200 million to £66,500,000.

On 11 January Major-General Sir Hugh Trenchard became Chief of Air Staff, and on 4 August new rank titles, ranging from Aircraftman 2nd Class to Marshal of the Royal Air Force, replaced the previous military rank titles. In December Mr Winston Churchill, Secretary of State for War and Air, submitted to both houses of Parliament a scheme proposed by Trenchard for the permanent organisation of the RAF. It provided for two squadrons at home to act as a striking force, later increasing to four, two training wings, an army co-operation and fleet reconnaissance squadron, one flight of shipborne fighters and one of flying boats, a flight of float seaplanes and half a squadron of torpedo aircraft, and a squadron for communications.

Overseas there were to be eight squadrons in India, seven in Egypt and three in Mesopotamia, plus one flight of seaplanes each for Malta and Alexandria and a flight of float seaplanes for the Mediterranean. An Air Force Cadet College and an Air Staff College were to be created.

Trenchard believed that the RAF could be used to settle rebellions and disputes in Britain's numerous overseas territories, and that air power would prove more efficient and cost-effective in this role than Army methods. He was able to prove his point in British Somaliland in January and February 1920, when a force of 12 DH9s, 36 officers and 183 airmen, commanded by Group-Captain Robert Gordon, cleared the fortresses of the self-styled Mullah of Somaliland in three weeks with no British casualties – a marked contrast to previous Army operations, which had been protracted, expensive and costly in lives.

This vindication of Trenchard's policy of 'air control' led Churchill to ask Trenchard to prepare a plan for policing Mesopotamia (later renamed Iraq) by air to counter widespread rebellions. By October 1920 the Service had been reduced to less than one-tenth of its wartime strength, but in March 1921 the scheme for the air control of Mesopotamia was approved. In June the Cairo-Baghdad air mail service was opened, with RAF aircraft operating a weekly service across the Syrian desert, following ploughed tracks over a 1,135-mile route.

In August 1922 it was announced that a further 15 Home Defence squadrons were to be raised, and on 1 October the military control of Iraq was handed over to the RAF. The Air Officer in Command was Air Vice-Marshal Sir John Salmond. On 9 February 1923, the Air Ministry announced the formation of the Reserve of Air Force Officers, and in June the Prime Minister, Mr Baldwin, advocated a Home Defence Force of 52 squadrons, 'to be created with as little delay as possible'. Late in the year the first fighter to replace the RAF's wartime Sopwith Snipes, the Gloster Grebe, began to enter service, followed by the Armstrong Whitworth Siskin the following May.

On 1 April 1924 the military and air forces in Palestine were placed under the command of an Air Officer of the RAF, and that same month saw the formation of the Fleet Air Arm (FAA), comprising RAF units normally operating from aircraft carriers and fighting ships. In May, when a confrontation arose between levies in Kirkuk and Moslems, a serious situation was avoided by the arrival of airborne troops, and, during frontier disputes between Turkey and Iraq in September, offensive patrols by the RAF prevented a Turkish occupation of Zakho. The aircraft used in Middle East operations were de Havilland DH9As, Sopwith Snipes, Bristol Fighters and Vickers Vernons and Vimys. By October there were 43 squadrons, including eight in Iraq, six in India and four in Egypt and Palestine, plus 18 flights of aircraft with the Navy.

In January 1925 the RAF checked repeated serious raids against the tribes of southern Iraq by Akhwan forces from the Najd territory, though the troubles were to persist until 1928. By March there was a total of 54 squadrons, including 18 for Home Defence. Two additional regular squadrons, one Special Reserve Squadron and four Auxiliary Air Force Squadrons were planned. That month the air defences of Great Britain, including anti-aircraft guns and searchlights, were unified under the command of Air Marshal Sir John Salmond, the command including three subordinate commands – Bombing Area, Fighting Area, and Special Reserve and Auxiliary Air Force. There were to be 35 bomber and 17 fighter squadrons. The new Air Defence Command had its headquarters at the Air Ministry in London until it was moved to Uxbridge in the middle of 1926.

In the early spring of 1925 Sheikh Mahmud again stirred up revolt in Iraq, but the RAF's DH9s and Bristol F2Bs were instrumental in forcing him into retreat. On India's North West Frontier DH9s and F2Bs again played a key role in the RAF's first independent air action, a 54-day bombing campaign against rebelling tribes in Waziristan which resulted in a peaceful settlement on 1 May. The Service lost only two men.

After remaining inactive in Persia during the winter of 1925–26, Sheikh Mahmud's rebels again began to cause trouble in the Sulaimaniya area of Iraq in

Hawker Furies of No. 43 Squadron, Tangmere, July 1935

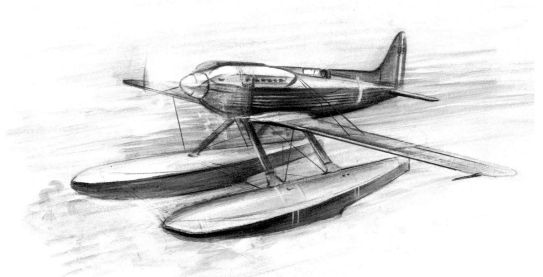

Supermarine S.6B, outright winner of the Schneider Trophy for Great Britain
in 1931

the spring of 1926. In mid-June intensive air action dispersed them, and the area quietened down.

On 1 March four Fairey IIID general-purpose aircraft set out from Cairo on a flight to the Cape, returning to Cairo on 27 May. Floats were then fitted in place of their land undercarriages and they flew to England, reaching Lee-on-Solent on 21 June, having flown some 14,000 miles. Also in March, home-based fighter squadrons began to receive the new Gloster Gamecock fighter in place of the Grebe. Another demonstration of the RAF's mobility was given by two Vickers Victoria bomber-transport aircraft of No. 216 Squadron, which made a successful flight from Cairo to Aden and back in September.

Sir Samuel Hoare announced in March 1927 that the strength of the RAF was being increased by ten per cent. On 30 March the first unit to be equipped with the Fairey IIIF general-purpose aircraft, No. 47 Squadron at Khartoum, took their new charges on an 11,000-mile round trip from Heliopolis to Cape Town and back under the leadership of Air Commodore C.R. Samson. They returned on 22 May, having completed the trip virtually without trouble and to a pre-arranged schedule. In July the Home Defence staffs and squadrons took part in day and night exercises in which four day-bomber squadrons, four night-bomber squadrons and 11 fighter squadrons participated. In Iraq, Sheikh Ahmad of Barzan, who had been displaying hostility towards the administration since 1919, was subdued by Iraqi levies assisted by RAF aircraft.

In September a team of RAF pilots flying seaplanes designed and built at Air Ministry expense competed in the Schneider Trophy contest at Venice. Flight Lieutenant A.M. Webster, flying a Supermarine S5, took the Trophy for Britain at a speed of 281 mph.

The same year saw two flying-boat cruises. The first, in the Baltic in September, was made by four aircraft of the Flying Boat Development Flight. Then, in October, four Supermarine Southamptons of the Far East Flight, led by Group Captain H.M. Cave-Brown-Cave, made a 27,000-mile cruise to Egypt, India, Australia, Japan and Singapore.

The success of the RAF's operations in Iraq was underlined in February 1928, when the Service became responsible for the defence of Aden and the surrounding territory. At the end of the year inter-tribal disorder in Afghanistan led to the Shiamwari tribe rebelling and cutting road and telegraph communications between Kabul and the Khyber Pass. As the rebellion spread, the British Legation at Kabul was cut off, and on 14 December rebel forces occupied the Asmai Heights, cutting off the Legation from the rest of the city. The British Commissioner requested that the women and children be evacuated by air, and the operation began on 23 December. When it ended on 25 February, no fewer than 586 persons of various nationalities had been rescued, along with some 24,000 lbs of baggage, the aircraft having flown a total of 28,160 miles over mountains 10,000 ft high during one of the severest winters on record. Only two aircraft were lost.

Improvements to RAF aircraft in 1929 included the fitting of Handley Page slots to improve slow-speed performance, and parachutes were installed in every suitable aircraft with the exception of sea-going types. It was also the year that the Bristol Bulldog fighter entered service. In April Squadron Leader Jones-Williams and Flight Lieutenant Jenkins flew non-stop from Cranwell to Karachi in a Fairey Long-range monoplane, a distance of 4,130 miles, achieving the first non-stop flight to India. In September Flag Officer Waghorn, flying a Supermarine S6 seaplane, won the Schneider Trophy for Great Britain for the second successive time, and on 12 September Squadron Leader Orlebar, also in an S6, set a new world absolute speed record of 357.7 mph.

In December 1929 Sir Hugh Trenchard, who had been promoted to Marshal of the Royal Air Force in early 1927, resigned his appointment as Chief of the Air Staff and was succeeded by Air Chief Marshal Sir John Salmond.

Trouble again broke out in Southern Kurdistan in the autumn of 1930 when Sheikh Mahmud crossed the Persian frontier into Iraq in a final attempt to establish himself as the leader of the Kurdish State. As Iraq was about to become an independent state, operations against the Sheikh were undertaken by the Iraqi Army with RAF co-operation. After indecisive ground action, the villages sheltering the rebels were bombed in March 1931. A series of air attacks with the Iraqi Army consolidating the gains then followed, and Sheikh Mahmud surrendered on 13 May.

On India's North West Frontier in 1930, the arrest of leader Abdul Ghaffar Khan in Peshawar led to rioting, and agitation spread to other tribes, including the Afridis. The RAF was heavily committed in operations against the rebels, bombing and strafing a force of some 7,000 in the Tirah area, and fighting a 48-hour battle with 2,000 men who advanced on Peshawar. In July 3,000 Mahsud tribesmen invested the South Waziristan Scout post, but were finally driven out and scattered after six weeks of daily RAF attacks. Attacks on army posts continued throughout August, but had petered out by the end of the month, though RAF operations continued until October 1931.

After 15 years with the RFC and RAF, the Bristol F2B was phased out of frontline service during 1931, to be replaced by the Westland Wapiti. The last squadron to part with the type, No. 20 Squadron, flew its final F2B formation on 13 March 1932. One of the great biplane fighters of the interwar years entered service in 1931, when the Siskin, which had been in service since 1924, began to be replaced by the elegant Hawker Fury. The first squadron to be fully equipped with Furies was No. 43 at Tangmere, which received them in May and June.

The Schneider Trophy was won outright for Britain on 12 September, when Flight Lieutenant J. Boothman flew his Supermarine S6B over the course unchallenged at 340 mph. Lady Houston had provided £100,000 to enable Britain to compete, and the Italian team had been forced to withdraw. On 29 September Flight Lieutenant G.H. Stainforth claimed the world speed record in an S6B, averaging 408 mph.

Operations in India and Iraq continued during 1932, though the responsibility for the administration, security and legal control of Iraq now devolved upon Iraq's own government. The RAF's prime role was the protection of British residents and properties, and the force was greatly reduced, though it played an important part in the subduing and occupation of the hostile Barzan district by the government. In Aden, No. 8 Squadron aircraft flew 761 hours on a survey of the Somaliland-Abyssinia border, and another 72 hours conveying the ground survey party from site to site.

After promotion to the rank of Marshal of the Royal Air Force in January 1933, Sir John Salmond was succeeded as Chief of the Air Staff on 1 April by Air Chief Marshal Sir Geoffrey Salmond. Tragically, Sir Geoffrey died on 27 April, and his place was taken by Air Chief Marshal Sir Edward Ellington on 22 May. The year saw further uprisings on the North West Frontier, where a planned attack on Kabul by the Mahsud and Wazir tribes in March was deterred by bombing their villages as a warning. Further uprisings north-west of Peshawar, led by a pretender to the Afghan throne, were quelled by four RAF squadrons. Later, feuding between the Upper and Lower Mohmand exploded into war and the Upper Mohmand had to be dispersed by aircraft.

In the House of Lords on 29 November Lord Londonderry declared that Britain's 'present relative weakness in the air cannot be allowed to continue'. In the Commons Rear-Admiral Sueter asked the Government to rearm up to the standard laid down in 1923. At this time there were only 74 squadrons, including 13 Reserve and Auxiliary squadrons and the units of the Fleet Air Arm. Forty of these squadrons were British-based. The programme of expansion laid down ten years earlier was still incomplete, partly owing to national economy and partly because of a general effort to limit armaments.

The Air Estimates for 1934 provided for only six new squadrons, but the failure to reach agreement about disarmament at Geneva obliged the British Government to strengthen the RAF. In July a programme was announced to bring first-line strength up to 128 squadrons in five years, and in November the process was accelerated by a decision to form 22 Home Defence squadrons and three more for the FAA in 1935–36.

On 22 May 1935 proposals for considerable expansion were announced. It was stated that the strength of the RAF based at home, exclusive of the FAA, would reach 1,500 first-line aircraft by March 1937. At the time of the announcement the RAF's strength stood at 580 aircraft: a total of 840 would have been reached in March 1937 under the earlier programme of July 1934. The new programme required that 71 new squadrons be formed, accompanied by a general expansion of training and all other services.

As part of the Royal Jubilee celebrations, on 6 July 1935, His Majesty King George V held a review of the RAF at Mildenhall and Duxford, which included a flypast of 350 aircraft.

On 3 October Italy declared war on Abyssinia (later Ethiopia), and was condemned as an aggressor by the League of Nations. Britain sent some 24 squadrons to Malta, Gibraltar, Egypt and Aden and prepared for a possible conflict with Italy, but by May 1936 the Italian conquest was completed.

The problems of rapid expansion and extra commitments were compounded by the wide variety of aircraft types in service or being introduced. There were three general-purpose aircraft: the Wapiti, Hardy and Vincent; five day bombers: the Hart, Hind, Wallace, Gordon and Overstrand; four night bombers: the Virginia, Hinaidi, Heyford and Hendon; no fewer than seven coastal-reconnaissance flying boats: the Southampton, Scapa, Stranraer, London, Perth, Singapore and Cloud; three army co-operation aircraft: the Hector, Audax and Wapiti, and four fighters: the Demon, Bulldog, Fury, and Gauntlet.

Hawker Hind of No. 602 Squadron over the Empire Exhibition, Glasgow, October 1938

Compared with the new aircraft coming into service in other countries, many of these were obsolete. Most were biplanes and, as far as the fighters were concerned, they were fast being outmoded by radical low-wing monoplanes such as Russia's I-16 and Germany's Messerschmitt Bf 109, both monoplanes with retractable undercarriages and enclosed cockpits.

In May 1936 the Home Defence Force was organised into four commands: Bomber Command, Fighter Command, Coastal Command, and Training Command. Conspicuous at the 17th Hendon Air Display were the prototypes of the new Hawker fighter, destined to win fame as the Hurricane, and Supermarine's Spitfire fighter. Other designs which would become familiar in succeeding years were the Hampden, Wellington (as yet unnamed), Battle, Whitley and Bristol 142, progenitor of the Blenheim. However, biplanes were by far the most numerous participants.

A significant feature of the air exercises carried out in July to give collective defence training to Metropolitan Air Force squadrons was the assumption, for the first time, that attacking forces would approach over the seaboard of south-east England. On 30 July 1936, Lord Swinton, Secretary of State for Air, announced the formation of the RAF Volunteer Reserve, to take 800 pilots a year.

By the end of March 1937 the RAF had 100 squadrons at home, 20 with the FAA, and 26 overseas, and the new-generation, all-metal, mass-produced aircraft were coming into service, Bomber Command receiving Battles, Blenheims, Harrows and Wellesleys. However, the latest fighter was the Gladiator, a fabric-covered biplane with a fixed undercarriage and only four guns, its greatest concession to modernity being an enclosed cockpit.

In July the FAA was placed under the control of the Admiralty, which was to supply all personnel for the air units of the Fleet. The following month 398 aircraft made a mock attack on London to give RAF pilots, new Observer Corps units and the staffs of Fighter and Bomber Command groups and stations operational practice. The first Hurricanes were delivered to No. 111 Squadron at Northolt in December.

By 1938 the total number of employees in the aircraft industry had grown from 30,000 in 1935 to almost 90,000. In April the Air Ministry adopted the policy of also buying military aircraft from the USA, and in June No. 19 Squadron became the first unit in the RAF to take delivery of Spitfires, to replace its obsolete Gauntlets.

When the Munich crisis came to a head in September 1938 the RAF was partially mobilised, but some time was gained at Czechoslovakia's expense. War preparations gathered pace, and in November RAF Balloon Command was formed to provide barrage protection for cities and strategic targets. In December it was announced that the FAA was to be enlarged from 3,000 to 10,000 officers and men, and that a further seven aircraft carriers were to be added to the six carriers and two seaplane carriers in service.

On 1 January 1939 the RAF's operational strength consisted of 74 bomber squadrons, 27 fighter squadrons, 12 army co-operation squadrons, 17 reconnaissance squadrons, four torpedo-bomber squadrons and a communications squadron. In addition, 20 auxiliary squadrons were working up to operational capability. It was estimated that, by the end of March, the Metropolitan Air Force would have 1,750 first-line aircraft, but this total still included outmoded Gauntlets and Gladiators.

The Women's Auxiliary Air Force was created on 28 June 1939. On 11 July

100 RAF bombers made a training flight over central France, followed a fortnight later by 240 bombers to Lyons and the Vosges. At the beginning of August 1,300 aircraft took part in large-scale exercises lasting four days and employing 53,000 men, 110 guns, 700 searchlights and 100 barrage balloons. On 31 August general mobilisation was proclaimed, all reservists were called up and the RAF was put on a war footing. The first RAF squadron to be despatched to France was No. 226 of the Advanced Air Striking Force, which comprised ten squadrons of Battle bombers and two squadrons of Hurricanes. On 3 September Great Britain declared war on Germany. The RAF was ready – but only just.

First Shots to the Auxiliaries – Spitfire I flown by Flight Lieutenant George Pinkerton of No. 602 Squadron attacking a Ju 88 of KG30 during the first successful air action of WWII in UK skies. The event took place off Crail in the Firth of Forth during the early afternoon of 16 October 1939 in which Spitfires of 603 Squadron also participated

The Early War Years and The Battle of Britain

AIR VICE-MARSHAL SANDY JOHNSTONE
CB DFC AE DL RAF (Retd)
(No. 602 Squadron 1934–1941)

'Glasgow's Own', as it quickly became known, had a proud history long before the outbreak of hostilities in September 1939.

Arising from Sir Hugh Trenchard's dream of creating, to use his own words, 'A *corps d'élite* of mechanical yeomanry organised on a territorial basis – men who in earlier times would have served on horseback', No. 602 (City of Glasgow) Squadron was the first of the newly-created Auxiliary Air Force squadrons to start flying operations, and when Squadron Leader C.N. Lowe, its Commanding Officer, flew the DH 9A H144 to Renfrew from Henlow on 7 October 1925, he little realised that his was the first aircraft ever flown in an Auxiliary Air Force unit. However the significance of the flight did not go unnoticed by the national press and from then on the exploits of the squadron were to provide much good copy for the gentlemen of Fleet Street for many years to come.

As an example, on 3 April 1933, at precisely 1005 hours, man first looked down on the summit of Mount Everest when two Westland biplanes of the Houston-Everest Expedition, flown by the Marquess of Douglas and Clydesdale and David MacIntyre, succeeded in clearing the famous peak with little to spare. At the time, Clydesdale was the Commanding Officer of No. 602 Squadron and David MacIntyre its senior Flight Commander, so it was not surprising that the high standards set by these illustrious gentlemen quickly permeated throughout the entire unit. Indeed it became one in which it was an honour and a privilege to serve and the standard it had continually achieved throughout its short life must have impressed the powers that be for, in the spring of 1939, No. 602 was the first squadron in the Auxiliary Air Force – and only the eighth in the entire country – to be equipped with Spitfire fighters. By the time war was declared four months later, No. 602 Squadron was well trained on these sophisticated aircraft both by day and by night and qualified to take its place in the front line of the air defences of the nation.

Members of the squadron were aware of the worsening political situation during the second and third quarters of 1939 when the undertakings given to Mr Chamberlain by the Axis leaders, promising 'peace in our time', were being ruthlessly disregarded, particularly by Hitler. They had become used to being summoned to Abbotsinch at regular intervals to test their call-up procedures and, on 23 August, when everyone was sent a strange blue envelope bearing the legend ON HIS MAJESTY'S SERVICE – URGENT, EMBODIMENT, they could be forgiven for assuming that this latest summons was nothing more than an elaborate extension of the drills already practised. However, when the lads turned up at the airfield in the dead of night to find the place a blaze of lights and a frenzy of activity, it was immediately apparent that it was no mere 'exercise'. This time it was the real thing.

'Sign here,' they were curtly ordered, 'and return to your homes to pick up enough clobber to last a week. Don't bring any civvies, you will be wearing uniform from now on!'

And so the weekenders prepared for the war they knew would come. The No. 269 Squadron Ansons which had been sharing the airfield with No. 602 had already left for their forward base at Montrose and No. 602 itself had investigated the possibility of a detachment moving forward to Grangemouth to be nearer the 'front line'. Drem, the officially designated forward base for No. 602 Squadron, was still occupied by a Flying Training School and it would take time to relocate such an important outfit.

When war was eventually declared, the news was received with a mixture of relief and apprehension by both pilots and ground crews alike.

Already dispersed in tents along the borders of the airfield, their Spitfires were parked nearby and ready to take off at a moment's notice. No one, least of all those controlling the fighters, could afford to drop their guard for a moment, with the result that crews spent many weary hours sitting by their aircraft, waiting for orders to scramble which never seemed to come. Granted the No. 602 boys were ordered into the air once or twice during that fateful September to tackle approaching unidentified raids but their targets generally turned out to be one of the Junkers 52 transports which British Airways had recently acquired from Lufthansa and had been injudicious enough to put into service in our area just as the nation decided to go to war. The smaller tri-motor Spartan Cruisers of Scottish Airways, although easier to identify, also put themselves at considerable risk by flying within the range of the waiting No. 602 Squadron Spitfires. Fortunately none were shot down.

The pilots soon became accustomed to hanging around their dispersals with little to do and several, among them Urie, Boyd and Jack, took the opportunity to slip off for a couple of days to make honest women of their long-time girlfriends believing, correctly, that the lull would not last much longer. So, within a week of being at war, a small colony of mobile caravans appeared in a corner of the field to form, for want of a better name, the No. 602 Squadron Married Patch. As the Romeos had foreseen, the lull was short-lived and, during the night of 30 September/1 October, I was sent off in a thick fog to intercept an unidentified plot reported to be approaching the Glasgow area. It was an episode I am not likely to forget for, having got airborne without the aid of a flarepath, I discovered that the radio was defective and that I had been left floundering in a fog with no one to tell me where to go or, indeed, what the hell I was meant to be doing. It was hardly surprising that I ended up by crashing on to the top of a hill, having previously mistaken a reservoir for a large field and all but ended up in a watery grave. It was of little consequence that the X-Raid turned out to be one of our own bombers which had gone astray; it was of greater significance to the squadron that this had been the first operational night patrol ever carried out by a Spitfire.

Things began moving from then on. After a short spell at Grangemouth, its interim forward base, No. 602 Squadron finally got orders to proceed on to Drem on Friday, 13 October 1939, the resident Flying Training School finally having been found an alternative base. It was fortunate the boys were not superstitious, for not only did 13 sit down to breakfast before flying 13 Spitfires to East Lothian, but the recently evacuated Flying Training School had been none other than No. 13 FTS and the squadron itself was operating under the command of No. 13 Group within Fighter Command! Indeed the number 13 became looked upon as a lucky number, for No. 602 was the first squadron to go into action over the British Isles a few days later and was to make its début in the Battle of Britain on 13 August the following year.

For No. 602, the war came to life on 16 October 1939 when nine Ju88s of I/KG30, led by Hauptmann Helmut Pohl, carried out a raid on a number of naval units anchored off the RN Dockyard at Rosyth and were promptly sent packing by the Spitfires of No. 602 Squadron and its sister squadron, No. 603, from Edinburgh. George Pinkerton, 'B' Flight Commander in No. 602, in company with Archie McKellar, were credited with despatching the unfortunate Pohl's aircraft, whilst Pat Gifford, No. 603 Squadron, meted out similar punishment to another Luftwaffe Ju88. It later came to light that several other raiders failed to return to their bases on the Continent and the action was recorded as yet another 'first' for the squadron to celebrate!

There followed a period when No. 602 was given the tedious task of providing air cover over convoys of small ships plying their trade up and down the coastal waters off south-east Scotland, but these sorties were not without their moments of excitement. Like all shipping in time of war, small coasters were forbidden to sail from port unless in convoy and escorted by units of the Royal Navy. Unfortunately those manning the escorting frigates and destroyers, although doubtless trained to identify the silhouettes of friendly and enemy warships, were woefully ignorant of the outlines of British fighter aircraft. This resulted in several of our patrols being met by a furious barrage of naval anti-aircraft fire as soon as they approached their charges. This uncomfortable state of affairs was to continue until the Admiralty was persuaded to carry an RAF officer in the Commodore's ship to help him identify friend from foe.

Whilst newspaper reports still talked of the 'phoney war', the reality had already arrived in the Firth of Forth. Almost daily, German Heinkels were making fleeting appearances over the region, mostly on reconnaissance flights, but few got away unscathed. On 28 November 1939 a pair of these aircraft were over Scotland, one circling North Berwick and the other over Rosyth. Archie McKellar was first to sight the former and waded in with all guns firing, whereupon the Heinkel came down in a sloping field near Haddington, with the pilot wounded, both gunners dead, and the observer unhurt. It was the first enemy aircraft to be brought down on the British mainland and another notable 'first' for No. 602.

The squadron's tally of enemy aircraft mounted as the winter wore on and it was not long before Luftwaffe pilots were referring to the Firth of Forth as 'Suicide Corner' and trying to find excuses for avoiding the area. It proved of little avail, for the Spitfires of No. 602 were able to seek out the raiders wherever they penetrated and, by the time the squadron flew south to face the Battle of Britain in August 1940, it had already accounted for 19 enemy aircraft destroyed and many more probably destroyed or damaged. Two of these engagements are worthy of mention for, being carried out by No. 602 Squadron, they were anything but orthodox.

On 22 February 1940 Douglas Farquhar, the Commanding Officer, was leading a section which included the only cannon-armed Spitfire in the RAF, currently attached to No. 602 Squadron, when he intercepted a Heinkel IIIK about 20 miles out to sea and heading for the Scottish coast. Having silenced the rear gunner, Farquhar called in the cannon-armed Spitfire to show its worth and stood off as the cannons took their toll and the stricken raider headed for a remote stretch of ground not far from St Abb's Head. Anxious to examine the effects the cannon fire had made on the Heinkel, Farquhar tried to land his Spitfire alongside his prey, which had by now made a successful wheels-up landing near the remote headland. Alas the Spitfire came down in a neighbouring bog and turned over, leaving Farquhar suspended by his safety harness and unable to get out. In the end he had to be rescued by the crew of the Heinkel bomber who, having first set their aircraft alight, did the decent thing and raised the Spitfire sufficiently to allow our gallant CO to crawl out from under. A few weeks later, when King George VI visited Drem to present Farquhar with a Distinguished Flying Cross, His Majesty could not contain his mirth when told of the exploit, although some in less exalted positions were less able to appreciate the joke and Farquhar was given a fair old ticking-off by his masters for unnecessarily hazarding the safety of his aircraft!

I also managed to figure in another unusual episode when, during the night of 26 June, I came upon a Heinkel III caught in the beams of searchlights just east of Edinburgh. As luck would have it I succeeded in delivering the coup de grâce immediately over Drem, thus giving the ground crews their first sight of a member of their squadron actually doing his stuff. It was also my own first recorded success and another 'first' for No. 602 Squadron.

The Nazi conquest of the low countries and Norway naturally posed additional problems for us, as we were required to operate from a waterlogged airfield in Aberdeenshire for several weeks to provide air cover for the British forces returning from the Norwegian campaign. Several weeks later we were all packed up and ready to fly south to cover the evacuation of our forces from Dunkirk when, at the eleventh hour, a signal came through, cancelling the move as most troops in France had been brought home. By now Farquhar had been promoted to the rank of Wing Commander and ensconced as Station Commander at Martlesham Heath, in Suffolk, and George Pinkerton had taken over No. 602. When France finally capitulated, we realised it would not be long before our services would be required to bolster the air defences along the south coast.

The call came on 13 August, by which time George Pinkerton had also gone and I had assumed the leadership of No. 602. We were to be based at Westhampnett, a small satellite airfield near Tangmere, so recently constructed that no one could tell us exactly where it was. In the event we managed to find the site, which consisted of two small fields hastily knocked into one larger one by the removal of the dividing hedgerow. It was to become the Goodwood motor racing track after the war.

The wreck of a Hurricane lay inverted in the middle of the field whilst, two fields beyond, a tell-tale pall of black smoke rose menacingly from the remains of the Messerschmitt with which it had been tangling minutes before. Johnny Peel, CO of

Spitfire Supreme – Squadron Leader Sandy Johnstone in Spitfire Ia, X4162 'LO-J' of No. 602 Squadron over London during the Battle of Britain, 7 September 1940, on which day he claimed the destruction of a Bf109

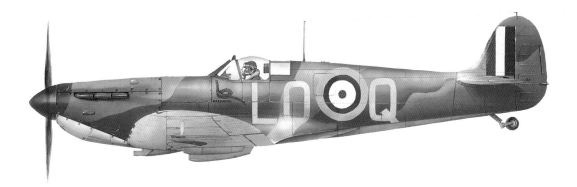

Spitfire I, L1004 'LO-Q', No. 602 (City of Glasgow) Squadron, Westhampnett, August 1940

the squadron we were to relieve, was there to greet us, arm in a sling and a bandage hastily tied round his head.

'Welcome to Westhampnett', he began. 'Sorry about my aeroplane cluttering up the airfield, but I had an aileron shot off whilst tangling with that bugger over there,' he went on, pointing to the distant pall of smoke. 'The rest of my boys have already left for the North so I had better go after them!'

With that peremptory welcome, Peel climbed into his small sports car and drove off, leaving us to take stock and sort ourselves out as best we could. It did not take long to discover that the facilities at Westhampnett were minimal – five Nissen huts and a couple of nearby farmhouses were the sum total – so all maintenance work would have to be done in the open. Nor did it help to discover that No. 602 was the only Spitfire unit operating in the area and no relevant spares were available. I need not have worried, of course, for No. 602's marvellous force of fitters and riggers, mostly from the Glasgow area, proved more than capable of overcoming any such temporary setback.

The squadron was in the thick of it two days later when scrambled from 'released', with no previous warning, to rush to the defence of the parent station, Tangmere, under attack by a large force of Ju87 Stuka dive bombers. Without waiting to form up in any organised fashion, the No. 602 Spitfires took off from all corners of the field, miraculously avoiding colliding with one another as they waded into the fray. Findlay Boyd was barely airborne when a Stuka swooped low ahead of him, whereupon he shot it down in flames even before retracting the undercarriage of his aircraft. Indeed Boyd completed his circuit, wheels still down, and was on the ground again within seconds of taking off. In the meantime the remaining No. 602 pilots were attacking any target of opportunity which presented itself – altogether a satisfactory baptism from the squadron's point of view for, besides Boyd's victory, Dunlop Urie, Andrew McDowall, Nigel Rose and myself were each credited with a victim on the score sheet whilst others could claim minor successes.

Two days later the squadron was engaged in a similar action when Ford was attacked. On this occasion they hit eight Stukas, five of which were destroyed, two returning damaged to their base and the eighth crashing in France, killing both occupants. But the escorting Bf109s soon got among our lads in an effort to settle the score, resulting in four Spitfires being badly shot up, although Mount and Urie managed to bring their damaged aircraft back to Westhampnett. Ferguson landed, slightly wounded, in a field near Littlehampton whilst Moody managed to set his damaged aircraft down amid the devastation at Ford. Urie's aircraft had been torn apart by cannon fire and had to be written off whilst Urie himself suffered such severe leg injuries that he was unable to take any further active part in the Battle of Britain.

On another occasion Hector Maclean, whose great-uncle had been one of the first instructors at CFS in 1912, received serious injuries when attacked by an Me109 a few miles south of the Isle of Wight yet, in spite of being in great pain, his right foot having been blown off by the enemy shell, he managed to fly his damaged Spitfire back to base before being whipped off to hospital to have the injured leg amputated below the knee. To be associated with such heroes was a humbling experience.

And so it went on throughout that hot and troubled summer, the crews of

No. 602 Squadron flying their hearts out, tangling with the enemy three, four and sometimes five times a day. It was not always possible to replace injured pilots immediately, so the burden of operations fell ever more on those who remained fit to fly. In time, the supply of trained replacements dried up altogether and we were sent Lysander pilots from hastily-disbanded Army Co-operation Units to fill the gaps – fellows with no experience whatever on high-speed fighters. Nevertheless they coped magnificently, learning 'on the job', and I have nothing but admiration for their guts and determination. The same goes for the ground crews who, working in spartan conditions day and night, never failed to provide machines on the line whenever they were required. These staunch fellows were the vital platform from which we operated and without them nothing could have been achieved. It was their job to supply the weapons. All we had to do was fire the bullets.

Little by little it seemed we were gaining the upper hand and by mid-September even believed we were coming out on top. It was not without loss, however, for Harry Moody and Roger Coverley failed to return to base on 7 September after the big action over Kent when Goering unleashed an enormous aerial armada to attack London. It was a sad blow, for they were two of our most experienced pilots and much-loved members of the squadron. They were, too, our first fatal casualties.

The sterling deeds of No. 602 Squadron during that fateful summer of 1940 have been chronicled at length by many other writers, so it would ill become me to attempt to gild further that particular lily: suffice to say No. 602 Squadron continued to acquit itself with flying colours throughout the Battle of Britain and returned to Scotland on 19 December, having served longer in the front line than any other squadron in Fighter Command. It had given of its best and, as history was later to show, its successes were of no mean order – 157 victories, the second highest score of any squadron in the Battle of Britain and achieved with the least number of casualties. By then, of course, most of the original pilots had either been wounded or posted to other units and its intrinsic 'auxiliary' make-up had gone. Nevertheless their successors, who included such illustrious names as Al Deere, Paddy Finucane, Pierre Closterman, Cupid Love and Raymond Baxter were to uphold the old unit's traditions and strove to ensure that No. 602 (City of Glasgow) Squadron's name would continue to be respected by the enemy throughout the rest of the war and admired by those who, through no fault of their own, were unable to join its honoured ranks.

Extract from flying log of Squadron Leader Sandy Johnstone DFC, Officer Commanding No. 602 (City of Glasgow) Squadron based in Westhampnett during the Battle of Britain in September 1940.

Attack on the Moehne Dam – Squadron Leader H. M. Young DFC and bar and crew in Lancaster B III (Special), ED877 'AJ-A'

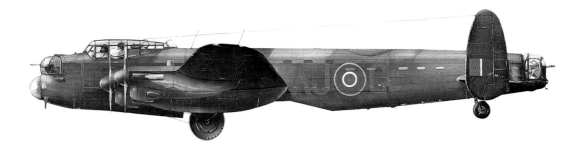

Lancaster B III (Special), ED932 'AJ-G', No. 617 Squadron, Scampton, May 1943

Operation Chastise –
the Dams Raid
DR JOHN SWEETMAN

As the dying sun dipped finally below the western horizon after a blisteringly-hot Sunday, 16 May 1943, a strange silhouette began to edge cautiously down the runway of RAF Scampton in Lincolnshire. Painfully slowly, Flight Lieutenant R.N.G. Barlow hauled his heavily-laden bomber off the grass, brushed the perimeter hedge and turned south-east towards the North Sea at 2128 hrs (Double British Summer Time). The modified Lancaster had no mid-upper turret, no bomb-bay doors and beneath its fuselage hung an unsightly garden roller held between two V-shaped arms.

Barlow was flying the first of 19 aircraft from No. 617 Squadron RAF to take off on Operation Chastise, which aimed to destroy selected dams in western Germany whose reservoirs contained water invaluable for the production and transportation of enemy war supplies. As the Chief of the Air Staff, Air Chief Marshal Sir Charles Portal, had exclaimed: 'If you want to win the war, bust the dams'.

Four of the target dams were grouped close to the Ruhr and its concentration of arms-producing factories; two controlled water supplies for the River Weser further east and ultimately the important Mittelland Canal. The Ruhr targets, the Moehne, Sorpe, Lister and Ennepe dams, together held back 254 million cubic metres of water; the Eder and Diemel 222 million cubic metres. All but the Sorpe were masonry dams, with a visible structure open to attack. The Sorpe had a central concrete core concealed between two sloping earth supports. Here the method of attack chosen for the other five dams, bouncing the 'garden roller' across the water, would not be used.

Operation Chastise was the culmination of six years of planning, experiment, hopes, disappointments and endless conferences. Government ministers, the Air Ministry, Admiralty and many civilian firms had been consulted and closely involved during this time. Incredibly, though, the final phase in which No. 617 Squadron had been trained to perfection, the Lancasters modified and the special weapon finalised lasted a mere eleven weeks. The lethal contraption suspended beneath Barlow's aircraft was scarcely more than its inventor's dream, despite exhaustive scientific tests, on 26 February 1943. Essentially, it had not left the drawing board. Nor had the squadron destined to deliver it yet been formed.

In 1937, the Air Staff identified the Moehne and Sorpe dams as primary targets in any effort to neutralise the might of Germany's war industry in the Ruhr once hostilities broke out. Several promising ideas for attacking either the air or water faces of the Moehne dam were examined: torpedoes, aerial mines, anti-submarine bombs, floating a seaplane packed with explosives down the reservoir, rockets directed from the air side, parachuting in men with charges strapped to their backs or using a drogue deposited on the water to drag a charge with the current to the dam. All failed to progress beyond the experimental stage.

Quite independently, when the Second World War started in 1939, the 51-year-old assistant chief designer at Vickers-Armstrongs works in Weybridge mused: 'What can an engineer do to win the war?' Barnes Wallis had established his reputation as an aeronautical engineer with construction of the R100 airship, Wellesley and Wellington bombers. He now believed that bombs and bombers would be decisive if directed at precise, crucial targets, not dropped on a wide variety of locations unconnected with one another. Initially, he argued for development of a massive six-engined aircraft capable of releasing a deep-penetration 10-ton bomb from 40,000 ft, which would quite literally undermine targets such as dams by exploding underground and causing their structure to collapse.

When this concept proved impracticable, he refused to be discouraged. Operation Chastise stemmed from his second, even more ingenious scheme. After three years of experiment, during which scaled-down charges had been used against models of the Moehne and an old dam in Wales, on bombing ranges in Dorset and off the Kent coast, the 9,250-lb cylinder containing 6,600 lbs of torpex underwater explosive (codenamed Upkeep) had evolved and thus hung underneath Flight Lieutenant Barlow's Lancaster on the late evening of 16 May 1943.

At the time, official documents referred to it as a 'mine'; ever after, Wallis's special creation has been called 'the bouncing bomb'. In fact, it was a depth charge. The trick was to make that depth charge sink in contact with the dam wall on the water side, so that three hydrostatic pistols set in it would explode the charge 30 ft below the surface of the water. If, for any reason, none of these worked, a fourth self-destructive device would activate after 90 secs. The Germans would not then be able to recover the complete, unexploded weapon, analyse it and build a similar one to threaten British dams.

No. 617 Squadron RAF had been formed under the command of Wing Commander G.P. (Guy) Gibson to carry out this attack. Initially as Squadron X, it came into existence on 17 March though the first practice flight did not occur until ten days later; and some of the 21 crews were not complete until a month later. Long, low-level, cross-country runs, attacks over simulated and actual dams and steep dives towards stipulated markings on Scampton's runway formed only part of the intensive training schedule devised and rigorously enforced by Gibson.

The all-up weight of the Chastise Lancasters was 63,000 lbs, which meant that they could fly at only 180 mph to the target. Loss of the mid-upper turret (to reduce drag) increased vulnerability to night fighters, so pilots were briefed to fly at a mere 100 ft. In the nose the bomb-aimer map read, passing information back to the navigator. The mid-upper gunner manned the forward-firing twin .303 Browning machine-guns, close to the bomb-aimer, and the only other protection came from the rear gunner. Pilot, flight engineer and wireless operator completed the crew. As one gunner remarked, every time they left England, 'it was seven men against the Reich'. Tonight, their task would be even more perilous, flying as they were without the protection of the usual bomber stream against a single target. Nor was the dropping of Upkeep straightforward. It must be released at 220 mph ground speed, which required aircraft to dive steeply from over 1,000 ft to gain the necessary momentum. To ensure that Wallis's weapon did not leap over the dam wall after striking it, a special machine driven by the hydraulic system (not required for the bomb-bay doors on this operation) back-spun it at 500 rpm. That machine would be activated by the wireless operator ten minutes before release.

Three waves of No. 617 Squadron Lancasters, flown by 91 RAF, 28 RCAF, 12 RAAF and two RNZAF personnel, were to execute Chastise. Barlow led the so-called second wave of five aircraft flying singly to the Sorpe. It ought to have been led by the American Flight Lieutenant J.C. McCarthy – an RCAF officer with twin shoulder flashes 'Canada' and 'USA' – but his Lancaster developed engine trouble prior to take-off. McCarthy would fly the reserve aircraft, but did not get airborne until the first wave had left Scampton. The first and second waves would cross the enemy coast 120 miles apart in an attempt to confuse the German defences. The Sorpe wave flew the longer route over the Frisian island of Vlieland, then across the Zuider Zee to skirt the Ruhr, touch the Moehne and fly on to the Sorpe. Hence it took off first. Meanwhile, Gibson led the first wave of nine aircraft, flying in three formations each of three aircraft at ten-minute intervals, to the Moehne. There he would direct the Lancasters to attack singly, allowing sufficient time to elapse between the attacks for turbulence in the water to settle after the previous explosion. Once the Moehne had been breached, those aircraft still carrying Upkeep, plus Gibson and Young (the deputy leader) would go to the Eder and, if that were breached, on to the Sorpe. The importance of destroying both the Moehne and the Sorpe, which together supplied almost two thirds of the Ruhr's water, was therefore underlined.

A third wave was to leave Scampton two hours after the other two. It also comprised five Lancasters flying individually. Once airborne, each of these aircraft would be directed to one of the six targets, depending upon the overall situation. In the event, one would be ordered to the Diemel, Lister and Ennepe, two to the Sorpe.

Few military operations go precisely according to plan. Operation Chastise was no exception. Barlow crashed short of his target near Rees on the Rhine at 2350 hrs and his loss was doubly unfortunate. The entire crew perished, but Upkeep did not explode. Once the embers cooled, the Germans recovered Wallis's invention and quickly analysed it. However, contrary to British fears, they did not develop a similar weapon to menace British dams. The second of the second-wave aircraft, piloted by New Zealander Flight Lieutenant J.L. Munro, was badly damaged by flak over the Frisian Islands and returned to Scampton. Pilot Officer V.W. Byers was less lucky. His Lancaster was shot down by flak in the same area at 2257 hrs. The fourth plane bound for the Sorpe flew too low over the Zuider Zee, hit the water and lost the 'mine'. It, too, returned early to Scampton. This left only McCarthy of that wave to attack the Sorpe. He eventually took off 34 mins late in the reserve aircraft, tickled the hedgerows of the continent at high speed and arrived unscathed at his target despite some uncomfortable exchanges with enemy gunners en route. The difficulty of diving over Langscheid village at one end of the Sorpe, flying along the crest of the dam, dropping Upkeep accurately in the middle (unspun) and clearing another hill beyond the dam became all too evident. There were, miraculously, no ground defences, though night-fighters might arrive at any moment. Nine times McCarthy flew along the dam and circled back before on the tenth run his bomb-aimer dropped Upkeep. It fell accurately, rolled down the earth bank on the water side and exploded 30 ft below the surface. Wallis's hope that the shock wave transmitted through the earth support would crack the dam would, however, prove groundless. The top of the dam crumbled. The wall did not crack. McCarthy left to fight his way back to base.

In the meantime, Gibson had reached the Moehne, though only eight of his wave had survived: Flight Lieutenant W. Astell succumbed to flak near Dorsten at 0015 hrs. At the Moehne, the attackers found three 20 mm flak guns mounted either on the towers or the dam wall. Each was capable of 120 rounds per minute at a range of 2,000 m, sufficient to hit the spit of land in front of the dam over which the Lancasters must turn to commence their attack run. Previously, they would dive to attain the necessary speed, hidden from the defenders, about 2,500 m beyond the spit and fly along the Moehne sleeve of the reservoir. Below the dam, three other flak guns were ideally placed to engage each Lancaster as it climbed to port after crossing the dam.

Gibson flew over the dam in a dummy run to test the defenders, then attacked himself. To ensure that Upkeep was released at exactly 425 yds from the target, the bomb-aimers used a triangular wooden sight especially fashioned to make use of the towers (639 ft apart) or appropriate marks on the clear vision panel in the nose of the Lancaster. Gibson attacked at 0028 hrs, but disappointingly his weapon exploded slightly in advance of the left-hand tower. Flight Lieutenant J.V. Hopgood went in next, was badly damaged and dropped the 'mine' late. Upkeep cleared the wall to land on the large power station below it on the air side. The self-destructive fuse did its job and the electricity plant went up in a gigantic blue flash – just as Hopgood's stricken aircraft crashed five miles to the north. Incredibly three men baled out at 700 ft. Two survived to become prisoners of war: one unscathed, the other with a broken back.

The third Lancaster to attack, flown by Flight Lieutenant H.B. Martin, was assisted by Gibson flying beyond the dam to engage the enemy gunners. Martin's Upkeep veered off course to explode near the left bank of the Moehne reservoir without cracking the dam. But, in exploding, it damaged the flak gun on the left-hand tower, which did not fire again that night.

Squadron Leader H.M. Young undertook the fourth attack, which Dugald Cameron's painting illustrates. Looking from the centre of the dam, Young approached unseen along the left-hand (Moehne) sleeve of the reservoir, skimmed the Delecke road bridge, and turned sharply to his right over the wooded spit (Hevers Berg) to fly straight ahead and line up his attack run. His navigator advised the pilot, according to practised procedure, to adjust his height so that the spotlights positioned in the front camera slot and rear of the bomb-bay met in a figure of eight forward of the leading edge of the starboard wing. Then the aircraft would be exactly 60 ft above the water.

With the moon behind him to port, Young dropped Upkeep which hit the water 200 yds after release and slowed to 55 mph behind the Lancaster as it lifted rapidly after shedding its burden. The red flare fired by the wireless operator as the aircraft crossed the dam after releasing Upkeep can be seen clearly. So too can artificial trees placed on the dam wall by the Germans in a vain attempt to conceal its nature before the operation. The flak gun knocked out by Martin is clearly shown on top of its tower. To the left, two other guns engage, one positioned on an extension beyond the second tower. The burning power station is clearly visible in the foreground. On Young's left, Martin provides additional protection, and Gibson circles to starboard. Young's front gunner can be seen engaging the enemy in the meadow below the dam, as the Lancaster flies over the compensating basin and begins to turn to port. Young's bomb-aimer is visible through the clear vision panel. Another small power station lies unseen to the right outside the area of the painting, as does the river Moehne down whose narrow valley floodwater would shortly surge.

Despite an enormous plume of water spurting skywards, when the water settled the dam apparently held. Flight Lieutenant D.J.H. Maltby began his attack. Suddenly, he realised that 'the crown of the wall was already crumbling' and that there was a 'breach in the centre of the dam'. Maltby therefore veered to port and dropped his Upkeep at 0049 hrs. Young had broken the Moehne Dam and Maltby enlarged the breach to 76 m × 20 m. 116 out of 132 million cubic metres of water would escape from the reservoir, and roar down the valley into the Ruhr, swelling it dangerously to cause extensive damage in that valley too.

The three remaining aircraft with Upkeep intact, Gibson and Young went on to the undefended Eder. There Flight Lieutenant D.J. Shannon and Squadron Leader H.E. Maudslay damaged the dam and Pilot Officer L.G. Knight dramatically and decisively breached it. A gap 70 m × 20 m released 154 million cubic metres of water to disrupt the Weser valley.

As Gibson and the first wave survivors headed back for England, the third wave flew along the southern inbound route. Pilot Officer L.J. Burpee scarcely crossed the enemy coast before being shot down over the German fighter base of Gilze Rijen in Holland. Pilot Officer W.H.T. Ottley, bound for the Lister, perished near Hamm, though his rear gunner escaped with extensive burns to become the third POW from Chastise. Flight Sergeant C.T. Anderson heading for the Diemel suffered mechanical failure and turned back short of the target. Like McCarthy, Flight Sergeant K.W. Brown found the Sorpe a difficult target, complicated by rising mist. He too needed several attack runs, some illuminated by flares, before dropping his 'mine' on the sixth. Although, like McCarthy, dropping Upkeep accurately, Brown failed to breach the dam. In truth, the method of delivery offered little hope of success. The last aircraft engaged in Operation Chastise was that of Flight Sergeant W.C. Townsend, which reported dropping Upkeep at the Ennepe at 0315 hrs without breaching the dam.

One aircraft (Hopgood) had been lost at a dam; five (Byers, Barlow, Astell, Ottley and Burpee) before their targets; and two (Young and Maudslay) on the way home. Fifty-three aircrew thus died; three were made prisoner.

Behind them, Chastise crews left a trail of destruction. Water flowed at a depth of 10 m through the Moehne valley, higher than the floods of 1890 which had prompted construction of the dam. Buildings up to 65 km from the dam were destroyed; and the Ruhr at its junction with the Rhine 148.5 km away ran 4 m above normal $25\frac{1}{2}$ hrs after the breach. The two generating stations at the Moehne, capable of 4,800 and 300 kW respectively had been destroyed; in Neheim-Huesten, where the Moehne flowed into the Ruhr, all 12 armament factories were damaged or destroyed.

Similar carnage occurred lower down the valley, where more factories, bridges and other buildings were devastated. One thousand two hundred and ninety-four people were killed and acres of valuable farming land ruined. The flood below the Eder was slower, due to the wider nature of the valley. But both power stations immediately beneath the dam were destroyed; and at one point a wave 12 m high and 8 m wide was reported in the valley. Towns like Kassel were inundated up to 2 m and considerable damage was done to the banks of rivers and compensating basins: 5½ km of the Weser's banks had to be rebuilt. At Karlshafen (139 km below the dam) on 18 May rowing boats were required to deliver milk supplies. Only 47 people died below the Eder, mainly because of a more effective warning system.

Extravagant claims of material damage were soon disproved by the enemy. Once the floods subsided, factories were cleaned, machinery restarted and bridges at least temporarily restored. The main effect, though, was on enemy morale. Thoroughly alarmed, German authorities diverted flak, balloons, searchlights, smokescreen apparatus and troops to many dams in addition to those attacked, besides installing extensive passive defences like fenders, torpedo nets and rows of acoustic mines. They also set about restoring the damaged Moehne and Eder walls. That both were repaired by September should not detract from the impact of Operation Chastise.

Eight out of 16 attacking aircraft were lost. Wallis was distraught, and could not be consoled by the assurance that 'percentage wise' it had all been worthwhile. Years later, when gently taxed about the losses, he replied abruptly: 'I don't want to talk about it'.

For their part in the operation, 34 of No. 617 Squadron aircrew were decorated, Gibson receiving the VC. Due to Upkeep's success, Wallis was encouraged to develop other special weapons – the earth-penetrating Tallboy and Grand Slam.

No. 617 Squadron RAF would continue the tradition of its first operation, by attacking the *Tirpitz*, helping to neutralise V1, V2 and V3 sites and bombing effectively road and rail communications. Under another of its commanders to earn a VC (Leonard Cheshire), the squadron pioneered a low-level marking technique which immensely increased main force bombing accuracy.

The 'Dambusters' Raid' may not have wrought the widespread, lasting damage to German industry, which its more enthusiastic protaganists claimed. But it gave the enemy a severe shock and it proved that precision targets could be hit. Pictures showing the Moehne dam and reservoir before and after the operation dramatically adorned newspapers and magazines throughout the English-speaking world including the United States within 48 hours. Stalin praised the results and called for full details of the operation. Leaflets dropped on occupied countries gave a much-needed boost to the civilian populations. At home, the First World War veteran Lord Trenchard declared: 'Wonderful work of Bomber Command is being recognised by all now'. Tersely and expressively, the Air Officer Commanding Coastal Command telegraphed: 'Well done Scampton. A magnificent night's work'.

Dugald Cameron's painting vividly and accurately portrays Squadron Leader H.M. Young carrying out his successful attack on the Moehne Dam, which began No. 617 Squadron's 'magnificent night's work', 16–17 May 1943.

THE FLYING UNITS OF THE
ROYAL AIR FORCE IN 1993
BADGES AND MARKINGS

From earliest times in WWI methods of aircraft identification were introduced. These consisted of geometic, numeric or alphabetic shapes and were devised as simple distinguishing marks for recognition purposes. Emblems were added so by the early 1930s the variety of markings was considerable and some form of standardisation was thought necessary. The position of Inspector of RAF Badges was introduced in March 1936 after which all badges had to be approved and conform to the official design. The content of the badge usually had some connection with the unit concerned and was contained in a standard frame, topped with a crown with the motto carried in a scroll at the base. All designs are registered at the College of Arms and have official heraldic descriptions. The aircraft identification marks were also formalised but the outbreak of war dictated that these colourful devices should be replaced by code letters or numerals and it was not until 1950 that the markings returned. Examples of the badges are contained in these pages and the colourful identification marks can be seen in many of the aircraft illustrations. With the squadron as the basic fighting unit within the RAF its achievements in battle are recognised by the awarding of Battle Honours. Some of these are displayed in true heraldic fashion on the Squadron Standard.

No. 111 Squadron

The Squadron Standard was granted by HRH King George VI and promulgated on
27 March 1952.
It was presented by Air Chief Marshal Sir Harry Broadhurst KCB KBE DSO DFC AFC,
Air Officer Commanding-in-Chief, Bomber Command, at North Weald on 30 April 1957.
A new Standard was presented by Air Chief Marshal Sir Patrick Hine KCB CBIM FRAeS at Leuchars on
2 August 1987 and the old Standard was laid up the same day in St Athernase Church, Leuchars.

FULL BATTLE HONOURS

PALESTINE 1917–1918   MEGIDDO   HOME DEFENCE 1940–1942
FRANCE & LOW COUNTRIES 1940   DUNKIRK   BATTLE OF BRITAIN 1940
FORTRESS EUROPE 1941–1942   DIEPPE   NORTH AFRICA 1942–1943   SICILY 1943
SALERNO   ANZIO & NETTUNO   GUSTAV LINE   FRANCE & GERMANY 1944

No. 1 Squadron

No. 1 Squadron was one of the first four squadrons in the Royal Flying Corps when it formed on 13 May 1912. Its origins, however, are in No. 1 Airship Company of the Air Battalion Royal Engineers which was formed in 1878. In 1914 the Squadron was reorganised as No. 1 Aeroplane Squadron and trained on various types before moving to France in March 1915 with Avro 504s and BE 8s. During the war it re-equipped with various other aircraft operating in the fighter, ground-attack and bomber escort roles over the Western Front. It returned to the UK in March 1919 but moved to India in 1920 and to Iraq in 1921 for policing duties in the desert but disbanded in November 1926. It reformed at Tangmere in February 1927 equipped with Siskins, receiving Furies in 1932 and Hurricanes in October 1938. At the outbreak of WWII the Squadron moved to France with the Advanced Air Striking Force but returned to the UK in May 1940 and took part in the Battle of Britain. It changed to the offensive role in 1941 flying fighter sweeps over France and then concentrated on night-fighter operations. Intruder sorties over enemy airfields early in 1942 were cut short when, in July, it converted to Typhoon IBs and flew in the fighter-bomber role on cross channel sweeps. The Spitfire IXs received in April 1944 were used with some success on anti-V1 patrols. Spitfire F21s were flown from May 1945 until the arrival of Meteor F3s in October 1946. These were, in turn, replaced by Meteor F4s, F8s, Hunter F5s, F6s and FGA9s and flown from Tangmere, Stradishall, Waterbeach and West Raynham. In August 1969 the Squadron began a new era in military aviation by converting to the Harrier, the world's first VTOL fighter. Based at Wittering in Cambridgeshire, No. 1 (Fighter) Squadron pioneered this revolutionary aircraft into front-line service and used it with outstanding success in the Falklands campaign in 1982. Initially equipped with the GR1 version which was subsequently upgraded to the GR3, it converted to the redesigned GR5 in November 1988 which, in turn, has been replaced in 1992 with the current GR7.

No. 2 Squadron

No. 2 Squadron was formed at Farnborough on 13 May 1912 as one of the original squadrons of the Royal Flying Corps. After training on a variety of types it moved to France in August 1914 as part of the British Expeditionary Force and later standardised on BE 2s. Flying from many locations in France during WWI the Squadron provided the vital reconnaissance information needed by the ground forces. After the war it operated in many areas but was based principally at Manston and later at Hawkinge. It flew Bristol Fighters, Atlas, Audax and Hector aircraft at this time and at the outbreak of WWII it was equipped with Westland Lysanders. It added some Tomahawks in August 1941 before re-equipping with Mustangs in April 1942. After D-Day the Squadron moved to France and advanced with the Army to the Netherlands where it received Spitfire XIVs in November 1944. After the war No. II (Army Co-operation) Squadron remained in Europe as a fighter-reconnaissance unit being part of the Second Allied Tactical Air Force. In December 1950 its Spitfire PR XIXs were replaced by Meteor FR9s which were supplemented with Meteor PR10s in March 1951. Swift FR5s were flown from March 1956 until replaced by Hunter FR10s in March 1961. Conversion to Phantom FGR2s took place at Bruggen in December 1970 but the Squadron moved to Laarbruch on 1 April 1971 where it re-equipped with Jaguar GR1s in April 1976. In January 1989 recce Tornado GR1As replaced the Jaguars and the Squadron relocated to Marham on 3 December 1991. These Tornados played an important part in the Gulf Operations. As well as integral engineering support, II (AC) Squadron has its own Reconnaissance Intelligence Centre (RIC) to interpret the Infra-Red Linescan imagery obtained by its aircraft. The Squadron badge contains the famous Wake Knot and the motto 'Hereward' is a combination of two old English words – 'Here' (Army) and 'Ward' (Protector).

No. 3 Squadron

Formed at Larkhill on 13 May 1912 from the Air Battalion of the Royal Engineers, No. 3 Squadron is the oldest aeroplane unit in the Royal Air Force. During WWI it pioneered aerial gunnery and photo-reconnaissance and was the first squadron to make a photo map of battle lines on the Western Front. In 1917, equipped with Camel aircraft, the Squadron took part in the first massed air-to-ground attacks in support of Allied troops. Between the wars No. 3 Squadron flew in India and also spent some time in the Sudan during the Abyssinian crisis in 1935/36. It flew Snipe, DH 9A, Walrus, Woodcock, Bulldog and Gladiator aircraft before equipping with Hurricanes in March 1938 when based at Kenley. Early in WWII the Squadron was in action over France and later took part in the Battle of Britain. It flew intruder operations over northern France and received Typhoon IBs in February 1943, which were replaced with Tempest Vs in February 1944. These aircraft were used in air defence with great success against the German V1 flying bombs, destroying 288 of these pilotless aircraft. In September 1944 a move was made to the continent of Europe and No. 3 (Fighter) Squadron became part of the Second Tactical Air Force. Continuing in the fighter role after the war the Squadron was equipped with Vampire, Sabre, Hunter and Javelin aircraft but in January 1961 its mission changed to that of a bomber unit when it received Canberra B(I)8s. Reverting to its traditional role No. 3 Squadron re-equipped with VTOL Harriers at Wildenrath in January 1971 and moved to Gütersloh in March 1977. The Harriers are frequently detached to off-station 'hides' where they can operate undetected and in comparative safety hidden from attacking aircraft. Their primary role is close support of ground forces armed with bombs, rockets and cannons. In May 1982 Squadron pilots saw action during the Falklands campaign and later manned a detachment at RAF Stanley for two months demonstrating the flexibility of the Squadron role, its aircraft and its personnel. In 1989 the Squadron converted to the new Harrier GR5 which has improved avionics, performance and weapons capability over the GR3 and in 1991 it further upgraded to the GR7. In November 1992 the Squadron moved to Laarbruch.

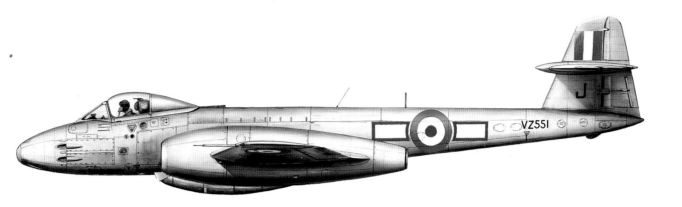

Meteor F8 – No. 1 (Fighter) Squadron
Tangmere – April 1951

Tornado GR1A – No. II (AC) Squadron
Laarbruch – May 1989

Harrier GR3 – No. 3 (Fighter) Squadron
Gütersloh – June 1986

NO. 4 SQUADRON

No. 4 Squadron formed at Farnborough in September 1912 and went into battle in France in August 1914. Soon standardising on BE 2Cs it provided air reconnaissance for the BEF upgrading to RE 8s in June 1917. Its close work with the British Army foreshadowed its present role of Army co-operation. In February 1919 it returned to the UK as a cadre but returned to strength in April 1920 at Farnborough with Bristol Fighters. It continued its role of Army support and, although based mainly in the UK, carried out tours of duty in Ireland and Turkey. Squadron aircraft of the time included the Bristol F 2B, Atlas, Audax, Hector and, by WWII, the Lysander. It was this type that 4 Squadron took to France in October 1939 in support of the BEF but was forced to retreat to Dunkirk. By May 1940, 4 Squadron Lysanders were the only BEF Air Component aircraft operating on the continent of Europe but soon returned to the UK. A period of coastal patrol and air-sea rescue duties ensued until the Squadron re-equipped with Mustangs and Tomahawks in April 1942, the role changing to tactical reconnaissance and fighter sweeps. A further change in task led to equipment with Spitfire PR XIs and Mosquito PR XVIs for high-level photo reconnaissance duties until the war's end. Since 1945 the Squadron has operated from numerous bases in Germany, firstly as a light bomber unit, then in the day-fighter role. Equipped with the Hunter FR10 fighter reconnaissance aircraft, it was based at Gütersloh during the sixties but, after moves to Jever and Wunstorf, it settled at Wildenrath in June 1970 to receive the first Harriers. The Squadron returned to Gütersloh in January 1977 operating in the twin role of attack and reconnaissance until losing its reconnaissance requirement on 31 May 1989. In November 1990 it re-equipped with the new Harrier GR7 and moved to Laarbruch in November 1992.

NO. 5 SQUADRON

No. 5 Squadron formed at Farnborough on 26 July 1913. It moved to France in September 1914 and in November achieved the distinction of being the first squadron to force down an enemy aircraft by gunfire. A variety of aircraft types were flown during the conflict including the BE 2C and RE 8. In 1918 the Squadron became associated with the Canadian Corps which is commemorated by the Maple Leaf as the Squadron's badge. After returning to England in September 1919 the Squadron disbanded on 20 January 1920 but was reformed in India on 1 April 1920 equipped with Bristol F 2B Fighters. It re-equipped with Wapitis in May 1931 for North West Frontier operations and later received Harts and Audaxes. On the outbreak of war in the Far East the Squadron moved to Calcutta for air defence duties. Based at Dum Dum, the Squadron flew Mohawks from December 1941 until moving to Assam in May 1942 for fighter escort duties. It re-equipped with the Hurricane IIC at Khargpur in June 1943 flying escort and ground-attack missions on the Japanese Front. Thunderbolts were received in September 1944 and these were put to good use providing close support for the Arakan Battle. No. 5 Squadron disbanded in India on 1 August 1947 but reformed at Pembrey in Wales on 11 February 1949. It flew Spitfires, Martinets, Oxfords, Beaufighters and Vampires on anti-aircraft co-operation duties but disbanded again on 25 September 1951. Reformed with Vampires at Wunstorf in Germany on 1 March 1952, the Squadron received Venoms in December 1952 and flew this type until disbanding on 12 October 1957. It reformed once more, this time at Laarbruch, and was equipped with Meteor NF11 night fighters. These were replaced by Javelin FAW5s in January 1960 and FAW9s in November 1962. The Squadron returned to the UK in October 1965 when it re-equipped with Lightning F6s at Binbrook as part of the UK Air Defence Force and flew this aircraft for 22 years. It is now equipped with the Tornado F3 which it received at Coningsby in May 1988. A combined No. 5/29 Squadron unit was the first RAF combat component in Saudi Arabia in August 1990 after the Iraqi invasion of Kuwait.

NO. 6 SQUADRON

No. 6 Squadron formed at Farnborough on 31 January 1914 and moved to France in October where it was soon engaged in reconnaissance duties. Flying BE2s, Martinsyde S 1s and Scouts the Squadron later had RE 8s and added artillery spotting and occasional bombing raids to its tasks. It remained in Europe after the war and moved to Iraq in April 1919 where it received Bristol Fighters flying policing patrols against rebels. The Squadron moved to Egypt in 1929 with a detachment in Palestine and received Fairey Gordons in 1931. These were replaced by Harts and Demons in 1935 and the Hawker Hardy in 1938. Gauntlets and Lysanders were added in August/September 1939 and by April 1940 the Squadron was fully equipped with the latter type. Flying on Army co-operation duties in the Western Desert, the Squadron also flew Gladiators, Hurricanes and Blenheims until redesignated a fighter unit in April 1942 equipped with Hurricane IIDs. This cannon-firing version was useful against tanks in the North African campaign but conversion to the rocket-firing Hurricane IVs in 1943 saw the Squadron flying from Italy against targets in the Balkans. In July 1945 the Squadron moved back to Palestine and began to receive Spitfire IXs in December but converted to Tempest F6s in December 1946 when based in Cyprus. A move to the Sudan was made in November 1947 and Egypt in May 1948 where Vampire FB5s arrived in 1949. Subsequent re-equipment included the Vampire FB9, Venom FB1 and FB4 with the Squadron moving between Egypt, Iraq and Jordan but a more permanent base at Akrotiri in Cyprus was found in April 1956. A change to the bomber role took place in July 1957 with the arrival of Canberra B2s and B6s in December 1959. Re-equipment with the specialised B16 was made in January 1962 which was flown until the Squadron disbanded on 13 January on 7 May 1969, the first time in the UK for 55 years, 6 Squadron was now flying Phantom FGR2s in the ground attack role. The Phantoms were replaced by Jaguar GR1s when the Squadron converted to that type at Lossiemouth in June 1974 and moved to its present Norfolk base of Coltishall in November 1974. Now part of the Coltishall Jaguar Wing, No. 6 Squadron was involved in Operation Desert Storm in 1991 and has since supplied aircraft and crews for Operation Warden.

Harrier GR7 – No. IV (AC) Squadron
Gütersloh – May 1991

Tornado F3 – No. 5 Squadron
Coningsby – December 1991

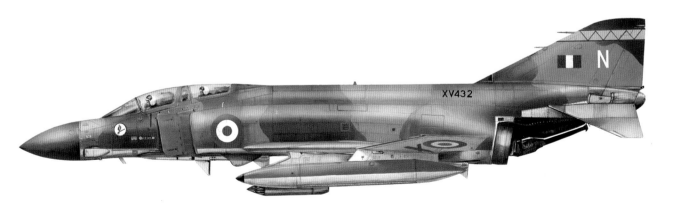

Phantom FGR 2 – No. 6 Squadron
Coningsby – December 1969

No. 7 Squadron

No. 7 Squadron formed at Farnborough on 1 May 1914, the last of the RFC squadrons to be formed before the outbreak of WWI. It was engaged in experimental flying until April 1915 when it deployed to France to perform reconnaissance and artillery spotting duties on the Western Front. After using a variety of aircraft it standardised on BE 2Cs during the summer of 1916. In July 1917 it received RE 8s, its equipment for the remainder of the war. The Squadron returned to the UK in September 1919 and disbanded on the last day of that year. After reforming on 1 June 1923 as a night-bomber squadron, the unit flew a succession of types: initially the Vimy, followed in 1927 by Virginias which were replaced by Heyfords in 1935, Wellesleys in 1937, Whitleys in 1938 and Hampdens in 1939. On 1 August 1940 No. 7 became the first squadron to be equipped with the Stirling, becoming operational on 10 February 1941. In 1942 the Squadron became part of the elite Pathfinder Force and converted to Lancasters in July 1943. For the rest of the war No. 7 Squadron spearheaded the night-bomber force in its attacks on Germany. In August 1949 it re-equipped with Lincolns which saw active service in 1954 against terrorist camps in the Malayan jungle. The Squadron joined the V-bomber force on 1 November 1956 when it was equipped with Valiants at Honington. It moved to Wittering in September 1960 before disbanding again on 30 September 1962. From 1 May 1970 until 5 January 1982 the Squadron flew Canberras in the target-towing role from St Mawgan. On 1 September 1982, 7 Squadron took on its present role as the Uk-based Chinook squadron, based at Odiham. While primarily operating in support of the United Kingdom Mobile Force and the Airmobile Brigade in Europe, the unit has supported operations in the Falkland Islands and during the evacuation of Beirut. More recently it was part of the Middle East Chinook Squadron in the Gulf conflict in 1991 and later flew relief missions to the Kurds in northern Iraq and Turkey.

No. 8 Squadron

Formed at Brooklands on 1 January 1915, No. 8 Squadron moved to France in April 1915 with BE2Cs for bombing and reconnaissance duties. The Squadron later specialised in tactical reconnaissance receiving FK 8s in August 1917. It returned to the UK in July 1919 prior to disbanding on 20 January 1920. On 18 October 1920, No. 8 Squadron reformed at Helwan in Egypt equipped with DH 9As but moved to Iraq in 1921 and to Aden in 1927 where it successively flew the Fairey IIIF and Vincent. At the outbreak of WWII the Squadron was flying Vincents and Blenheim Is and later in the war it received Blenheim IVs, Vs, Hudsons and Wellingtons before disbanding in Aden on 1 May 1945. No. 8 was reformed again on 15 May 1945 at Jessore in India equipped with Liberator VIs for special duties operations over Burma and South East Asia, but disbanded again on 15 November 1945. It reformed again at Khormaksar in Aden on 1 September 1946, now flying Mosquito FB6s and subsequently received Tempest F6s, Brigand B1s, Vampire FB9s, Venom FB1s and FB4s, Meteor FR9s and Hunter FGA9s and FR10s. The Squadron was based in the Middle East throughout this period, leaving Aden in September 1967 before disbanding at Sharjah on 15 December 1967. Operating in an entirely new role and based in the UK for the first time in over 50 years, No. 8 Squadron reformed at Kinloss on 8 January 1972 to fly in the airborne early warning role with the Shackleton AEW2 and moved to Lossiemouth on 17 August 1973. The Shackleton was the RAF's last operational piston-engined aircraft and on 1 July 1991 the Squadron re-equipped with the Sentry AEW1 at Waddington in Lincolnshire.

No. 9 Squadron

No. 9 Squadron formed at St Omer in Northern France on 8 December 1914. Initial tasks included artillery direction and reconnaissance but the Squadron soon became a specialist bomber unit. Returning to the UK in July 1919, it disbanded on 31 December. It reformed at Upavon as a night-bomber unit on 1 April 1924 equipped with the Vickers Vimy followed, in turn, by the Virginia and Handley Page Heyford. The Squadron received its first monoplane, the Wellington Mk I, in February 1939 and subsequently provided six crews for the first offensive operation of WWII. It later flew other marks of Wellington but re-equipped with the Lancaster in August 1942 and flew strategic bombing raids until the end of the war. Armed with 12,000 lb Tallboy bombs, the Squadron's Lancasters were involved in the raids which sank the German warship *Tirpitz* at Tromso on 12 November 1944. After the war the Squadron spent a short time in India before returning to Binbrook and converting to Lincolns. Canberras were received in May 1952 and these aircraft were used successfully against Malayan terrorists in 1956. The Squadron became part of the V-bomber force in April 1962 when it received Vulcan B2s at Coningsby, moving to Cottesmore in November 1964. In February 1969 9 Squadron moved to Akrotiri in Cyprus as part of the Near East Air Force before returning to Waddington in January 1975. On 1 June 1982 the Squadron moved to Honington in Suffolk to become the RAF's first operational Tornado squadron and deployed to Brüggen in Germany on 1 October 1986. The Squadron was deeply involved in Operation Desert Storm in the Gulf in 1991.

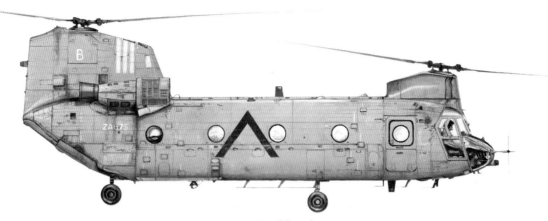

Chinook HC1 – No. 7 Squadron
Gulf – February 1991

Sentry AEW1 – No. 8 Squadron
Waddington – November 1990

Tornado GR1 – No. IX Squadron
Brüggen, Germany – February 1987

No. 10 Squadron

No. 10 Squadron formed at Farnborough on 1 January 1915 and moved to France in July for tactical reconnaissance and light bombing duties. It returned to the UK in February 1919 and disbanded on 31 December that year. No. 10 reformed at Upper Heyford on 3 January 1928 as a bomber squadron, initially equipped with Hyderabads. It later flew Hinaidis, Virginias, Heyfords and Whitleys prior to the outbreak of WWII. The Whitleys were used on night-bombing raids over Germany until replaced with Halifaxes in December 1941 and the Squadron continued with this type of aircraft as part of the main force of Bomber Command for the remainder of the war. On 7 May 1945 No. 10 Squadron transferred to Transport Command and took its Dakotas to India in October 1945 for transport duties, but disbanded on 20 December 1947. The Squadron reformed again at Oakington on 5 November 1948 and flew Dakotas until disbanding again on 20 February 1950. Reforming as a bomber unit at Scampton on 15 January 1953, 10 Squadron was now equipped with Canberra B2s and flew this aircraft in the Suez operation in 1956 before disbanding on 15 January 1957. It reformed again at Cottesmore on 15 April 1958 as part of the V-bomber force equipped with Victor B1s but disbanded once again on 1 March 1964. No. 10's current commission began on 1 July 1966 when it reformed at Brize Norton with VC10 C1 long-range transport aircraft to fly the trunk routes of RAF Transport Command. In the spring of 1982 the Squadron was involved in the Falklands campaign and later provided the transport for the return of the British hostages from the Middle East. The VC10s, which are currently being upgraded to C1K configuration, continue in service with the Squadron as part of RAF Strike Command.

No. 11 Squadron

Formed at Netheravon on 14 February 1915, No. 11 Squadron moved to France on 25 July equipped with the Vickers FB 5 Gunbus to become the first unit ever to be tasked specifically with fighter duties on the Western Front. During early combat engagements a Victoria Cross was won by Lieutenant G.S.M. Insall – the fourth to the Royal Flying Corps. The Squadron served as a fighter and reconnaissance unit during the war and re-equipped with Bristol Fighters in 1917. It served as part of the occupation force in Germany before returning to the UK in September 1919 and disbanding on 31 December 1919. 11 Squadron reformed at Andover on 13 January 1923 in the bomber role and moved to India on 29 December 1928 where it remained until the outbreak of WWII when it took its Blenheims to Singapore. In May 1940 it went to Egypt, but the following month moved to Aden to support the Abyssinian campaign. The Squadron remained in the Middle East until March 1942 when it arrived in Ceylon for operations against the Japanese. A further move to Burma took place in January 1943 where the Squadron received Hurricane IICs in September. Re-equipment with Spitfires took place in June 1945 and in May 1946 the Squadron moved to Japan as part of the occupation force where it disbanded in February 1948. The Squadron returned to service on 4 October 1948 when it reformed in Germany with Mosquito FB6s as a fighter-bomber unit. These aircraft were replaced with Vampire FB5s in August 1950 and the Squadron continued in fighter operations as part of the 2nd ATAF, re-equipping later with Venoms, Meteors and Javelins before disbanding again on 12 January 1966. It reformed with Lightning F6s on 1 April 1967 at Leuchars – its first UK base in 38 years – and moved to Binbrook in March 1972. With the Lightning it formed an element of the air defence of the UKADR and was the last RAF Lightning Squadron. On 1 July 1988 it re-equipped with the Tornado F3 at Leeming as the first element of the Leeming Air Defence Wing and adopted the unofficial title of 'North Yorkshire Air Defence'. Between August and December 1990 the Squadron deployed to Dhahran in Saudi Arabia as part of Operation Desert Shield – the multi-national effort to liberate Kuwait. With the Tornado the Squadron has returned to its original role as a two-seat fighter unit symbolised by the two eagles in the Squadron badge.

No. 12 Squadron

Formed at Netheravon on 14 February 1915, No. 12 Squadron moved to St Omer in France in September equipped with BE 2Cs for bombing and reconnaissance duties on the Western Front. From early 1916 the Squadron confined its activities to reconnaissance and re-equipped with BE 2Es at the end of that year. RE 8s were received in August 1917 when night bombing was added to its duties. After the Armistice the Squadron moved to Germany with the Army of Occupation and flew Bristol Fighters until disbanding at Bickendorf on 27 July 1922. No. 12 reformed as a bomber squadron at Northolt on 1 April 1923 equipped with DH 9As, but these were soon replaced by Fawns which, in turn, gave way to Foxes, Harts and Hinds. The Squadron moved to Andover in March 1924 remaining there until going to Aden in October 1935 for ten months. Fairey Battles were received in February 1938 and the Squadron took these aircraft to France at the outbreak of WWII. During this difficult time, Flying Officer D. E. Garland and Sergeant T. Gray were each posthumously awarded the Victoria Cross for their efforts in stemming the enemy advance. Back in England the Squadron continued attacks on Channel Ports but re-armed with Wellingtons in October 1940 and spent the remainder of the war as part of the main force of Bomber Command. Lancasters were received in November 1942 and were retained until the arrival of Lincolns in August 1946. Canberra B2s were taken on strength in April 1952, but these were replaced by the improved B6s in May 1955, being flown in the Suez campaign in 1956 from Malta. After returning to Binbrook the Squadron moved to Coningsby in July 1959 where it disbanded on 13 July 1961. It reformed there on 1 July 1962 flying the Vulcan B2 as part of the V-bomber force but stood down on 31 December 1967. No. 12 Squadron's current commission began on 1 October 1969 when it reformed at Honington as the RAF's first Buccaneer maritime strike squadron. It moved to its present base at Lossiemouth in October 1980. Although now a relatively old aircraft, the Buccaneer has been progressively updated adding new dimensions to its already broad range of capabilities, as was seen by the laser designating skills demonstrated in the Gulf War of 1991.

VC10 C1 – No. 10 Squadron
Brize Norton – July 1991

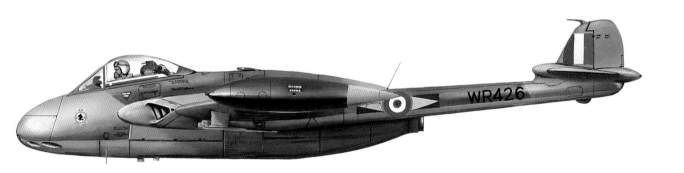

Venom FB4 – No. XI Squadron
Fassberg – June 1953

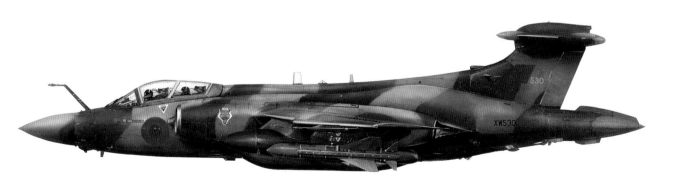

Buccaneer S2B – No. 12 Squadron
Lossiemouth – March 1988

No. 13 Squadron

No. 13 Squadron formed at Gosport on 10 January 1915 and operated BE 2Cs in France on Army co-operation duties (recce and artillery 'shoots') until it went over to the offensive with bombing raids during the Somme fighting being one of the first squadrons to bomb in formation. The Squadron received RE 8s in 1917 when the accent was on photographic duties. The Squadron flew Bristol Fighters, Atlas Is, Audaxes and Hectors during the inter-war years in England. The onset of WWII saw the squadron equipped with Lysanders which it took to France, before returning to England in May 1940. Between 1940 and the end of WWII the Squadron operated several different types of aircraft; Blenheim IVs, Blenheim Vs, Martin Baltimores and Bostons from various bases in Gibraltar, Algiers, North-West Africa, Italy and Greece. The Squadron then equipped with Mosquitos operating from Egypt in 1946. Its primary role was now photographic surveying to assist in the mapping of North Africa, Arabia and the Eastern Mediterranean and as far south as Southern Rhodesia. At the end of 1951 the first jet aircraft was received, the Meteor PR10, operating from Egypt and Cyprus. In 1956 the Squadron re-equipped with the Canberra which was used operationally in the Suez campaign. Several marks of Canberra were operated before transferring to Malta. In 1978 the Squadron returned to England where it was based at RAF Wyton until its disbandment in 1982. 13 Squadron reformed at RAF Honington on 1 January 1990 equipped with the Tornado GR1A operating in the tactical reconnaissance and ground-attack roles. During the 1991 Gulf War, 13 Squadron crews deployed to Dhahran and Tabuk in Saudi Arabia, operating in both the reconnaissance and laser designating roles.

No. 14 Squadron

No. 14 Squadron formed at Shoreham on 3 February 1915 and moved to Egypt with BE 2s for Army co-operation duties in Palestine, Arabia and the Western Desert. It flew a number of other types but re-equipped with RE 8s in November 1917 and retained these until January 1919 when it returned to the UK to disband the following month. Reformed on 1 February 1920 in Palestine by renumbering No. 111 Squadron at Ramleh, its Bristol F 2Bs patrolled Transjordan and Palestine for the next 20 years. DH 9As, Fairey IIIFs, Gordons and Wellesleys were later received and it was during this time that the Squadron gained its Arabic script motto meaning 'I spread my wings and keep my promise'. At the outbreak of WWII the Squadron moved to Egypt but soon returned to Amman. Conversion to Blenheims began in September 1940 and these were used on bombing operations over the Western Desert from Egyptian bases. Marauders were received in August 1942 which were used for bombing, minelaying and shipping reconnaissance missions. The Squadron moved to Algeria in March 1943 for anti-submarine duties but returned to the UK in October 1944 where it re-equipped with Wellington XIVs at Chivenor. It moved to Banff on 1 June 1945 to fly Mosquito VIs and transferred to Wahn on 31 March 1946 where it changed to Mosquito FB16s. It received Mosquito B35s in December 1947 and converted to Vampire FB5s in February 1951, Venom FB1s in May 1953 and Hunter F4s in May 1955. During this period the Squadron moved to Celle, Fassberg, Oldenburg, Ahlhorn and Gütersloh where it converted to Canberra B(I)8s in December 1962. On 30 June 1970 the Squadron moved to Brüggen and re-equipped with Phantom FGR2s, followed by Jaguar GR1s in April 1975 and Tornado GR1s in November 1985. In common with all Tornado GR1 squadrons No. 14 played a significant part in the Gulf War in 1991.

No. 15 Squadron

Formed on 1 March 1915 at South Farnborough with BE 2Cs, No. 15 Squadron moved to France in December. It performed reconnaissance, bombing and Army co-operation duties on the Western Front, receiving Bristol Scouts in 1916 and RE 8s in 1917. During the latter stages of the war it carried out ground-attack missions and in February 1919 it returned to the UK to disband at the end of the year. The Squadron reformed in March 1924 as part of the A&AEE at Martlesham Heath, and in June 1934 it moved to Abingdon as a bomber unit, receiving Harts which were superseded by Hinds in 1936 and Fairey Battles in 1938. In September 1939 the Squadron went to France, but returned to England in December when it re-equipped with Blenheim IVs. In November 1940 it received Wellington ICs for night-bombing operations, but converted to Stirling Is five months later. One such aircraft was presented to the Squadron by Lady MacRobert in memory of her three sons, all killed in the war, and named 'MacRobert's Reply'. Lancasters were flown from December 1943 and 15 Squadron continued as part of the main force of Bomber Command for the rest of the war. Based at Wyton from August 1946 it later flew Lincolns, Washingtons and Canberras from Marham, Coningsby, Cottesmore and Honington where it disbanded on 15 April 1957. It had deployed to Cyprus in 1956 for the Suez campaign. The Squadron reformed with Victor B1s at Cottesmore on 1 September 1958 but disbanded on 31 October 1964. Remaining in retirement until 1 October 1970, 15 Squadron reformed at Honington with Buccaneer S2s, moving to Laarbruch on 11 January 1971 as part of the strike force. On 31 October 1983 it became the first of RAF Germany's units to receive Tornado GR1s and these were flown in action during the Gulf War in 1991. It disbanded on 18 December 1991 but on 1 April 1992 the Tornado Weapons Conversion Unit (TWCU) was granted reserve status as No. 15 Squadron. The TWCU was formed at RAF Honington in Suffolk on 1 August 1981 and all British Tornado crews undergo weapons and tactics training with the unit before proceeding to their operational squadrons. The Unit's aircraft now display both the TWCU emblem, the crossed arrows and crown of St Edmunds with the vertical sword, and the white XV on the fin. The 'MacRobert's' Coat of Arms and the name continue to be carried by 15 Squadron aircraft.

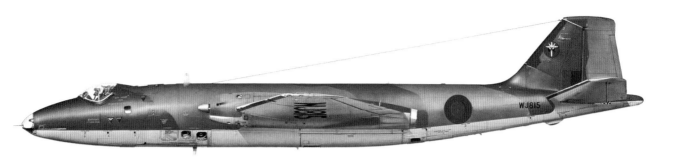

Canberra PR7 – No. 13 Squadron
Wyton – April 1979

Tornado GR1 – No. 14 Squadron
Brüggen – January 1989

Tornado GR1 – No. XV Squadron
Honington – April 1992

NO. 16 SQUADRON

No. 16 Squadron formed on 10 February 1915 at St Omer in France and subsequently became known as 'The Saints'. The Squadron's main role in the WWI was photographic reconnaissance and artillery ranging and it served on the Western Front in support of the Canadian Corps. Equipped with BE 2 and later RE 8 aircraft during the conflict, 16 Squadron returned to the UK in February 1919 and disbanded on 31 December. It reformed at Old Sarum on 1 April 1924 equipped with Bristol Fighters and during the next 15 years it flew in the tactical reconnaissance, photographic, gunnery and bombing roles with Atlas and Audax biplanes. Lysanders were received in June 1938 and the Squadron flew various marks of this aircraft during the early years of WWII on observation and bombing patrols. In April 1942 re-equipment with Mustangs commenced and these were used until Spitfire PR XIs arrived and the role changed to photographic reconnaissance. The Squadron's last war sortie was flown on 7 May 1945 when the liberation of Denmark was photographed. Between 1945 and 1958 the Squadron was successively equipped with Spitfire, Tempest, Vampire and Venom aircraft while based at Celle, Fassberg and Gütersloh, where it disbanded in June 1957. On 1 March 1958 'The Saints' reformed at Laarbruch, flying the Canberra B(I)8 interdictor and retained this aircraft until 6 June 1972 when it re-equipped with the Buccaneer S 2B. Still at Laarbruch as part of RAF Germany, No. 16 Squadron received the Tornado GR1 in March 1984 and became familiar with this aircraft's wide and varied capabilities, all of which were put to good use in the Gulf War of 1991. As part of the 'Options for Change' policy, No. 16 Tornado Squadron disbanded on 11 September 1991 but its number was applied in Reserve status to the Jaguar Operational Conversion Unit at Lossiemouth on 1 November 1991.

NO. 17 SQUADRON

No. 17 Squadron was formed at Gosport on 1 February 1915 equipped with BE 2 aircraft. The Squadron moved to Egypt in November 1915 and operated in support of troops over the Turkish lines in Sinai. It later flew a variety of aircraft in this region before disbanding at Constantinople on 14 November 1919. Reforming with Snipes on 1 April 1924 at Hawkinge as a fighter squadron, No. 17 received Woodcocks in March 1926 before moving to Upavon in October that year and later flew Gamecocks, Siskins, Bulldogs, Harts and Gauntlets before re-equipping with Hurricanes in June 1939. By then No. 17 (Fighter) Squadron was based at North Weald as part of the UK Air Defence Force and was soon engaged in operations against enemy intruders in WWII. Flying from Debden and Tangmere the Squadron was in the Battle of Britain before spending some time in northern Scotland in 1941. It was sent to the Far East in November 1941 and flew from bases in Burma until May 1942, when it moved to India and flew its Hurricane IIs in the air defence role. A change to ground-attack was made in February 1943 and the Squadron moved to Ceylon in August where it converted to Spitfire VIIIs in March 1944. It returned to India in November where it flew escort and ground-attack missions on the Burma Front. In June 1945 it was withdrawn to prepare for the invasion of Malaya but eventually moved to Japan with its Spitfire XIVs as part of the occupation force, disbanding on 23 February 1948. It reformed at Chivenor on 11 February 1949 as an Army co-operation unit flying Spitfire LF16Es, Oxford T2s, and Beaufighter TT10s but was again disbanded on 13 March 1951. On 1 June 1956 No. 17 (F) Squadron was reformed at Wahn in Germany in the photo-recce role equipped with Canberra PR7s and moved to Wildenrath on 3 April 1957, where it disbanded on 12 December 1969. Still in Germany and now equipped with Phantom FGR2s, the Squadron reformed on 16 October 1970 at Brüggen flying in the ground-attack role as part of the Second Tactical Air Force. Jaguar GR1s were flown in the same role from December 1975 until re-equipment with Tornado GR1s in March 1985 which were flown in the Gulf War in 1991.

NO. 18 SQUADRON

No. 18 Squadron Royal Flying Corps formed at Northolt on 11 May 1915 and operated with distinction during WWI in the fighter, reconnaissance, Army co-operation and night-bombing roles. Initially equipped with Vickers FB 5s, it later received FE 2Bs and DH 4s. Just before the Armistice it took delivery of DH 9As but returned to the UK in September 1919 and disbanded at the end of that year. It was not until 20 October 1931 that No. 18 Squadron reformed as a bomber unit at Upper Heyford equipped with Harts. Hinds were flown from April 1936 until Blenheim Is arrived in May 1939, which it took to France at the outbreak of WWII. The Squadron suffered heavy losses before returning to the UK in May 1940 where it regrouped and continued in the bombing of enemy targets in Europe. It moved to the Mediterranean in January 1942 but returned to the UK in May where it prepared for a permanent move to the North African Front in November. The Blenheim Vs were exchanged for Boston IIIs in March 1943 and these were superseded by Mk IVs and Vs in July 1944. No. 18 moved through Sicily to Italy where it was engaged in bombing operations in the Balkans and attacking coastal shipping. In September 1945 the Squadron moved to Hassani in Greece where it disbanded on 31 March 1946. No. 18 Squadron briefly emerged in Palestine flying Lancaster GR3s from 1–15 September 1946, but reformed at Butterworth in Malaya on 15 March 1947 with Mosquito Met 6s for meteorological work. It disbanded again on 15 November 1947 only to reform in the transport role at Waterbeach on 8 December 1947, equipped with Dakota C4s. These were flown in the Berlin Airlift before disbanding again on 20 February 1950. The Squadron reverted to the bomber role when it reformed with Canberra B2s at Scampton on 1 August 1953 and moved to Upwood in May 1955 where it disbanded on 1 February 1958. As part of the V-bomber force, No. 18 appeared at Finningley equipped with Valiant B1s on 16 December 1958, but disbanded yet again on 31 March 1963. On 27 January 1964 the Wessex Trials Unit at Odiham became No. 18 Squadron to operate in the tactical helicopter support role providing transport for the Army. It relocated to Gütersloh in January 1965 and, apart from a spell in the UK from January 1968 until August 1970, it has remained in Germany ever since. It disbanded with the Wessex in 1980, but re-equipped at Gütersloh with the Boeing-Vertol Chinook HC1 in 1981, the Squadron seeing service in the Falklands and Gulf campaigns using the versatile Chinook to its limits. In 1992 the Squadron added Puma HC1s to its strength and moved to Laarbruch in March 1993.

Jaguar T2 – No. 16 Squadron
Lossiemouth – July 1992

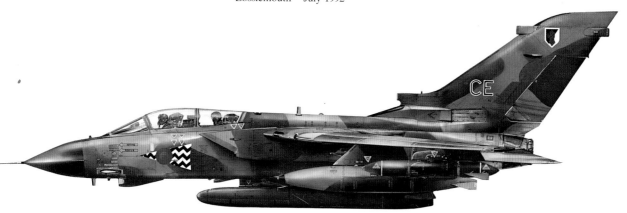

Tornado GR1 – No. 17 (Fighter) Squadron
Brüggen – October 1985

Chinook HC1 – No. 18 Squadron
Gütersloh – March 1985

NO. 19 SQUADRON

Formed at Castle Bromwich on 1 September 1915, 19 Squadron trained on various types of aircraft before moving to France with BE 12s in July 1916 as a fighter unit. Spads were received at the end of the year for fighter and ground-attack missions but these were replaced with Dolphins in January 1918. The Squadron returned to the UK in February 1919 and disbanded on the last day of that year having destroyed 281 enemy aircraft during the war. Reforming with Snipes at Duxford on 1 April 1923, No. 19 Squadron continued in the fighter role with Grebes, Siskins, Bulldogs and Gauntlets before being chosen as the first squadron to be equipped with Spitfires in August 1938. Covering the evacuation from Dunkirk, the Squadron later took part in the Battle of Britain. Mustangs were received in February 1944 and 19 Squadron provided close support for the Army during the invasion of Europe, but reverted to fighter escort duties later in the year. By the end of WWII the Squadron had accounted for 145½ enemy aircraft destroyed with 24 probables and 57 damaged. Spitfires were flown for a few months in 1946 but the Squadron's first twin-engined aircraft, Hornets, were taken on charge at Wittering in October. A move to Church Fenton was made in July 1947 where Meteors and, later, Hunters were flown until moving to Leconfield in June 1959. No. 19 Squadron received Lightning F2s in November 1962 and became part of No. 2 Allied Tactical Air Force in September 1965 when it moved to Gütersloh in Germany. Conversion to Phantom FGR2s started in July 1976 and the Squadron moved to Wildenrath in January 1977. The Squadron took part in Operation Granby/Desert Storm when it defended the Sovereign Base areas of Cyprus from August 1990 until the ceasefire in February 1991. On 9 January 1992 the Squadron disbanded but reappeared as a Reserve unit with No. 7 FTS at Chivenor on 23 September 1992, equipped with Hawks.

NO. 20 SQUADRON

No. 20 Squadron formed at Netheravon on 1 September 1915 and trained on various aircraft before moving to France in January 1916 with FE 2Bs for fighter and reconnaissance duties. Bristol Fighters were received in August 1917 and this type was flown for the remainder of the war. After the Armistice it remained in France until May 1919, when it moved to India to police the North-West Frontier area. The Bristol F 2Bs were retained until January 1932 when Wapitis arrived and these were replaced with Audaxes in December 1935. One flight equipped with Blenheim Is in June 1941, but the Squadron was completely equipped with Lysanders in December for Army co-operation, reconnaissance and liaison duties in support of Chinese forces. Hurricane IIDs arrived in February 1943 and these were used for anti-tank sorties as well as tactical reconnaissance. Rocket-firing Hurricanes were used from November 1944 but the Squadron converted to Spitfire VIIIs at Bangkok in September 1945 and Spitfire XIVs in December, prior to returning to India in May 1946. It received Tempest F2s in June 1946 but disbanded at Agra on 1 August 1947. The Squadron reformed at Llanbedr on 11 February 1949, but moved to Valley on 19 July flying in the anti-aircraft co-operation role but relinquished this task on 16 October 1951. Reformed again at Jever in Germany on 1 July 1952 with Vampire FB9s, 20 Squadron changed to the day-fighter role in October 1953 with the arrival of Sabre F4s, having moved to Oldenburg in July 1952. Hunter F4s replaced the Sabres in November 1955 which, in turn, were exchanged for Hunter F6s in August 1957 but the Squadron disbanded on 30 December 1960. It reformed on 3 July 1961 at Tengah with Hunter FGA9s in the ground-attack role and in 1969 it added four Pioneer CC1s for forward air control duties, but disbanded again on 13 February 1970. No. 20 Squadron reformed at Wildenrath in Germany on 1 December 1970 with Harriers, but re-equipped with Jaguar GR1s at Brüggen on 1 March 1977 flying this type until 30 June 1984, when it received Tornado GR1s at Laarbruch. After playing a major role in the Gulf War of 1991 20 Squadron disbanded on 1 September 1992 but transferred the same day in Reserve status to the Harrier OCU at Wittering.

NO. 22 SQUADRON

No. 22 Squadron formed at Gosport on 1 September 1915 and trained on a variety of aircraft before standardising on FE 2Bs which it took to France to join the British Expeditionary Force in April 1916. The Squadron's tasks were reconnaissance and surveillance of enemy movements behind the Western Front. It received Bristol F 2Bs in July 1917 with fighter missions now becoming the main role. After the Armistice in 1918 the Squadron returned to the UK in September 1919 and disbanded at Ford in December. No. 22 Squadron reformed at Martlesham Heath on 24 July 1923 and was attacked to the Aeroplane and Armament Experimental Establishment flying Gamecock, Jockey, Tutor, Bulldog, Hart and Fairey Postal Monoplane aircraft. In May 1934 the Squadron re-equipped with Vildebeest torpedo bombers and was based at Donibristle moving to Malta in October 1935, but returned to Donibristle in August 1936. It moved to Thorney Island in March 1938 where it received Beauforts in November 1939 and later flew from North Coates, Thorney Island and St Eval before relocating to the Far East in March 1942. Now flying from bases in Ceylon the Squadron was engaged on convoy escort and anti-submarine patrols until re-equipping with the Beaufighter X in June 1944 which was used for rocket delivery in addition to torpedo attack. A move to the Burma Front began in December 1944 in the ground attack role. The Squadron disbanded at Gannavaram in India on 30 September 1945, but reformed at Seletar in Singapore on 1 May 1946 equipped with Mosquito FB6s. This commission was short-lived as 22 Squadron disbanded again on 15 August 1946. Reformed as a search and rescue squadron at Thorney Island on 15 February 1955, it was initially equipped with Sycamore helicopters but Whirlwind HAR2s arrived in June. The headquarters moved to St Mawgan on 4 June 1956 with detachments at Martlesham Heath (later moving to Felixstowe), Valley and Thorney Island. The turbine-powered HAR10 replaced the earlier Whirlwinds from August 1962 and the present Wessex HC2s were received in May 1976. The Squadron's headquarters and engineering facilities, latterly at Finningley, are now at St Mawgan and detached flights operate from Chivenor, Leuchars, Valley and Coltishall. Although not a corporate part of 22 Squadron, the Search and Rescue Training Unit operates from Valley alongside 'C' Flight.

Lightning F2A – No. 19 (Fighter) Squadron
Gütersloh – April 1974

Harrier T4 – No. 20 Squadron
Wittering – September 1992

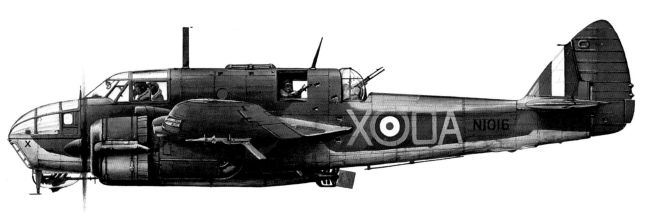

Beaufort I – No. 22 Squadron
North Coates – April 1941

NO. 23 SQUADRON

No. 23 Squadron formed at Gosport on 1 September 1915 and flew a number of different aircraft before equipping with FE 2Bs in January 1916. It moved to France in March 1916 where it flew fighter-reconnaissance patrols, adding ground attack with the arrival of Spads in February 1917. Conversion to Dolphins took place in March 1918 and these aircraft were used with considerable success for the remainder of the war. The Squadron returned to the UK in March 1919 and disbanded on 31 December. Reforming with Snipes as a fighter squadron at Henlow on 1 July 1925, No. 23 received Gamecocks in April 1926 which it displayed to good effect in the late 1920s. Bulldogs arrived in April 1931 and in October, a flight of Harts was added for two-seat trials. The Squadron finally parted with biplanes in December 1938 when it re-equipped with Blenheim IFs for night-fighter operations. In WWII early duties centred around shipping protection and in 1940 intruder missions were also flown. In March 1941 Havocs arrived which were supplemented by Bostons in February 1942, but the Squadron converted to Mosquito IIs in July and relocated to Malta in December. It flew from Mediterranean bases on missions over Sicily, Italy, Tunisia and southern France. In June 1944 the Squadron returned to the UK where it was attached to Bomber Command with Mosquito VIs on intruder missions from East Anglian airfields. It disbanded on 25 September 1945 but reformed at Wittering with Mosquito NF30s on 11 September 1946, upgrading to NF36s in February 1947. Vampire NF10s arrived in September 1951 which were replaced with Venoms in November 1953 and Javelins in April 1957. During this time the Squadron was based at Coltishall, Church Fenton, and Horsham St Faith but a move to Leuchars in March 1963 also marked the change to single-seat aircraft when Lightning F3s arrived in August 1964. The improved F6 was flown from May 1967 until the Squadron disbanded on 31 October 1975. It reformed at Coningsby with Phantom FGR2s on 1 December and transferred to Wattisham on 25 February 1976. It deployed to Stanley in the Falkland Islands on 1 April 1983 and moved to Mount Pleasant airfield on 21 April 1986. On 1 November 1988 it re-equipped with Tornado F3s at Leeming as part of the UK Air Defence Force. The Squadron provided air cover in the early stages of Operation Granby in 1990.

NO. 24 SQUADRON

No. 24 Squadron formed at Hounslow Heath on 1 September 1915 and, after training, moved to France in February 1916, its DH 2s being the first of the type on the Western Front. It re-equipped with DH 5s in May 1917 and SE 5As in December 1917. The Squadron flew fighter and ground-attack missions during the war and returned to the UK in February 1919 disbanding at Uxbridge on 1 February 1920. Inactivity was short lived, however, as 24 Squadron reformed on 1 April 1920 at Kenley as a communications and training unit. It was initially equipped with Bristol Fighters but gained a wide selection of aircraft over the following 24 years. It moved to Northolt in January 1927 and to Hendon in July 1933 and flew such types as Wapiti, Fairey IIIF, Audax, Tomtit, Tutor, Hart, Flamingo, Ensign, Proctor, Anson, Oxford, Tiger Moth, Magister, DH 86, DH 89A, Wellington and Dakota. Early in WWII it received many of the civilian aircraft impressed into the RAF, which were used for general communications work on the Continent and later within the UK. The smaller aircraft were acquired by other units and 24 concentrated on longer distance route flying. By 1943 it had received Yorks to add to the work already being done by the Dakotas, although this type was temporarily phased out of 24 Squadron service. Dakotas returned in February 1944 and soon almost fully equipped the Squadron. In 1945 it became a VIP transport unit and moved to Bassingbourn in February 1946, where it acquired Lancastrians in June. It moved to Waterbeach in June 1949 and Lyneham in November 1950 where Hastings were received the following month. This aircraft became the standard equipment for the next 18 years and was flown worldwide on the many and varied transport duties within the RAF. The Squadron moved to Topcliffe in February 1951, Abingdon in May 1953 and to Colerne in January 1957. In January 1968 conversion to the Lockheed C-130H Hercules took place and this coincided with a move back to Lyneham on 9 February 1968. Since then 24 Squadron has been involved in all the major operations throughout the world in both military and humanitarian roles. In particular its efforts in the Falklands and Gulf campaigns were most significant.

NO. 25 SQUADRON

No. 25 Squadron formed at Montrose on 25 September 1915 and flew FE 2Bs on fighter reconnaissance patrols over the Western Front. It re-equipped with DH 4s in June 1917 and then concentrated on long-range photo-reconnaissance and high-level bombing. After the Armistice it remained in Germany but returned to the UK in September 1919. It re-equipped with Snipes at Hawkinge on 1 February 1920 and left for Turkey in September 1922, returning to Hawkinge in October 1923. It received Grebes in October 1924, Siskins in May 1929, Furies in February 1932, Demons in October 1937 and Gladiators in June 1938. It equipped with Blenheim IFs in December 1938 and Blenheim IVFs in August 1939 and became the first squadron to fly with air interception radar. At the beginning of WWII the Squadron flew night-fighter missions from various bases in England receiving Beaufighters in October 1940 and Mosquitos in October 1942. Intruder missions were flown from February 1943 and the Squadron was later involved in bomber support sorties over Germany against enemy night fighters. Latterly flying Mosquito 30s from Castle Camps, it moved to Boxted in January 1946 and to West Malling in September, where it received Mosquito NF36s. Vampire FB5s were received in February 1951 followed by NF10s in July and Meteor NF12s and NF14s in March/April 1954. These were taken to Tangmere in September 1957 where the Squadron disbanded on 23 June 1958. It reformed at Waterbeach on 1 July 1958 with Meteor night fighters and converted to Javelin FAW7s in March 1959. On 23 October 1961 it moved north to Leuchars, where it disbanded on 30 November 1962. No. 25 Squadron reformed at North Coates on 1 October 1963 as a Bloodhound ground-to-air missile unit but reverted to manned flight on 1 October 1989 when it equipped with Tornado F3s at Leeming. In the autumn of 1990 it formed part of the air defence wing in the Gulf.

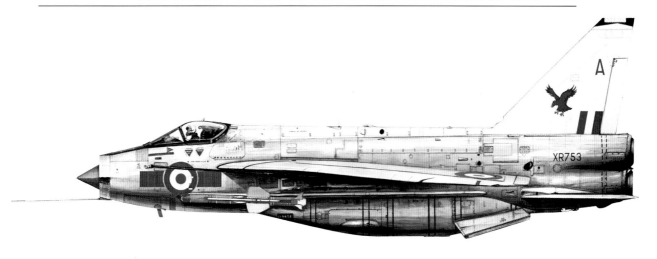

Lightning F6 – No. 23 Squadron
Leuchars – September 1975

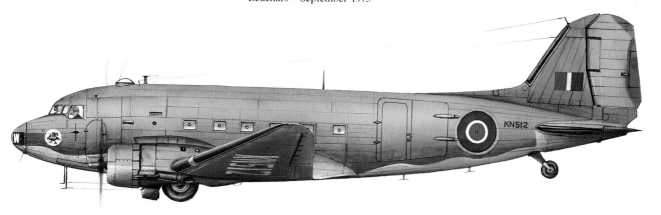

Dakota IV – No. 24 Squadron
Hendon – September 1945

Tornado F3 – No. 25 Squadron
Leeming – April 1990

NO. 27 SQUADRON

No. 27 Squadron formed at Hounslow Heath on 5 November 1915 equipped with the Martinsyde G 100 Elephant. The Squadron moved to France in March 1916 where it concentrated on reconnaissance and bombing operations and took part in many battles – notably the Somme, Ypres and Amiens. During this period it was also responsible for two outstanding pieces of development flying, namely high-altitude reconnaissance and all-weather flying. In September 1917 it received DH 4s and DH 9s in May 1918, but the Squadron returned to the UK in March 1919 and disbanded in January 1920. Reformed in India with DH 9As on 1 April 1920, it operated on the North West Frontier between the wars, receiving Wapitis in May 1930. These aircraft were retained until October 1940, by which time some Harts and Tiger Moths had been added for training purposes. Re-equipment with Blenheim IFs was effected in November 1940 and the Squadron moved to the Far East in February 1941. During the fall of Singapore it was almost wiped out by the invading Japanese but some survivors escaped to India where the Squadron was reformed in September 1942 to fly Beaufighter VIs. Mosquito IIs arrived in April 1943 and were followed by Mk VIs in December but rocket-firing Beaufighter Xs took over in March 1944 and with No. 47 Squadron, it formed a strike wing which concentrated on ground attack against targets in Burma. In April 1945 the Squadron became an air-jungle rescue unit, but was disbanded on 1 February 1946. No. 27 Squadron reformed at Oakington on 27 November 1947 and flew Dakotas in the transport role. It participated in the Berlin Airlift but disbanded again on 1 November 1950. The Squadron reformed at Scampton on 15 June 1953 with Canberra B2s in the light-bomber role. After four years and participation in the Suez crisis it was disbanded in December 1956 and did not reform until 1 April 1961 when it equipped with Vulcan B2s at Scampton, operating first in the Blue Steel and later in the medium-bomber role, but disbanded on 29 March 1972. It reformed again on 1 November 1973 with Vulcan SR2s in the maritime radar reconnaissance role, which ended when the Squadron disbanded on 31 March 1982. Reformed at Marham on 1 May 1983, 27 Squadron became the third UK Tornado squadron operating in the all-weather strike/attack role, principally in the European theatre. In 1991 the Squadron played a valuable part in the Gulf War.

NO. 28 SQUADRON

No. 28 Squadron formed at Gosport on 7 November 1915 and spent its first 18 months as a training unit. It moved to Yatesbury in July 1917 and re-equipped with Camels, moving to France in October. Before becoming involved on the Western Front it was hastily sent to serve in Italy, where it spent the remainder of the war flying offensive patrols in support of the Army. It returned to the UK in February 1919 and disbanded on 20 January 1920. It reformed again on 1 April 1920 by the renumbering of No. 114 Squadron at Ambala in India and flew Bristol Fighters on the North West Frontier as an Army co-operation unit. Wapitis were received in September 1931 and Audaxes in June 1936, with Lysanders arriving in September 1941. These aircraft were taken to Burma in January 1942 in an effort to stem the Japanese advance through Malaya, but the country was soon overrun. No. 28 Squadron reformed at Lahore in March 1942 still with Lysanders and continued in the Army co-operation role until receiving Hurricanes in December 1942. These were used on tactical reconnaissance operations over Burma from January 1943 and continued until the end of the war in the Far East. The Squadron received Spitfires in July 1945 and moved to Penang in Malaya in November. After a spell at Kuala Lumpur from April 1946, the Squadron moved to Tengah in February 1947 where it re-equipped with Spitfire FR18s. On 11 May 1949, the Squadron's long association with Hong Kong began when it moved to Kai Tak operating in the Colony from this airfield and Sek Kong until a temporary disbandment from 31 December 1966 until 1 April 1968. During this period 28 Squadron flew Vampire FB5s and FB9s, Venom FB1s and FB4s, and Hunter FGA9s. Conversion to helicopters coincided with the break in service and Whirlwind HAR10s were flown from 1 April 1968 until replaced by Wessex HC2s in January 1972. These aircraft provide transport and search and rescue facilities in the Hong Kong area.

NO. 29 SQUADRON

Formed at Gosport on 7 November 1915, No. 29 Squadron moved to France in March 1916 for fighter and escort duties over the Western Front. After the War it was reduced in size and returned to the UK to disband on 31 December 1919. No. 29 reformed at Duxford on 1 April 1923 as a fighter squadron equipped with Snipes. It later flew Grebes, Siskins and Bulldogs, but the arrival of Demons in March 1935 marked the change to a two-seat squadron. Blenheims were received in December 1938, these being used for shipping patrols and night-fighter duties during the early part of WWII, the Squadron later taking part in the Battle of Britain. Beaufighters arrived in 1941, but these were exchanged for Mosquitos in May 1943 for use on night intruder missions. The Squadron was the first to be equipped with the Meteor NF11 in August 1951, at Tangmere. It moved to Acklington in January 1957 and converted to Javelin FAW6s in November, before moving again, this time to Leuchars, in July 1958. Uprated Javelin FAW9s were flown to Cyprus in February 1963 and used in the Zambian detachment in 1965/66. No. 29 Squadron returned to the UK in May 1967 and re-equipped with Lightning F3s at Wattisham. The Squadron moved to Coningsby on 31 December 1974 with Phantom FGR2s in the air defence role. On 1 January 1980 the Squadron increased in size and took on additional responsibilities as one of the two UK Maritime Air Defence Squadrons. In 1982, 29 Squadron supported the Falklands Campaign and provided the first land-based fighters at Port Stanley. In April 1987 it became the first operational squadron to be equipped with the Tornado F3 and was one of two air-defence squadrons to see active service in the Gulf War of 1991 having previously been in the region with the joint No. 5/29 Squadron in August 1990.

Wapiti IIA – No. 27 Squadron
Kohat – March 1934

Hunter FGA9 – No. 28 Squadron
Kai Tak – July 1965

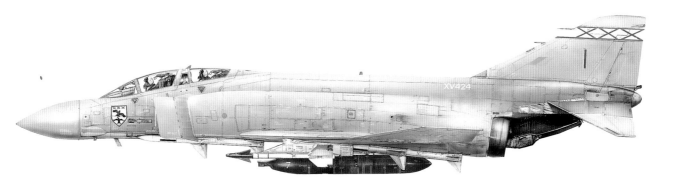

Phantom FGR2 – No. 29 (Fighter) Squadron
Coningsby – April 1981

NO. 30 SQUADRON

No. 30 Squadron formed at Farnborough in October 1914 for service in Egypt but did not adopt its number until 24 March 1915. Its principal task was the defence of the Suez Canal but a detached flight at Basra was formed in August 1915 and eventually the whole Squadron moved to this area flying reconnaissance and bombing missions plus occasional supply dropping. A variety of aircraft types were flown, but 30 Squadron settled on RE 8s in October 1917. It was reduced to a cadre in April 1919 while based in Baghdad, but brought back to full strength in February 1920 when it became a permanently based unit. DH 9As were received in January 1921 and flown until replaced by Wapitis in April 1929. The Hardy was in use from April 1935, and Blenheims from January 1938, but just before the outbreak of WWII the Squadron moved to Ismailia to fly bomber escorts over the Western Desert. In November 1940 it moved to Greece and was redesignated a fighter squadron in March 1941. It transferred to Crete in April but retired to Egypt in May, when it re-equipped with Hurricanes which were used for night air defence of Alexandria. The Squadron returned to the desert in October but in February 1942 it sailed for Ceylon, arriving on 6 March. It used its Hurricanes for the air defence of Colombo and continued in this role until February 1944 when it moved to the Burma Front. In July it re-equipped with Thunderbolts and resumed operations in October as a fighter-bomber unit. Tempests were flown from June 1946 and the Squadron disbanded on 1 December. It reformed at Oakington on 24 November 1947 as a transport squadron equipped with Dakotas, which were used in the Berlin Airlift before re-equipment with Valettas in November 1950, which coincided with a move to Abingdon. Further moves were made to Benson in May 1952 and to Dishforth in April 1953. Beverleys were taken on strength in April 1957 which were taken to Eastleigh in Kenya in November 1959. The Squadron moved to Muharraq in September 1964 in support of British Forces in the Gulf where it disbanded on 6 September 1967. No. 30 Squadron reformed at Fairford on 10 June 1968 equipped with the Hercules C1 and moved to its present base at Lyneham on 24 September 1971. It was heavily engaged in the Falklands campaign in 1982 and provided the Hercules tankers for the journey to the South Atlantic. In 1990/91 it was equally committed to the Gulf War.

NO. 31 SQUADRON

No. 31 Squadron formed at Farnborough on 11 October 1915 for service in India. 'A' Flight left on 27 November and arrived at Risulpur on 26 December, being joined by two more Flights in May 1916. Flying the BE 2C and a few Henri Farmans, the Squadron flew Army co-operation patrols over the North West Frontier for the remainder of the war. Bristol F 2Bs were received in September 1919 and flown until the arrival of Wapitis in February 1931. In April 1939 the role was changed to bomber-transport when Valentias were taken on strength. 'Impressed' DC 2s arrived in April 1941, which later replaced the ageing Valentias. DC 3s and Dakotas were flown from April 1942 and 31 Squadron rendered service in the transport field from bases in India in support of the 14th Army in Burma. It disbanded in Java on 30 September 1946, but re-appeared the next day by the renumbering of No. 77 Squadron at Mauripur. Still flying Dakotas, it continued with transport duties in India until disbanding on 31 December 1947. It next appeared at Hendon on 19 July 1948 when the Metropolitan Communications Squadron was renumbered and now had Ansons and Proctors on strength. Devons were added in 1950, but the unit reverted to its former title on 1 March 1955 and 31 Squadron was established at Laarbruch in Germany equipped with Canberra PR7s in the photo-recce role as part of 2 ATAF. Disbanding on 31 March 1971, the Squadron reformed at Brüggen on 7 October 1971 with Phantom FGR2s as a strike/ground-attack unit, converting to Jaguar GR1s in December 1975. Another change of type took place in July 1984 when the first Tornado GR1s arrived and the Squadron was fully operational on 1 November. Now part of the Brüggen strike wing, 31 Squadron's aircraft and crews were part of the RAF Tornado force in the Gulf War of 1991.

NO. 32 SQUADRON

No. 32 Squadron RFC formed at Netheravon on 12 January 1916. After training it equipped with DH 2 biplanes and deployed to France on 28 May. Re-equipping with DH 5s and, later SE 5s, the Squadron remained in France until the end of the war, returning to the UK in March 1919 to disband on 29 December. No. 32 Squadron reformed at Kenley on 1 April 1923 with Sopwith Snipes and during the inter-war years became one of the RAF's premier fighter squadrons. In 1924 it re-equipped with Grebes which, in turn, gave way to Gamecocks, Siskins and Bulldogs. In September 1932 the Squadron moved to Biggin Hill, where it received Gauntlets in 1936, but in October 1938 it converted to Hurricanes. Its first action in WWII was in May 1940 when seven enemy aircraft were destroyed over Dunkirk. The Squadron acquitted itself with honour during both the Battle of France and the Battle of Britain after which it was employed on convoy patrol duties and took part in the Dieppe Raid. In November 1942 it moved to North Africa and, equipped with Spitfires, participated in operations in Algeria, Tunisia, Italy, Greece and Palestine. During WWII the Squadron added a further seven Battle Honours to the five gained in WWI. After the war 32 Squadron remained in the Middle East, moving to Nicosia in 1948. In March 1949 it converted to Vampires subsequently flying Venoms, it served in Iraq, Malta, Jordan and the Canal Zone. In 1957 it returned to Cyprus to operate Canberras in the light-bomber role changing to the communications role in February 1969 when it assumed the VIP/Communications duties of the Metropolitan Communications Squadron based at Northolt. It now operated Pembrokes, Bassets, Sycamores, Andovers and, later, Whirlwinds and is presently equipped with Andovers, BAe 125s and Gazelles. The Squadron operates within the UK into Europe, Africa, North America and the Caribbean, the Middle East and the Far East.

DH 9A – No. 30 Squadron
Hinaidi – June 1928

Tornado GR1 – No. 31 Squadron
Dhahran – March 1991

BAe 125 CC3 – No. 32 Squadron
Northolt – March 1989

No. 33 Squadron

No. 33 Squadron formed at Filton on 12 January 1916 equipped with BE 2s and moved to Yorkshire in March for home-defence duty against airship raids. It received FE 2s in November 1916, Bristol F 2Bs in June 1918 and Avro 504Ks in August 1918. During the war 33 Squadron flew from airfields in Lincolnshire and Yorkshire but disbanded on 13 June 1919. Reforming at Netheravon on 1 March 1929, the Squadron was initially equipped with Horsley IIs, but received Harts in February 1930 which it took to Egypt in October 1935 during the Abyssinian crisis. Gladiators arrived in February 1938 and on 1 March its role changed to that of a fighter squadron, operating in Palestine on policing duties. The Squadron returned to Egypt in May 1939 and was soon engaged in patrols over the Western Desert. Hurricane Is were received in September 1940 for ground attack sorties and in early 1942 the Squadron received Hurricane IIBs and Cs. A few Spitfire Vs arrived in January 1943, but it was the end of the year before this type fully equipped the Squadron. In April 1944, 33 Squadron returned to the UK and received Spitfire IXs. It covered the invasion of Europe flying ground-attack sorties from airfields on the Continent. Conversion to Tempest Vs was made in England, but the Squadron returned to Europe in February 1945 as part of Second TAF. Spitfire XVIs arrived in November 1945, by which time the Squadron was based in Germany, and these were replaced by Tempest F2s in October 1946 moving with the Squadron to Changi in the Far East in August 1949. Hornets were received in April 1951, the Squadron disbanding on 31 March 1955. It reformed at Driffield on 15 October 1955 with Venom NF2s, but disbanded again on 3 June 1957, reforming in the same role with Meteor NF14s at Leeming on 30 September 1957. 33 Squadron continued as an air defence night-fighter unit flying Javelin FAW7s and 9s from July 1958 until disbanding on 17 November 1962. It reformed as a Bloodhound surface-to-air missile unit at Butterworth in Malaya on 1 March 1965 and this operation lasted until 30 January 1970. Back in the air again, 33 Squadron reformed at Odiham on 14 June 1971 equipped with Puma HC1s as a helicopter support unit. It has commitments within NATO, supports the Pumas in Belize and was fully committed to the Gulf operations in 1991 as part of the RAF Puma (Middle East) Squadron.

No. 39 Squadron

No. 39 Squadron formed at Hounslow on 15 April 1916 as a home-defence unit equipped with BE 2s. It added BE 12s in August 1916, but re-equipped with Bristol F 2Bs in September 1917 and moved to France in November 1918, where it disbanded later that month. It reformed on 1 July 1919 at Biggin Hill but remained as a cadre until February 1923 when, at Spittlegate, it received DH 9As as a day-bomber unit. Departing for India in December 1928 the Squadron flew patrols on the North West Frontier with Wapitis, which were exchanged for Harts in November 1931. The Squadron was transferred to Singapore in January 1938 where it received Blenheims in August 1939, but returned to India in April 1940 on its way to Egypt, arriving at Heliopolis in May. Flying from Aden the Squadron carried out bombing raids on Italian East Africa, but in November, it returned to Egypt converting to Marylands in January 1941. With these aircraft 39 Squadron began strategic reconnaissance missions in April and added some Beauforts to its strength in August for anti-shipping duties, which gradually became the Squadron's main role. Beaufighter Xs were received in June 1943 to cover the central Mediterranean from North African bases and, later, Sardinia. Marauders replaced the Beaufighters in February 1945, and the Squadron moved to the Sudan in October where it flew some Mosquito VIs from February 1946 until disbanding on 8 September 1946. It reformed at Nairobi on 1 April 1948 equipped with Tempest F6s converted to Mosquito night-fighters at Fayid in Egypt on 1 March 1949 for defence of the Suez Canal. Meteor NF13s were flown from March 1953 until 1 July 1958, when the role was changed to photographic reconnaissance with Canberra PR3s. The uprated PR9 was received in October 1962 and some PR7s were flown between October 1970 and March 1972. The Squadron moved to Wyton on 30 September 1970, where it retained the same role until disbanding on 28 May 1983. Its activities were rekindled on 1 July 1992 by changing the designation of No. 1 PRU at Wyton with Canberra PR9s, to No. 39 (1 PRU) Squadron.

No. 41 Squadron

No. 41 Squadron formed at Gosport on 14 July 1916 and trained on a variety of aircraft. Equipped with FE 8 fighters, it moved to St Omer in France in October for duties over the Western Front. DH 5s were received in July 1917 but SE 5As were flown on ground-attack, fighter and escort duties from November 1917 until the Squadron disbanded in the UK on 31 December 1919. No. 41 Squadron reformed at Northolt on 1 April 1923 equipped with Snipes as a fighter unit. Siskins were received in May 1924 and Bulldogs in October 1931, but the Squadron took Demons to Aden in October 1935. Returning to Catterick in September 1936, it received Fury IIs in October 1937 and re-equipped with Spitfire Is in January 1939. Flying defensive patrols in the early months of WWII, the Squadron moved to Hornchurch in the late spring of 1940 to cover the evacuation from Dunkirk and take part in the Battle of Britain. After this it flew offensive sweeps over France receiving later marks of Spitfire as the war progressed. The Squadron added fighter-bomber attacks, shipping reconnaissance and bomber escort to its fighter activities and later became involved in the anti-V1 flying bomb attacks. In October 1944 it joined the Second TAF and flew from airfields in Belgium as part of No. 125 Wing for the remainder of the war. On 1 April 1946 it moved to Dalcross and transferred with Spitfire F21s to Wittering two weeks later. As an instrument flying training unit based at Church Fenton it flew Harvards and Oxfords from August 1947 but, in June 1948, it reverted to a fighter squadron, equipping with Hornets. These were replaced by Meteors in January 1951, Hunter F5s in August 1955 and Javelins in February 1958 flying from Biggin Hill, Coltishall and Wattisham where it disbanded on 6 December 1963. From 1 September 1965 it operated as a Bloodhound surface-to-air missile unit at West Raynham, but returned to manned flight when reformed at Coningsby on 1 April 1972 as a Phantom FGR2 fighter-reconnaissance ground-attack unit. Jaguar GR1s were received at Coltishall on 1 April 1977 and No. 41 (Fighter) Squadron took these aircraft to war in the Gulf in 1991. It was also part of the combined Jaguar detachment in Operation Warden.

Puma HC1 – No. 33 Squadron
Odiham – November 1986

Hart – No. 39 Squadron
Risalpur – April 1932

Jaguar GR1A – No. 41 (Fighter) Squadron
Coltishall – February 1989

NO. 42 SQUADRON

No. 42 Squadron formed at Filton on 1 April 1916 and, after training, moved to France in August with BE 2D and BE 2E aircraft for reconnaissance duties over the Western Front. In April 1917 the Squadron re-equipped with RE 8s and moved to northern Italy to cover the Austro-Italian Front, but returned to France in March 1918. In February 1919 it came back to the UK and disbanded at Netheravon on 26 June 1919. No. 42 Squadron reformed at Donibristle on 14 December 1936 from 'B' Flight of No. 22 Squadron equipped with Vildebeest IIIs and became one of only two torpedo strike units in the UK. After a number of moves the Squadron settled at the new airfield at Thorney Island, but relocated to Bircham Newton on 12 August 1939. It exchanged its Vildebeests for Beauforts in April 1940 with which it specialised in anti-shipping and mine laying along the coasts of northern Europe. On 18 June 1942 it left for the Far East but delayed in the Middle East for operations there until December, when it finally arrived in Ceylon. It converted to Blenheim Vs in India in March 1943 but re-equipped with Hurricane IICs in October for ground-attack duties, adding Mk IVs in November 1944. A change to Thunderbolt IIs took place in July 1945, and the Squadron disbanded at Meiktala in Burma on 30 December 1945. It reformed with Beaufighter Xs at Thorney Island on 1 October 1946 as part of Coastal Command's Strike Wing, but disbanded again on 15 October 1947. No. 42 Squadron's current commission started on 28 June 1952 when it reformed at St Eval in Cornwall equipped with Shackleton MR1s for maritime reconnaissance duties. The MR2s were received in April 1954 and the Squadron moved to St Mawgan on 8 October 1958, where MR3s were accepted in December 1965. It converted to the Nimrod MR1 in April 1971 and received the upgraded MR2 in 1983. No. 42 (Torpedo Bomber) Squadron has been involved in numerous overseas detachments and operations including Operation Corporate in 1982 and Operation Granby in January 1991. Disbanded as a front-line unit on 1 October 1992, No. 42 (TB) Squadron continues as the Nimrod OCU No. 42 (Reserve) Squadron, formerly No. 236 OCU, at Kinloss in Scotland.

NO. 43 SQUADRON

No. 43 Squadron formed at Stirling on 15 April 1916 within the Royal Flying Corps and trained on BE 2Cs and Avro 504Ks. It moved south in August and equipped with Sopwith 1½ Strutters before going to France in January 1917 for fighter and reconnaissance duties. It later flew Camels and Snipes before returning to the UK in August 1919 and disbanding on 31 December. The Squadron reformed at Henlow on 1 July 1923 equipped with Snipes, but replaced these with Gamecocks in 1926 before moving to Tangmere in December of that year. Siskins were received in 1928 and Furies in 1931 and the first monoplane, the Hawker Hurricane, arrived in November 1938. Initially engaged in defensive duties, the Squadron covered the Dunkirk evacuation and later took part in the Battle of Britain when it was credited with the destruction of 43 enemy aircraft. After the Dieppe raid and the North African invasion the Squadron re-equipped with Spitfires in March 1943 and joined the Desert Air Force to cover the landings in Sicily, Anzio and Salerno. It later covered the landings in southern France, but returned to Italy in October 1944 and concentrated on fighter-bomber duties for the remainder of the war. After being part of the occupation forces in Austria and Italy the Squadron disbanded on 16 May 1947. The 'Fighting Cocks' reformed at Tangmere on 11 February 1949 equipped with Meteors and moved to Leuchars in November 1950 where, in August 1954, it became the first squadron to fly the Hawker Hunter. It moved to Cyprus in June 1961 and to Aden in March 1963, where it disbanded on 14 October 1967. The Squadron reformed again at Leuchars on 1 September 1969 equipped with Phantom FG1s as part of the UK Air Defence Force and flew this aircraft for nearly 20 years. In July 1989 it started to re-equip with Tornado F3s and was declared operational on 1 July 1990. It deployed to the Gulf in November 1990 as part of the RAF's air defence component and returned after the cessation of hostilities in March 1991.

NO. 45 SQUADRON

No. 45 Squadron formed at Gosport on 1 March 1916 and, after training, moved to France in October. Flying Sopwith 1½ Strutters on fighter patrols it re-equipped with Nieuport 12s in April 1917 and Camels in July. In December 1917 the Squadron moved to northern Italy for offensive patrols and ground-attack operations, returning to France in September 1918 for the remainder of the war. It came back to the UK in November 1919 disbanding the following month. It reformed in Egypt on 1 April 1921 flying DH 9As but soon received Vimys which were replaced by Vernons in 1922 for bomber and transport duty. The Squadron moved to Iraq for policing duties in May 1922 disbanding on 17 January 1927 only to reform on 25 April equipped with DH 9As. Again flying on policing duty in Egypt and Palestine, it changed to Fairey IIIFs in September 1929, Harts in September 1935 and in November some Vincents were added, but complete re-equipment with Wellesleys was carried out by December 1937. These were exchanged for Blenheim Is in June 1939 and the Squadron moved to the Western Desert before the outbreak of war. It operated in the bomber role until being sent to Burma in February 1942 before going to India where it equipped with Vengeance dive bombers in December. It converted to Mosquito VI fighter-bombers in February 1944, but problems with this wooden aircraft prevented its operational use until September. In May 1946 the Squadron moved to Ceylon and in November received Beaufighter Xs. These were used in Operation Firedog in Malaya in 1948, and the Squadron moved to Kuala Lumpur in May 1949 where Brigands were taken on charge. In December it went to Singapore and Hornet F3s were flown from January 1951. A move to Butterworth in 1955 coincided with the arrival of Vampire FB9s. Venom FB1s took over in December and were flown until November 1957 when the Squadron converted to Canberra B2s at Tengah, disbanding on 13 January 1970. Reformed at West Raynham on 1 August 1972 with Hunter FGA9s in the ground-attack role, 45 Squadron provided tactical weapons experience until 4 June 1976. The number came to the fore again on 1 December 1983 when it was allocated 'shadow' status for the Tornado Weapons Conversion Unit at Honington, retaining this position until 31 March 1992. On 1 July 1992 the Multi-Engine Training Squadron at Finningley was redesignated No. 45 (Reserve) Squadron, flying Jetstream T1s.

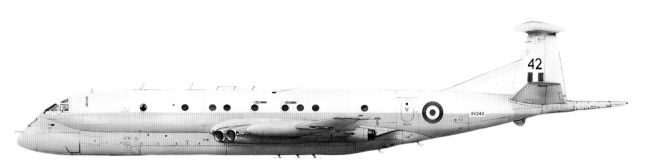

Nimrod MR1 – No. 42 (Torpedo Bomber) Squadron
St Mawgan – July 1978

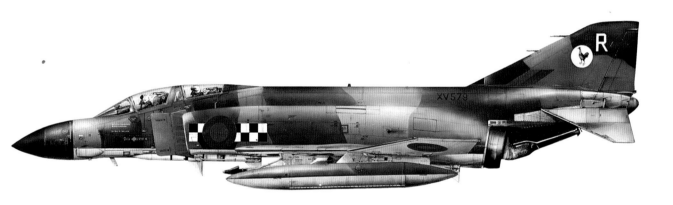

Phantom FG1 – No. 43 (Fighter) Squadron
Leuchars – June 1975

Jetstream T1 – No. 45 (Reserve) Squadron
Finningley – August 1992

No. 47 Squadron

No. 47 Squadron formed at Beverley on 1 March 1916 as a local air defence unit but left for Greece in September. Flying Bristol Scouts in the reconnaissance and fighter roles it supported the Allied armies in Macedonia. Other types flown included DH 2s, Vickers FB 19s, SE 5As, FK 8s, Bristol M1Cs and DH 9s. In April 1919 the Squadron moved to southern Russia where it was redesignated 'A' Squadron in October. Flying DH 9 day-bombers, the Squadron reformed at Helwan on 1 February 1920 replacing them with DH 9As in 1921. It moved to Khartoum in October 1927 where it received Fairey IIIFs in December. It co-operated with the Sudan Defence Force in policing the area and from February 1929 some of the IIIFs were fitted with floats and operated from the Nile. Some of the Gordons which arrived in January 1933 were similarly fitted. Three flights were equipped with Vincents in July 1936 with Wellesleys starting to take over in June 1939. The Squadron began bombing raids on Italian airfields in Eritrea in June 1940 and moved to Egypt in December 1941. Flying anti-submarine patrols off the Egyptian coast the Squadron converted to Beaufort torpedo-bombers in July 1942. In June 1943 it moved to Tunisia where it changed to Beaufighter Xs using them on anti-shipping strikes and as torpedo-carrying fighters. It moved to Libya in October but left for India in March 1944 to join a Mosquito strike wing. The tropical climate caused problems with this aircraft's wooden construction and Beaufighters returned in November. Ground-attack operations over Burma started in January 1945 and modified Mosquitos arrived in February. After the war the Squadron remained in the Far East flying from Butterworth, disbanding on 21 March 1946. It reformed in Palestine with Halifaxes on 1 September 1946 in the airborne support role and moved to Fairford at the end of the month. A move to Dishforth in September 1948 coincided with the arrival of Hastings transport aircraft which were used in the Berlin Airlift. From May 1949 the Squadron started flying Transport Command's scheduled routes and moved to Topcliffe in August 1949. It went to Abingdon in May 1953 where, in March 1956, it became the first squadron to fly the Beverley. The Squadron disbanded on 31 October 1967 but returned to operations again on 25 February 1968 when it reformed at Fairford with the Hercules moving to Lyneham in September 1971. With this versatile aircraft it has flown in all the major operations since that date and participated in many of the humanitarian and relief missions organised by the RAF.

No. 51 Squadron

No. 51 Squadron formed at Thetford on 15 May 1916 as a home defence unit. Initially flying a mixed group of BE 2s and BE 12s from East Anglian bases, it later specialised on night-fighter duties with FE 2Bs. In January 1918 it received Avro 504Ks for training and later added some Camels to its strength. Having operated in the defence of London and the Midlands, the Squadron disbanded on 13 June 1919. It reappeared on 5 March 1937 when 'B' Flight of No. 58 Squadron at Driffield was renumbered 51 Squadron. Equipped at first with Virginia Xs and Anson Is, it received Whitleys in February 1938 and trained in the bomber role. On the first night of WWII the Squadron aircraft were over Germany on a leaflet raid, but real action started in May 1940 when it took part in the first attack on a land target, bombing the seaplane base at Hornum. In May 1942 the Squadron was transferred to Coastal Command flying Whitley Vs on patrols over the Bay of Biscay but a reversion to Bomber Command coincided with the arrival of Halifax IIs in November 1942. Halifax IIIs arrived in January 1944 and 51 Squadron continued in No. 4 Group for the remainder of the war. In May 1945 the Squadron was transferred to Transport Command and equipped with Stirling Vs for trooping flights to the Far and Middle East. Yorks were added from February 1946 and fully equipped the Squadron from January 1948 being used in the Berlin Airlift. The Squadron disbanded on 30 October 1950 and reformed again at Watton on 21 August 1958 in another new role, now carrying out routine radar and communications research. Initially equipped with Canberra B2s, B6s and Comet 2Rs in Signals Command, it moved to Wyton in March 1961 and transferred to Bomber Command in March 1963. Nimrod R1s were received in July 1971 and these are used on the Squadron's special duties.

No. 54 Squadron

No. 54 Squadron formed on 16 May 1916 at Castle Bromwich and moved to France for fighter duties in December flying Pups for bomber escort and balloon attack duties. Camels were received in November 1917 when ground-attack was added to the Squadron's role. In January 1919 the aircraft were transferred to No. 151 Squadron and No. 54 returned to the UK where it disbanded on 25 October. It reformed at Hornchurch on 15 January 1930 as a fighter squadron equipped with Siskins, but these were soon replaced by Bulldogs in April, with Gauntlets arriving in September 1936. Gladiators were received in April 1937 and Spitfire Is in March 1939 and at the outbreak of war the Squadron went on patrol over Kent on defensive duties. In the spring of 1940 the Squadron was providing air cover for the evacuation at Dunkirk and was soon involved in the Battle of Britain. For the next year and a half it took part in offensive sweeps over France and convoy patrol duties and had progressed to Spitfire Vs. In June 1942 the Squadron left for Australia, arriving in Richmond in August. Equipped with Spitfire VCs it flew on air defence duties in north west Australia. Conversion to Spitfire VIIIs was made in March 1944 and the Squadron remained in Australia, disbanding in Melbourne on 31 October 1945. It reformed at Chilbolton on 15 November 1945 with Tempest IIs which were replaced by Vampire F1s in October 1946, F3s in April 1948 and FB5s in October 1949 by which time the Squadron was based at Odiham. Meteor F8s were received in April 1952 and the swept-wing Hunter F1s arrived in March 1955. These were upgraded to F4s in September 1955 and F6s in January 1957 with the Squadron moving to Stradishall in July 1959. Hunter FGA9s were received in March 1960 and taken to Waterbeach in November 1961 and West Raynham in August 1963. The fighter role was changed to ground-attack in March 1960 when 54 Squadron transferred to No. 38 Group as part of Transport Command's Offensive Support Wing. On 1 September 1969 the Squadron re-equipped with Phantom FGR2s at Coningsby and changed to Jaguars at Lossiemouth in March 1974, moving to its present base at Coltishall on 8 August 1974. The Squadron continues in its specialist ground-attack role which it demonstrated to good effect in the Gulf War in 1991.

Hercules C3P – No. 47 Squadron
Lyneham – August 1982

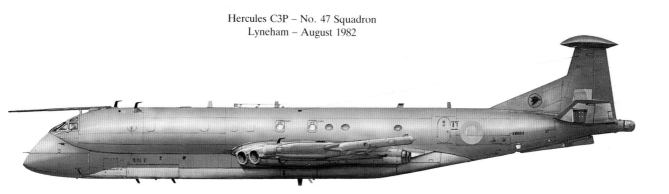

Nimrod R1P – No. 51 Squadron
Wyton – May 1987

Jaguar GR1A – No. 54 (Fighter) Squadron
Bahrain – February 1991

No. 55 Squadron

No. 55 Squadron formed at Castle Bromwich on 27 April 1916 as a training squadron moving to France in March 1917 as the DH 4 day-bomber unit. In June 1918 it began strategic raids on targets in Germany as part of the Independent Force and operated on mail-carrying duties after the end of the war. It returned to the UK in January 1919 and disbanded at Shotwick on 22 January 1920. Inactivity was short-lived as the Squadron reformed on 1 February 1920 at Suez flying DH 9s and began 19 years of air-control operations against raiding tribes in Iraq. It re-equipped with Wapitis in 1930 and Vincents in 1937, with Blenheim Is arriving in March 1939. The Squadron moved to Ismailia in Egypt in August 1939 and, after flying shipping patrols in the Gulf of Suez, it began bombing raids on targets in Libya. In September 1941 it transferred to anti-shipping sweeps, but converted to Baltimores in May 1942 and resumed its bombing activities in support of the 8th Army. It progressed through Libya, Tunisia and Italy, where it received Bostons in October 1944. The Squadron moved to Hassani in Greece on 20 September 1945, re-equipping with Mosquito FB26s in June 1946, disbandment coming on 1 November 1946. No. 55 Squadron reformed at Honington on 1 September 1960 equipped with Victor B1s as part of the V-bomber force. In May 1965 it moved to Marham, where it became the first Victor in-flight refuelling squadron. Initially flying modified Victor K1s, it received K2s from July 1975. During the Falklands campaign in 1982, No. 55 flew unarmed reconnaissance sorties over South Georgia as well as numerous vital tanking missions in support of the Vulcan raids against Port Stanley. Nimrod maritime patrols and Hercules supply missions were also refuelled. In 1990 and 1991, 55 Squadron Victors were in action again supporting the coalition forces in the Gulf.

No. 56 Squadron

No. 56 Squadron formed at Gosport on 9 June 1916 and flew a variety of aircraft before moving to France in April 1917 with SE 5s. For the remainder of the war the Squadron flew patrols over the Western Front and returned to England in December 1919, disbanding on 22 January 1920. Only 12 days later, on 1 February 1920, 56 Squadron reappeared in Egypt equipped with Snipes, but disbanded again on 23 September 1922. The Squadron reformed at Hawkinge on 1 November 1922 and was equipped successively with Snipes, Grebes, Siskins, Bulldogs, Gauntlets and Gladiators. Receiving Hurricanes at North Weald in May 1938, the Squadron was detached to France in May 1940 before taking part in the Battle of Britain. Typhoons were delivered in September 1941 and the Squadron was the first to fly this type on ground-attack and anti-shipping missions. Spitfires were flown from April until June 1944 when it re-equipped with Tempest Vs these aircraft being used to good effect against V1 flying bombs over southern England. The Squadron moved to Belgium in September 1944 and, for the remainder of the war, was engaged in armed reconnaissance sweeps over Germany. Returning to England on 1 April 1946, 56 Squadron was equipped with Meteor F3s but these, in turn, were replaced with Meteor F4s, Meteor F8s, Swifts, Hunters and Lightnings, with which type the Squadron formed 'The Firebirds' aerobatic team. After a period in Cyprus as part of the Near East Air Force, the Squadron returned to the UK in July 1976 to re-equip with the Phantom FGR2 at Wattisham, as part of the UK Air Defence Force. The Phantom era ended on 1 July 1992 when 56 (Reserve) Squadron moved to Coningsby to become the Tornado F3 OCU.

No. 57 Squadron

No. 57 Squadron was formed at Copmanthorpe on 8 June 1916 and moved to France in December for fighter and reconnaissance duties. In May 1917 it re-equipped with DH 4s for high-altitude and photo-recce operations. The Squadron suffered heavy losses between 1917 and 1918 such that, at one period, the entire flying personnel were casualties but, with replacements from various other sources, it managed to remain in action. This period inspired the Phoenix badge and motto. In May 1919 DH 9As were received prior to returning to the UK to disband on 31 December 1919. No. 57 Squadron reformed at Netheravon on 20 October 1931 in the bomber role, flying Hawker Harts. It re-equipped with Hinds in May 1936 and with Blenheims in March 1938. The Squadron moved to France in September 1939 but returned in May 1940. The following month it moved to Lossiemouth where it was attached to Coastal Command for shipping strikes off Norway. The Squadron returned to East Anglia in November 1940 where it equipped with Wellingtons and joined No. 3 Group for attacks on Germany. Lancasters were received in September 1942 and this type was flown for the remainder of the war. Lincolns were received in August 1945, B-29 Washingtons in May 1951 and Canberras in May 1953, which were flown until the Squadron disbanded on 9 December 1957. On 1 January 1959, 57 Squadron reformed at Honington as part of the V-bomber force, equipped with Victor B1s. A move to Marham in December 1965 signalled a new role and 57 became a flight refuelling squadron on 1 June 1966, re-equipping with Victor K2 tankers in 1976. 57 Squadron moved to Ascension Island on 18 April 1982 and played a major part in the operations to recover South Georgia and the Falkland Islands, but returned to Marham after the conflict, where it disbanded in June 1986. On 1 July 1992, No. 242 OCU at Lyneham was renumbered No. 57 (Reserve) Squadron and is responsible for the training of all RAF Hercules crews.

Victor K2 – No. 55 Squadron
Marham – June 1992

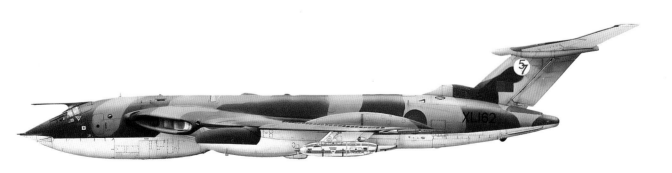

Lightning F1A – No. 56 (Fighter) Squadron
Wattisham – July 1963

Victor K2 – No. 57 Squadron
Marham – January 1979

No. 60 Squadron

No. 60 Squadron formed at Gosport on 30 April 1916 taking Moranes to France in May. It soon suffered heavy losses and re-equipped with Nieuport fighters. In July 1917 it received SE 5s for fighter and ground-attack duties and returned to the UK in February 1919 to disband on 22 January the following year. The Squadron reformed in India on 1 April 1920 equipped with DH 10As which were exchanged for DH 9As in April 1923 and Wapitis in July 1930 and was engaged in policing duties on the North West Frontier. Just before the outbreak of WWII it converted to Blenheims for use on coastal patrols. In February 1941 the Squadron moved to Burma, adding some Buffalos in July for a few months, before it returned to India in March 1942 to concentrate on bombing raids. It converted to Hurricane IIs in August 1943 using these for ground-attack duties. Thunderbolts arrived in July 1945 but in September the Squadron moved to Java in support of the Army. Spitfire FB 18s were flown from January 1947 on fighter-bomber sorties during the Malayan emergency when some Spitfire PR XIXs were added. A move to Tengah in Singapore was made in January 1950 where conversion to Vampire FB 5s took place in December and FB 9s arrived in February 1952. Venom FB 1s were flown from April 1955, the FB 4 version equipping the Squadron from April 1957 until the arrival of Meteor NF14s in October 1959. Now operating in the all-weather role, 60 Squadron equipped with Javelin FAW9s in July 1961 and operated this type in the Far East theatre until disbanding on 30 April 1968. The RAF Germany Communications Squadron was renumbered 60 Squadron on 3 February 1969 and flew Pembrokes from Wildenrath in the transport field until disbanding again on 31 March 1992. Initially, some Heron C4s were also flown and latterly a few Andovers were added to the unit's strength. Reformed in an entirely new guise on 1 June 1992, No. 60 Squadron now flies Wessex HC2s in the helicopter support role from Benson.

No. 70 Squadron

No. 70 Squadron formed at Farnborough on 22 April 1916. Flying as a fighter unit it was equipped with Sopwith 1½ Strutters and was fully established in France by the end of July. It also flew reconnaissance and bombing missions but re-equipped with Sopwith Camels in July 1917 for use in fighter and ground-attack duties for the rest of the war. It returned to the UK in September 1919 and disbanded on 22 January 1920. It reappeared on 1 February by the renumbering of No. 58 Squadron at Heliopolis in Egypt and flew Handley Page 0/400s and Vimys in the bomber-transport role. A move was made to Iraq in December 1921, where it re-equipped with Vernons in November 1922 and later Victorias and Valentias. Back in Egypt in August 1939, 70 Squadron did not receive Wellingtons until September 1940 with which attacks were made on targets in Libya, Italy and Greece. The Squadron moved forward with the advancing Army into Italy and replaced its Wellingtons with Liberators in January 1945. In October 1945 it returned to the Middle East and disbanded there on 31 March 1946. Two weeks later it reformed in Egypt with Lancasters only to disband once more on 1 April 1947. Reformed as a transport unit on 1 May 1948, No. 70 Squadron was now flying Dakotas from Kabrit in Egypt. Valettas arrived in January 1950 and the Squadron moved to Nicosia in Cyprus in December 1955, where it re-equipped with Hastings. It participated in the Suez campaign in 1956, dropping parachute troops. In July 1966 it moved to Akrotiri where, the following year, it converted to Argosy C1s. The Hercules began to equip the Squadron from November 1970 but conversion was not complete until February 1972. On 1 February 1975 the Squadron returned to the UK to be based at Lyneham from where it has operated ever since. It forms part of the Transport Wing and has played significant roles in the Falklands and Gulf Wars as well as operating in the humanitarian relief fields throughout the world.

No. 72 Squadron

No. 72 Squadron formed at Upavon on 2 July 1917 flying a variety of aircraft. It moved to Mesopotamia in December where it assembled at Basra in March 1918 equipped with Spad S VIIs, Martinsyde G 100s, Bristol M 1Cs and SE 5s. With these types the Squadron operated with the Army as detached flights on fighter-protection and reconnaissance duties. After the war the Squadron reduced to a cadre in February 1919 and returned to the UK where it disbanded on 22 September. Reformed at Tangmere on 22 February 1937 and equipped with Gladiator Is, 72 Squadron was established as a fighter squadron. It moved to Church Fenton in June 1937 and received Spitfire Is in April 1939. These were used to cover the withdrawal from Dunkirk in 1940 and in the Battle of Britain, until replaced by Spitfire IIs in April 1941. The Squadron flew fighter sweeps over France from July 1941 but left for the North African Front in November 1942 operating in Tunisia before proceeding to Malta, Sicily and Italy by the end of the war. It moved to Austria in 1945 where it was part of the occupation forces, disbanding at Tissano on 30 December 1946. No. 72 Squadron reformed at Odiham on 1 February 1947, by the renumbering of No. 130 Squadron equipped with Vampire F1s. These were exchanged for F3s in June 1948 and FB5s in November 1949, before the Squadron moved to North Weald in March 1950. A change to Meteor F8s was made in July 1952 and a move to Church Fenton took place in May 1953. In February 1956 its role changed to night-fighter with the arrival of two-seat Meteor NF12s and NF14s these being exchanged for Javelin FAW4s in April 1959. No. 72 Squadron moved to Leconfield in June 1959 where it added some Javelin FAW5s and disbanded on 30 June 1961. Reformed in the helicopter support role at Odiham on 15 November 1961, 72 Squadron was now flying twin-rotor Belvedere HC1s as part of No. 38 Group in Transport Command. Wessex HC2s were received in August 1964 and this useful medium-lift helicopter still equips the Squadron. It has operated in many parts of the world but moved to Northern Ireland on a permanent basis in November 1981 where its headquarters is at Aldergrove.

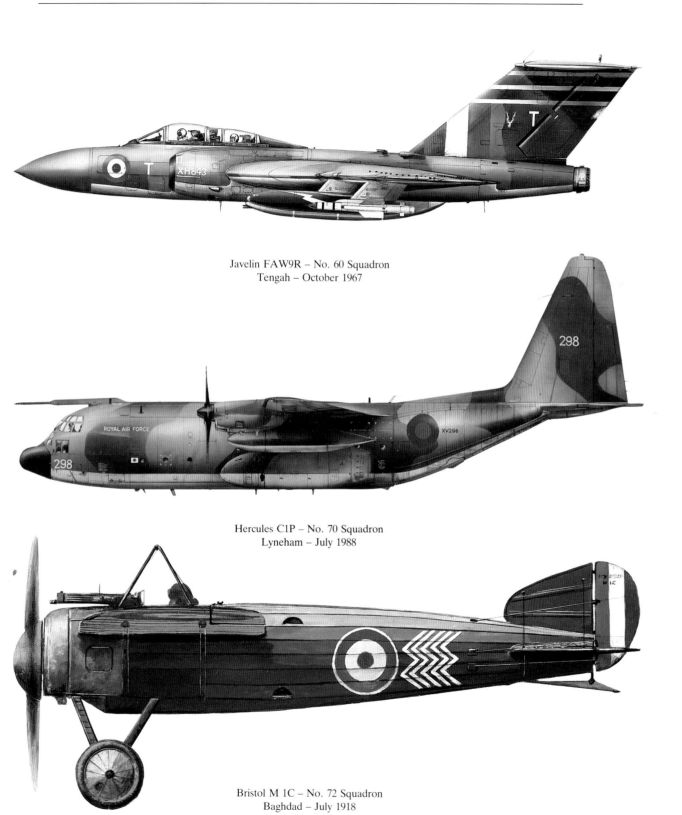

Javelin FAW9R – No. 60 Squadron
Tengah – October 1967

Hercules C1P – No. 70 Squadron
Lyneham – July 1988

Bristol M 1C – No. 72 Squadron
Baghdad – July 1918

NO. 74 SQUADRON

No. 74 Squadron formed at Northolt on 1 July 1917 and trained on Avro 504Ks before receiving SE 5s in March 1918 and moving to France. It flew fighter patrols and was also engaged in ground-attack during the war, but returned to the UK in February 1919 and disbanded on 3 July. No. 74 Squadron reformed at sea on board the troopship *Neuralia* bound for Malta where it arrived on 11 September 1935. It equipped with Demons for the defence of the island but returned to Hornchurch in September 1936 where Gauntlets were received in April 1937. It converted to Spitfire Is in February 1939 using them on defensive patrols in the early stages of WWII. The Squadron covered the withdrawal from France and flew in the Battle of Britain, thereafter commencing offensive sweeps over France from January 1941. Spitfire IIs were received in September 1940 and Spitfire Vs in May 1941 and the Squadron was sent to the Middle East in April 1942, arriving in Egypt in June. It was some months before any aircraft were received with Hurricane IIBs arriving in December but reversion to Spitfire Vs began in August 1943 and some Spitfire IXs were added in October. The Squadron operated in the Eastern Mediterranean area until it returned to the UK, arriving at North Weald on 24 April 1944. Equipped with Spitfire IXEs, 74 Squadron was involved in the D-Day operations in the fighter-bomber role. It later flew from bases in Europe from late August 1944, returning to the UK in May 1945. It converted to Spitfire XVIEs in March 1945 and changed to Meteor F3s in June. It moved from Colerne to Horsham St Faith in October 1946, where it upgraded to Meteor F4s in December 1947 and F8s in October 1950. Hunter F4s arrived in March 1957, but the improved F6 soon displaced them. At Coltishall from June 1959, the 'Tigers' were selected as the first squadron to receive Lightning F1s in June 1960. It moved to Leuchars in February 1964 and upgraded to the F3 in April 1964 and the F6 in November 1966. In June 1967 the Squadron transferred to the Far East where it disbanded on 31 August 1971. No. 74 Squadron reformed at Wattisham on 31 July 1984 uniquely equipped with ex-US Navy F-4J Phantoms as an additional air-defence squadron. It operated this version of the Phantom until receiving the FGR2 early in 1991 and was the last RAF unit to fly the F-4, standing down on 1 October 1992. Its number, however, continues in Reserve status as a Hawk T1A squadron within 4 FTS at Valley.

NO. 78 SQUADRON

No. 78 Squadron formed at Harrietsham in Kent on 1 November 1916 as a home defence unit. It moved to Hove in December and flew BE 2 and BE 12 aircraft until the arrival of Sopwith 1½ Strutters in October 1917. Its prime role was the defence of London from Zeppelin and Gotha attacks. Sopwith Camels were flown from April 1918 and Snipes from November 1918, the Squadron disbanding on 31 December 1919. Reformed as a bomber unit at Boscombe Down on 1 November 1936 and equipped with Heyfords, the Squadron moved to Dishforth in February 1937 where it received Whitleys in July. During March 1942 the later Mk V Whitleys were replaced by Halifax IIs and these aircraft were utilised in notable operations such as the first 1,000 bomber raid on Cologne and attacks on the *Scharnhorst*. It remained part of the Main Force in No. 4 Group, Bomber Command flying the Mk III and Mk VI versions of the Halifax until July 1945, when the Squadron was transferred to Transport Command and received Dakotas. Operating from Almaza in Egypt on general transport duties in the Mediterranean and Middle East, it moved to Kabrit in September 1946 where it converted to Valettas in August 1950. A further move to Fayid was made in February 1951, but 78 Squadron disbanded on 30 September 1954. It reformed at Khormaksar in Aden on 24 April 1956 to operate Pioneer CC2s in support of the Army. The larger Twin Pioneer CC1s and CC2s were flown from October 1958 until June 1965 when the Squadron changed to the helicopter role and received Wessex IIC2s maintaining its Army co-operation duties. It moved to Sharjah in October 1967 disbanding on 1 December 1971. On 22 May 1986 the Squadron reformed at Mount Pleasant airfield in the Falkland Islands by the renumbering of No. 1310 (Chinook) Flight and No. 1564 (Sea King) Flight. Now tasked in the twin roles of heavy lift and SAR, 78 Squadron supports the British Forces in the South Atlantic.

NO. 84 SQUADRON

No. 84 Squadron formed at Beaulieu, Hampshire in January 1917 and, after training, moved to France on 23 September 1917 equipped with SE 5As. The Squadron was engaged on offensive patrols, ground attack and bomber escort duties over the Western Front and became adept at destroying enemy observation balloons. After the Armistice in November 1918, the Squadron spent a period with the occupation forces before returning to the UK on August 1919. It disbanded on 30 January 1920, reforming at Baghdad on 13 August 1920 with DH 9As for policing duties in Iraq. It moved to Shaibah on 20 September 1920 and remained there for the next 20 years. During this time it re-equipped with Wapitis in July 1928, Vincents in January 1935 and Blenheim Is in February 1939. After the outbreak of WWII the Squadron moved to Egypt on 24 September 1940 and later flew on operations in Greece, Albania and Crete. Blenheim IVs were received in March 1941, and the Squadron moved to the Far East in January 1942. After heavy losses in Sumatra, remaining personnel regrouped in India in March where Blenheims arrived the following month although they were withdrawn in June pending the arrival of Vengeances in December. The Vengeance was not successful in this theatre of operation and Mosquito VIs were received in February 1945. Remaining in the Far East after the end of the war the Squadron converted to Beaufighter Xs in November 1946, based at Seletar. In October 1948 it returned to Iraq, where Brigand B1s replaced the Beaufighters in February 1949 moving back to Singapore in April 1950. Changing to a transport unit, the Squadron relocated to Fayid in Egypt on 20 February 1953 equipped with Valettas. It transferred to Aden in January 1957 where it received Beverleys in June 1958, although the last Valettas did not leave until August 1960. A move to Sharjah in Oman in August 1967 coincided with the conversion to Andovers and the Squadron relocated to Muharraq in December 1970 where it disbanded on 31 October 1971. On 17 January 1972 No. 84 Squadron reformed at Akrotiri in Cyprus from No. 1563 Flight and a detachment of No. 230 Squadron. Equipped with Whirlwind HAR10s, it provided support for the United Nations force on the island and also flew in the SAR role. Wessex HC2s were received in March 1982, and the Squadron has flown ex-Fleet Air Arm Wessex HC5Cs since 1984, maintaining its dual role in the Mediterranean.

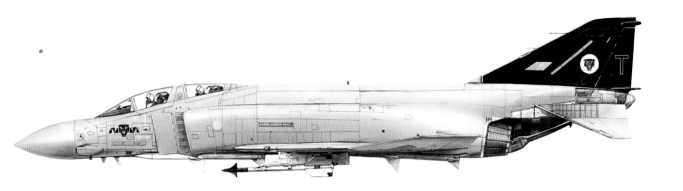

Phantom F-4J – No. 74 (Fighter) Squadron
Wattisham – December 1985

Sea King HAR3 – No. 78 Squadron
Mount Pleasant – February 1987

Wessex HC5C – No. 84 Squadron
Akrotiri – November 1987

NO. 92 SQUADRON

No. 92 Squadron formed at London Colney on 1 September 1917 and, after training, moved to France in July 1918 equipped with SE 5As. It was engaged in fighter and ground-attack operations on the Western Front and, after the Armistice, moved to Belgium and then to Germany where it disbanded at Eil on 7 August 1919. The Squadron reformed at Tangmere on 10 October 1939 as a night-fighter unit equipped with Blenheim IFs, but these were replaced by Spitfire Is in March 1940 which were used for offensive fighter patrols over France. The role changed to defence in June when the Squadron moved to South Wales and later took part in the Battle of Britain. It returned to offensive operations later in 1940, moving to the Middle East in February 1942 equipped with Spitfire VBs. These were used on fighter sweeps and bomber-escort missions over the desert as the Squadron followed the 8th Army to Tunisia. Flying Spitfire IXs and VIIIs from Malta in June 1943, the Squadron covered the landings in Sicily and from there moved to Italy, where it became a fighter-bomber unit in July 1944. After the war it moved to Austria, where it disbanded on 30 December 1946. No. 92 Squadron reformed with Meteor F3s at Acklington on 31 January 1947 as part of the UK Air Defence, moving to Duxford the following month where it received Meteor F4s in May 1948. In October 1949 it transferred to Linton-on-Ouse where it upgraded to Meteor F8s in October 1950. Sabre F4s were flown from February 1954 until the arrival of Hunter F4s in April 1956 and the F6 in February 1957, a move being made to Middleton St George in October 1957. A further move to Leconfield was made in May 1961 with Lightning F2s being received in April 1963. No. 92 Squadron transferred to Gütersloh in Germany in January 1968 to reinforce the Second ATAF and converted to Phantom FGR2 aircraft in April 1977, coinciding with relocation to Wildenrath. The Squadron took part in Operation Granby/Desert Storm when it defended the Sovereign Base areas of Cyprus from August 1990 until the ceasefire in February 1991, but disbanded in July 1991. On 23 September 1992 the Squadron reformed in Reserve status at Chivenor as part of No. 7 FTS, flying Hawk T1As in the advanced training role.

NO. 100 SQUADRON

No. 100 Squadron formed at South Farnborough on 23 February 1917 equipped with FE 2Bs as the first specialised night-bomber squadron in the Royal Flying Corps. During the closing stages of WWI it operated Handley Page 0/400s. In 1920 the Squadron was in Ireland, where it co-operated with the local security forces until the formation of the Irish Free State. Returning to the UK as a day-bomber squadron, it moved to Donibristle in November 1930 to undertake the specialised role of torpedo-bombing. It received the RAF's first Vildebeests in November 1932 and transferred to the Far East in December 1933 as a torpedo-bomber unit for the defence of Singapore. Re-equipment with Beauforts in 1941 was thwarted by the Japanese attack on Malaya and the Squadron was almost annihilated in February 1942. Its remnants then merged with No. 36 Squadron. On 15 December 1942 the Squadron was reborn at Waltham, taking part in the bomber offensive against Germany equipped with the redoubtable Lancaster. As part of No. 1 Group's heavy-bomber force, 100 Squadron contributed to the offensive against Germany until the end of the war. Retained as a peacetime unit, the Squadron received the new Lincoln in 1946 and in 1950 was detached again to Singapore for anti-terrorist operations in Malaya. In 1954 it moved from Wittering for similar operations against the Mau-Mau in Kenya. The Lincolns gave way to Canberras in April 1954 to form the Bomber Command Development Unit and these aircraft were flown until disbanding on 31 August 1959. On 1 May 1962 No. 100 Squadron reformed at Wittering as part of the Victor force equipped with Blue Steel missiles, disbanding again on 30 September 1968. When reformed on 1 February 1972, No. 100 Squadron flew Canberras in the target facilities role for both air and ground live firing, or acting as silent targets to test air and ground radar defence units. The Squadron moved to Wyton in January 1982 with Canberra B2, PR7, E15 and TT18 aircraft. On 1 January 1992 100 Squadron re-equipped with the Hawk T1/T1A.

NO. 101 SQUADRON

No. 101 Squadron was formed on 12 July 1917 as the Royal Flying Corps' second specialised night-bomber unit equipped with FE 2Bs. In August of that year the Squadron moved to France and mounted operations over the Western Front until the Armistice. Between the wars the Squadron flew DH 9As, and later, Boulton Paul Sidestrands and Overstrands. Interestingly, the tower on the badge represents the gun turret fitted to the Squadron's Overstrands whilst the lion symbolises fighting spirit. The Squadron motto, 'Mens Agitat Molem' translates as 'Mind Over Matter'. Throughout WWII, 101 Squadron served within Bomber Command flying Blenheims, Wellingtons and Lancasters both in the bombing role and, from 1943 onwards, in radio counter-measures operations with specially modified Lancasters. Since the war the Squadron has operated a variety of aircraft – Lincolns, Canberras and Vulcans – and achieved several 'firsts', including the longest-range bombing mission in the history of air warfare – the attack on Port Stanley airfield by a Vulcan during the battle for the Falkland Islands. The Squadron disbanded on 4 August 1982 but reformed on 1 May 1984 at Brize Norton with VC10 tanker aircraft. The Squadron's primary role is the in-flight refuelling of Britain's Air Defence fighters. There are two marks of the VC10 tanker aircraft, the K2 and K3. The K2s were standard VC10s whilst the K3s were Super VC10s, both types being passenger aircraft previously owned by airlines. Both marks have been fitted with additional fuel tanks in the fuselage and three hoses for air-to-air refuelling using the 'probe and drogue' technique. In Operation Desert Storm, No. 101 Squadron was based at King Khalid International Airport near Riyadh, Saudi Arabia. The Squadron mounted a total of 390 missions in support of the coalition air defence and attack aircraft during January and February 1991 and the aircrews flew a total of 1,371 hours. Following the Gulf War, No. 101 Squadron has been extensively involved in Operation Warden, the Coalition effort to protect the Kurds and to monitor Iraqi military movements. For this task aircraft were based at Incirlik Air Base in Turkey.

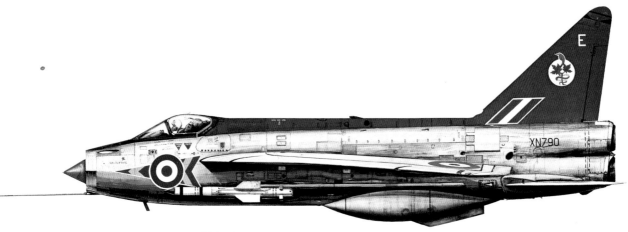

Lightning F2 – No. 92 (Fighter) Squadron
Leconfield – September 1964

Hawk T1A – No. 100 Squadron
Wyton – April 1992

VC10 K2 – No. 101 Squadron
Brize Norton – May 1992

No. 111 Squadron

No. 111 Squadron formed at Deir-el-Belah in Palestine on 1 August 1917 as a fighter squadron. Flying a variety of aircraft the Squadron supported the Army against the Turks in Palestine and Syria. In October 1918 it moved to Egypt where it re-equipped with Bristol Fighters in February 1919 disbanding on 1 February 1920. On 1 October 1923 No. 111 reformed at Duxford as a fighter squadron, equipped with Grebes. Snipes were added the following year and it subsequently flew Siskins, Bulldogs and Gauntlets. In January 1938 No. 111 was chosen as the RAF's first Hurricane squadron and flew these on defensive duties at the beginning of WWII, before taking part in the Battle of Britain where it was credited with 65 victories. It received Spitfires in April 1941 which were used for offensive sweeps over France and bomber-escort duties. In November 1942 the Squadron moved to Gibraltar to cover the North African landings and thereafter supported the 1st Army in Algeria and Tunisia before moving to Malta in June 1943 to cover the invasion of Sicily. It was later based in Italy and Corsica but disbanded at Treviso with Spitfire IXs on 12 May 1947. The Squadron reformed at North Weald on 2 December 1953 equipped with Meteor F8s. These were replaced with Hunters in June 1955 with which the Squadron achieved international fame with their Black Arrows aerobatic team, flying 22 aircraft. The Squadron moved to Wattisham in June 1958 where it converted to the Lightning F1A in April 1961. Upgrading to the F3 in December 1964, it flew this type until September 1974. It re-equipped with Phantom FGR2s at Coningsby on 1 October 1974 and moved to Leuchars on 3 November 1975 changing to the FG1 version in 1979. The last Phantom sortie was flown on 30 January 1990 and, after re-equipping with the Tornado F3, 'Treble-One' was declared operational again on 31 December 1990.

No. 115 Squadron

No. 115 Squadron formed at Catterick on 1 December 1917 and, after training on a variety of types, it received Handley Page 0/400 night bombers at Castle Bromwich in July 1918. It moved to France in September where it joined the Independent Force for bombing operations. It attacked various targets in Germany and lost only one aircraft by the war's end. Remaining in France until 4 March 1919, it returned to the UK and disbanded on 18 October 1919. No. 115 Squadron reformed at Marham on 15 June 1937 equipped with Harrow IIs. Still in the bomber role, it converted to Wellingtons in April 1939, using these early in the war for attacks on enemy shipping off Norway and on enemy airfields. Raids on targets in France and Germany soon followed and the Wellington IIIs were replaced by Lancasters in March 1943, with the Squadron being part of the main force of Bomber Command. After the war the Squadron received Lincolns in September 1949 before disbanding at Mildenhall on 1 March 1950. It reformed at Marham on 13 June 1950 with Washington B1s and flew this type until converting to Canberras in February 1954, only to disband again on 1 June 1957. Reformed at Watton on 21 August 1958 by renumbering No. 116 Squadron, 115 was now flying Varsity T1s. It moved to Tangmere four days later as part of No. 90 Group Signals Command and operated in the checking and calibration of airfield radio and radar equipment in the UK and Europe. Some Valettas were added in October 1963 and these were supplemented by Argosy E1s from February 1968. The Squadron returned to Watton in October 1963 and moved to Cottesmore in April 1969. In February 1976 it transferred to Brize Norton where it received the present Andover E3s in November 1976. Since January 1983 the Squadron has been based at Benson.

No. 120 Squadron

No. 120 Squadron formed at Cramlington in Northumberland on 1 January 1918 equipped with DH 9 aircraft. It was intended that the Squadron should join in the bombing of Germany but the Armistice was signed before the Squadron became operational and its role changed to mail-carrying between Hawkinge in Kent and France. In May 1919 the Squadron re-equipped with DH 10 aircraft and earned considerable publicity by flying mail non-stop from Hawkinge to Cologne in the then unheard-of time of three hours. With the post-war contraction of the RAF the Squadron disbanded on 28 August 1919. It reformed in WWII on 2 June 1941 and was tasked with protecting trans-Atlantic convoys. Equipped with long-range Liberator aircraft the Squadron flew anti-U-boat and convoy patrols initially from Northern Ireland and, after April 1943, from Reykjavik in Iceland. During the war 120 was the RAF's top-scoring anti-submarine Squadron, being credited with 14 U-boats destroyed, half shares in three others and eight damaged. The Squadron badge shows an Icelandic falcon standing on top of a globe to provide a permanent reminder of its wartime operations. After a short disbandment 120 Squadron reformed in October 1946 and, in the ensuing years, saw service in Palestine, Canada, Australia, the Far East, the Caribbean and Norway flying Lancaster GR3 and ASR3 aircraft and Shackleton MR1s, MR2s and MR3s. From December 1970 onwards Nimrods replaced the Shackletons and, since that date, the Squadron has flown worldwide in anti-submarine, surface surveillance and search and rescue operations. In January 1977 the Squadron began a new task of patrolling the UK's 200-mile fishing limits. It re-equipped with the improved MR2 version of the Nimrod in 1981. As a result of the Argentinian seizure of the Falkland Islands in April 1982, 120 Squadron soon became involved in the campaign. Its aircraft operated from Ascension Island and were progressively fitted for air-to-air refuelling, with Sidewinder air-to-air missiles and Harpoon air-to-surface missiles. In October 1983, Her Majesty the Queen awarded the Battle Honour 'South Atlantic 1982' to the Squadron.

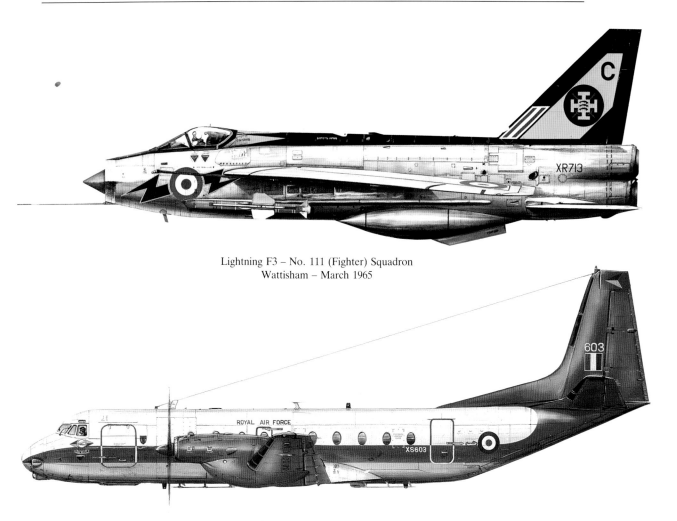

Lightning F3 – No. 111 (Fighter) Squadron
Wattisham – March 1965

Andover E3 – No. 115 Squadron
Benson – April 1986

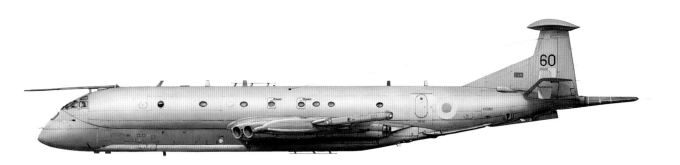

Nimrod MR2P – No. 120 Squadron
Kinloss – July 1992

NO. 201 SQUADRON

No. 201 Squadron was originally formed at Gosport on 16 October 1914 as No. 1 Squadron of the Royal Naval Air Service. During the early part of WWI it took part in the first ever engagement against a submarine and later flew fighter patrols over the Western Front. Initial equipment was the Bristol Scout but other types of aircraft were flown by the Squadron at this time. On 1 April 1918 it was renumbered 201 Squadron by which time it was equipped with Sopwith Camels. Snipes were received in September 1918 but the Squadron returned from France on 15 February 1919 and disbanded on 31 December. No. 201 Squadron reformed at Calshot on 1 January 1929 equipped with Southamptons and began the flying boat era which was to last for over 28 years. Re-equipment with Londons started in April 1936 and the Squadron's annual 'cruises' allowed it to visit many far-off locations. The affiliation with Guernsey was announced in 1939 in recognition of the many visits made to the island. Visits to Invergordon and Sullom Voe in 1938 and 1939 saw 201 preparing for war and it was soon flying on submarine patrol over the North Sea. The first Sunderland arrived with the Squadron in April 1940 and it continued with successive marks of this type until February 1957. A move to Castle Archdale in October 1941 allowed the Sunderlands to carry out anti-submarine patrols over the North Atlantic and a similar move to Pembroke Dock in April 1944 was made to prevent U-boats from entering the English Channel prior to the Normandy landings. The Squadron returned to Northern Ireland in November 1944 to continue the North Atlantic regime for the remainder of the war. No. 201 returned to Pembroke Dock in August 1945 and moved to Calshot in March 1946 but returned to south Wales in January 1949. During this post-war period it took part in the Berlin Airlift and supported the North Greenland Expedition, disbanding on 28 February 1957. It reformed at St Mawgan on 1 October 1958 with Shackleton MR3s and moved to Kinloss on 14 March 1965, where it received the Nimrod MR1 in October 1970. The MR2 version was accepted in 1981 and the Squadron used this 'Mighty Hunter' with considerable success in the Falklands and Gulf Wars.

NO. 202 SQUADRON

No. 202 Squadron's origins may be traced back to No. 2 Squadron RNAS which formed at Eastchurch on 17 October 1914. Equipped with a variety of aircraft it moved to Dover in February 1915 but lost its identity in June when it became No. 2 Wing. Reformed again at Dunkirk in November 1916, No. 2 Squadron RNAS flew reconnaissance, bombing and escort sorties for the remainder of the war and was renumbered No. 202 Squadron on 1 April 1918. It returned to the UK in March 1919 and disbanded on 22 January 1920. The Squadron reformed at Alexandria on 9 April 1920 as a naval co-operation unit, disbanding on 16 May 1921. It reformed on 1 January 1929 at Kalafrana in Malta equipped with Fairey IIID seaplanes which were replaced with Fairey IIIFs in 1930. Supermarine Scapas, the Squadron's first flying boats, were received in May 1935 and these were replaced in September 1937 with Saro Londons. A move to Alexandria was made in September 1938 but, at the outbreak of WWII, the Squadron moved to Gibraltar to patrol the approaches to the Mediterranean. In September 1940 Swordfish floatplanes were added for local patrol duties, but 1941 saw the arrival of Catalina and Sunderland flying boats. The Squadron moved to Northern Ireland in September 1944 for U-boat patrols off the west coast, disbanding on 12 June 1945. No. 202 Squadron reformed at Aldergrove on 1 October 1946 equipped with Halifaxes for meteorological flights over the Atlantic. Hastings were received in October 1950 and flown until the Squadron disbanded on 31 July 1964. On 1 September 1964, the Squadron took over the duties of No. 228 Squadron at Leconfield operating Whirlwind HAR10s in the search and rescue role. SAR flights were operated from Coltishall, Acklington and Leuchars as well as at the HQ at Leconfield. In January 1976 the HQ moved to Finningley where, with HQ 22 Squadron, SAR Wing was formed. The Whirlwinds were replaced by Sea King HAR3s in 1978/9 and these aircraft then equipped detached flights at Boulmer, Brawdy, Coltishall and Lossiemouth. Immediately after the South Atlantic campaign in 1982, 'C' Flight was sent from Coltishall to provide SAR cover in the Falkland Islands, being later renumbered No. 1564 Flight as an independent unit. On 2 September 1985 'C' Flight was reformed at Coltishall and on 1 September 1988, this Flight moved to Manston. 'E' Flight later formed at Leconfield. In December 1992 the Squadron's second-line engineering facility moved to St Mawgan and its Headquarters joined 'A' Flight at Boulmer.

NO. 206 SQUADRON

No. 206 Squadron formed in December 1916 at Petite Synthe in France as No. 6 Squadron Royal Naval Air Service and flew several fighter aircraft of the time: Nieuport Scouts, Sopwith Strutters, Triplanes and Camels. It was disbanded in August 1917 but reformed at Dover on 1 January 1918 as a day-bombing, reconnaissance and photographic squadron. The Squadron returned to Petite Synthe on 14 January 1918 and became No. 206 Squadron RAF on 1 April 1918, the day the Royal Air Force was formed. It carried out numerous bombing raids (dropping 116 tons of bombs, destroying 29 enemy aircraft and damaging 23 others) with reconnaissance flights producing 12,000 photographs. At the end of hostilities the Squadron became part of the occupying forces of the 2nd Army. After a period of policing in Heliopolis, Egypt, the Squadron was disbanded on 1 February 1920. It reformed at RAF Manston on 15 June 1936 as a general reconnaissance squadron flying the Avro Anson, but in August it was transferred to Coastal Command. In March 1938 the Squadron badge was presented – the octopus being symbolic of the maritime role. The Squadron successively re-equipped with Hudsons, Fortress IIs and Liberators during the war and was credited with the destruction of ten U-boats. In June 1945 it transferred to Transport Command and flew on long-haul operations to India. It disbanded on 25 April 1946 but reformed at Lyneham on 17 November 1947 flying Yorks which were used on the Berlin Airlift, disbanding again on 20 February 1950. No. 206 resumed its maritime role on 27 September 1952 when it reformed at St Eval with Shackleton MR1s. On 10 January 1958 it moved to St Mawgan and received Shackleton MR3s. The Squadron took up residence at Kinloss on 7 July 1965 where, in November 1970, the Nimrod MR1 entered service. In 1979 it became the first Squadron to convert to the Nimrod MR2, which served in the Falklands and Gulf Wars.

Sunderland MR5 – No. 201 (Flying-Boat) Squadron
Pembroke Dock – June 1954

Sea King HAR3 – No. 202 Squadron
Finningley – March 1987

Nimrod MR2P – No. 206 Squadron
Kinloss – April 1989

NO. 208 SQUADRON

No. 208 Squadron formed as No. 8 Squadron Royal Naval Air Service at Dunkirk on 26 October 1916 to reinforce the RFC. Flying Sopwith Pups, Nieuport Scouts and Sopwith 1½ Strutters, the Squadron operated with the 5th Brigade near Amiens but moved frequently. It later re-equipped with other types. On 1 April 1918, the day on which 'Naval 8' was embodied into the newly-formed Royal Air Force, it was flying Camels on the Western Front and was engaged in fighter and ground-attack duties until the end of the war, when it received Snipes. After a spell with the occupation forces it returned to the UK in September 1919 and disbanded on 7 November. It reformed at Ismailia in Egypt on 1 February 1920 with RE 8s and began an unbroken period of 51 years in and around the Middle East. It re-equipped with Bristol Fighters in November 1920 for Army co-operation duties but in 1922 it was sent to Turkey for a year. Returning to Egypt it received Atlases in May 1930 which were replaced by Audaxes in August 1935 although some Demons were flown from September 1935 until March 1936. In January 1939 conversion to the Lysander was effected. During WWII, 208 Squadron was equipped with Hurricanes, Tomahawks and Spitfires and saw action in Greece, Palestine, the Western Desert and Italy. After the war it was involved in almost continuous operations until September 1971 based in Palestine, the Canal Zone, Eritrea, Sharjah, Cyprus, Aden, Iraq and Kuwait flying Spitfires, Meteor FR9s, Hunter F6s, Venoms and Hunter FGA9s. No. 208 reformed at Honington on 1 July 1974 with Buccaneer S2As and was the first RAF participant in Exercise Red Flag. On 1 July 1983 it changed from the overland to the maritime role and moved to Lossiemouth. In September 1983 the Squadron flew operational sorties over Beirut in support of the British peacekeeping force in Lebanon. No. 208 added the Sea Eagle anti-ship missile to its inventory in 1986. In 1991 the Squadron was part of the highly successful Buccaneer Gulf Detachment designating laser-guided bombs for delivery from Tornado and other Buccaneer aircraft. When the Buccaneer is retired from service in 1994, 208 Squadron is scheduled to continue in reserve status at Valley as part of No. 4 FTS.

NO. 216 SQUADRON

No. 216 Squadron, RAF, had its origins in No. 16 Squadron, Royal Naval Air Service, at Villeneux in France, equipped with Handley Page 0/400 night bombers. On 1 April 1918, 'B' Flight of that Squadron became part of the newly formed Royal Air Force and was renumbered 216; however, to commemorate its lineage the Squadron has been referred to ever since as 'Two-Sixteen'. After WWI it went to Egypt and, during the next two decades, flew DH 10s, Vimys, Valentias, Victorias and Bombays. During WWII the Squadron saw active service in Greece, the Middle-East and Africa where it flew first Wellingtons, then Hudsons, before re-equipping with the ubiquitous Dakota. The Squadron's tasks included the resupply of besieged Tobruk and Habbaniya and of the 14th Army in the Aegean, and keeping open the reinforcement supply route across Africa. In 1949 'Two-Sixteen' re-equipped with Valettas which it operated until 1955. In 1955, after 38 years service overseas, the Squadron returned to the United Kingdom to re-equip with the de Havilland Comet C2 at Lyneham, and so became the world's first military jet-transport squadron. With the introduction of the larger Comet C4 in 1962 the Squadron assumed a Royal, and VIP, flight commitment. No. 216 Squadron disbanded on 30 June 1975, but reformed at Honington on 1 July 1979 in a totally new role, as a strike/attack squadron, equipped with the Buccaneer S2. This was short-lived however, and with a rationalisation of the Buccaneer's role, the Squadron once again disbanded in 1980. As a result of the Falklands conflict the Ministry of Defence identified a requirement for a strategic tanker squadron and accordingly the Squadron reformed on 15 August 1983 equipped with Tristar Series 500 aircraft. These aircraft underwent conversion to give them a tanker capability and now serve with 'Two-Sixteen' in the dual role of air-to-air refuelling and air transportation.

NO. 230 SQUADRON

No. 230 Squadron formed at Felixstowe in August 1918 from Nos. 327 and 328 Flights equipped with F 2A flying boats for maritime reconnaissance duties. A separate unit, No. 487 Flight equipped with Camels, was added to the Squadron in September for escort duty. A few F 5 flying boats were received in 1920 but the Squadron was renumbered No. 480 Flight on 1 April 1923. It reformed at Pembroke Dock on 1 December 1934 and did not receive its first aircraft, Singapore IIIs, until April 1935, taking them to Egypt in September to cover the Abyssinian crisis. It returned to Pembroke Dock in August 1936, but departed for the Far East in October, arriving at Seletar in January 1937. Short Sunderlands were received in June 1938 and the Squadron was fully equipped by the end of the year. Maritime patrols were flown from the outbreak of war and a detachment in Ceylon became a permanent base in February 1940, but in May the Squadron left for Egypt for operations in the Mediterranean. Convoy protection followed but 230 moved to Dar-es-Salaam in Tanganyika in January 1943 for patrols over the Indian Ocean. It returned to Ceylon in February 1944 and, in February 1945, provided a detachment in Calcutta for freight transport and casualty evacuation from Burma. The Squadron moved to Burma in April and returned to Singapore in December before returning to the UK in April 1946. Initially based at Calshot, it later joined the Berlin Airlift. In February 1949 it moved to Pembroke Dock where it resumed its maritime operations with Sunderland MR5s until disbanding as one of the RAF's last two flying boat squadrons on 28 February 1957. No. 230 Squadron reformed at Dishforth on 1 September 1958 equipped with Pioneer CC1S, flying in support of the Army. It moved to Upavon on May 1959 where it added Twin Pioneer CC1s in January 1960 and relocated to Odiham in May. In September 1960 it detached 'A' Flight to the Cameroons for security operations, returning in September 1961. A radical change of equipment began in June 1962 with the arrival of Whirlwind HC10 helicopters and these were taken to Gütersloh in January 1963. The Squadron moved to Odiham in January 1965 but transferred to Borneo in March returning to Odiham in December 1966 and provided detachments in Cyprus until 1971. Conversion to the Puma HC1 started in November 1971 with a move to Gütersloh in October 1980. The Squadron played a prominent role in the Gulf during 1990/1991, but moved its field of operations to Northern Ireland on 4 May 1992.

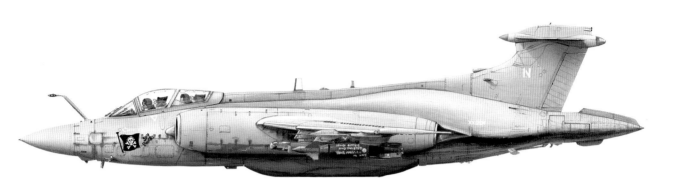

Buccaneer S2B – No. 208 Squadron
Bahrain – March 1991

Tristar KC1 – No. 216 Squadron
Brize Norton – January 1990

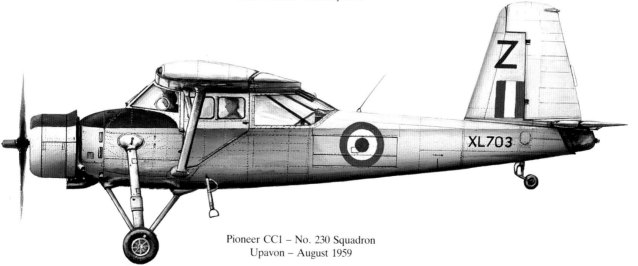

Pioneer CC1 – No. 230 Squadron
Upavon – August 1959

NO. 234 SQUADRON

No. 234 Squadron formed at Tresco Seaplane Base in the Scilly Isles on 26 February 1917. It had a mixed complement of Curtiss H 12 and Felixstowe F 2A and F3 flying-boats which were used on submarine patrols over the Atlantic. The Squadron destroyed one submarine but was disbanded on 15 May 1919. It did not reform until 30 October 1939 when it equipped with a mixed bag of Battles, Blenheim IFs, Gauntlets, Magisters and Tutors at Leconfield. In March 1940 it converted to Spitfire Is and moved to Church Fenton in May but moved again in June to St Eval in Cornwall. As part of No. 10 Group it flew in the Battle of Britain, moving to Middle Wallop on 13 August but returning to St Eval on 11 September. Spitfire IIAs were received in November 1940 which were used on convoy escort and defensive patrols. These were exchanged for Spitfire VBs in September 1941 and the Squadron continued in this role until 1942 when fighter sweeps over northern France and bomber escort became the order of the day. In January 1943 it moved north to the Orkney Islands where some Spitfire VIs were added but by late June it was in England again engaged in convoy escort. It covered the Normandy landings and went on offensive operations thereafter but in September 1944 it converted to Mustangs when based at North Weald. These aircraft were used for long-range bomber escort missions and retained until August 1945 when Spitfire IXs were received. Meteor F3s arrived in February 1946 but the Squadron disbanded on 1 September 1946. It reformed at Oldenburg on 1 August 1952 as part of the Second Tactical Air Force equipped with Vampire FB5s and FB9s but exchanged these for Sabre F4s in November 1953. These were replaced by Hunter F4s in May 1956 but the Squadron disbanded again on 15 July 1957. On 30 November 1958 No. 234 emerged as a 'shadow' squadron within No. 229 OCU at Chivenor equipped with Hunter F6 and FGA9 aircraft. In January 1966 it received reserve squadron status and moved to Brawdy in September 1974 where Hawk T1s arrived from August 1978. With the closure of Brawdy in August 1992 the Squadron moved to Valley to become part of No. 4 FTS.

NO. 360 SQUADRON

No. 360 Squadron formed at Watton on 1 April 1966 as a joint Royal Navy/Royal Air Force Electronic Warfare squadron. During its early months it was without any aircraft but in October it absorbed 'B' Flight of 97 Squadron together with its Canberra B2s, T4s and B6s. However, with delivery of specially modified T17s the earlier equipment departed. The role of the Squadron is to provide electronic counter-measure training for the warships, radar stations, missile units and air-defence fighters operated by the Royal Navy, Army and Royal Air Force. Although embodied in the Royal Air Force, 360 Squadron is one quarter funded by the Royal Navy and every fourth CO is from that Service. As the RAF's youngest squadron it has no battle honours but its badge and motto, approved by HM Queen Elizabeth II in September 1973, are significant of its specialised role. Its heraldic description reads – 'In front of a trident erect, a moth, wings displayed'. The moth uses its own ultrasonic emissions to confuse predators and the motto – 'Confundemus' – means 'We shall throw into confusion'. The Squadron moved to Cottesmore in April 1969 and to its present base at Wyton in June 1974. From 1987, six of the Squadron's Canberras were further modified to T17A standard. The very nature of the unit's task means that its aircraft are regularly seen at other airfields where they work with locally based squadrons. The original green and grey camouflage of the Canberras was changed to low visibility 'hemp' in the mid-80s but all now carry the Squadron's red rectangle embodying a yellow lightning flash on either side of the fuselage roundel.

NO. 617 SQUADRON

No. 617 Squadron formed at Scampton on 21 March 1943 as a heavy-bomber unit. Formed specifically for the special task of breaching the Möhne, Eder and Sorpe Dams by the use of the now legendary Wallis 'bouncing bombs', the Squadron was equipped with modified Lancasters (B III Special). After training on simulated targets, 19 Lancasters took off on the night of 16 May for the targets in the Ruhr, the details of which are described elsewhere. Its first leader, Wing Commander G.P. Gibson DSO DFC, was awarded the Victoria Cross for his gallantry during the attack. After the raid it was decided to retain the Squadron for other special operations and it went on to deliver weapons like the 12,000 lb 'Tallboy' and 22,000 lb 'Grand Slam' bombs. It also became well known for its target marking abilities under the leadership of Wing Commander G.L. Cheshire DSO DFC, who was awarded the Squadron's second Victoria Cross for his outstanding leadership. The Squadron later operated from Coningsby and Woodhall Spa, moving to Waddington in June 1945 when it equipped with Lancaster VIIs. It remained in Bomber Command after the war, receiving Lincolns in September 1946 and Canberras in January 1952, disbanding at Binbrook on 15 December 1955. Earlier that year it had been on detachment in Malaya operating against Communist terrorists. On 1 May 1958 the 'Dam Busters' reformed at Scampton with Vulcan B1s as part of the RAF's V-bomber force. In September 1961 it re-equipped with the B2 version which was modified to carry the Blue Steel 'stand-off' bomb. After the withdrawal of this weapon the Squadron continued in the long-range bombing role until disbanded on 31 December 1981. For its third life it reformed as a strike squadron at Marham on 1 January 1983, flying the Tornado GR1. It has since continued in its precision bombing vein, winning many prizes in national and international competitions. During the Gulf War in 1991, the Squadron flew in its established strike role but also pioneered the use of new target marking and laser designation equipment. In 1992 it was again in the Gulf in Operation Jural as part of the UN force monitoring the 'no fly' zone in southern Iraq.

Hawk T1A – No. 234 Squadron
Brawdy – January 1987

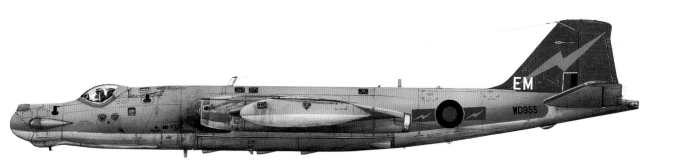

Canberra T17A – No. 360 Squadron
Wyton – May 1991

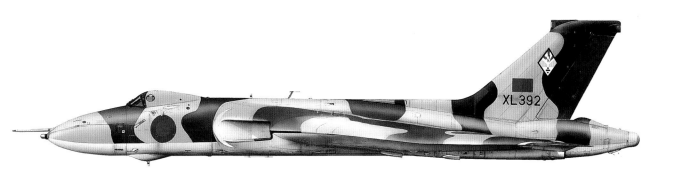

Vulcan B2 – No. 617 Squadron
Scampton – October 1978

No. 1312 Flight

No. 1312 Flight originally formed on 19 April 1944 with Dakota aircraft as part of No. 46 Group Transport Command before being transferred to 2 ATAF. The Flight moved to Abingdon in 1954 operating the Hastings until its disbandment in April 1957. The Falkland Islands Hercules Detachment was formed in July 1982 and renamed No. 1312 Flight in September 1983. The Flight aircrews are drawn from Nos. 24 and 30 Squadrons based at Lyneham and ground-crew are drawn from RAF stations throughout the UK and Germany. No. 1312 Flight's primary task is to provide air-to-air refuelling support for the Tornado F3s of No. 1435 Flight but other tasks include maritime reconnaissance cover for the Falkland Islands Protection Zone, airborne resupply and mail drops to South Georgia, airbridge support and search and rescue duties. The Lockheed C-130 Hercules C1K aircraft entered service with the RAF during the Falklands campaign. They were modified by Marshall of Cambridge (Engineering) Ltd to incorporate a flight refuelling probe, a Mk 17B hose drum unit and four internal 900-gallon fuel tanks in the fuselage.

No. 1417 Flight

The origins of 1417 Flight date back to July 1940 with the formation of No. 417 (General Reconnaissance) Flight at St Athan equipped with six Ansons. In March 1941 it was renumbered No. 1417 Flight and disbanded in June 1941. It reformed at Chivenor on 18 January 1942 equipped with Wellingtons in No. 19 Group, Coastal Command for developing the Leigh Light night-attack system for work against submarines. Such was the success of the unit that it was expanded and upgraded to become No. 172 Squadron on 8 March 1942 and continued its wartime operations in the anti-submarine role. 1417 Flight next reformed in November 1953 at Bahrain as a light transport, communications and operational reconnaissance flight equipped with Ansons, supporting a detachment at Muharraq. It later received Pembroke C1s but was absorbed into No. 152 Squadron in October 1958. In March 1963, 'C' Flight of No. 8 Squadron based at Khormaksar in Aden was designated No. 1417 (Fighter Reconnaissance) Flight. Equipped with four Hunter FR10s and a Hunter T7, its primary role was to provide photographic and visual reconnaissance in support of counter-rebellion operations throughout the Air Forces Middle East area of responsibility and particularly in the troublesome Radfan district in the North of Aden. After more than four years of exciting and demanding operations over the deserts and mountains of the Arabian peninsula, the Flight was absorbed back into No. 8 Squadron in August 1967 during the gradual withdrawal of British Forces from Aden. The current commission of the Flight in Belize is its longest to date. Harriers first arrived in 1975, initially as a detachment of No. 1 (Fighter) Squadron. By 1978 the presence had developed into 'Hardet', a detachment provided from all the RAF's Harrier squadrons, and on 18 April 1980 the detachment was designated No. 1417 Flight. It is currently equipped with four Harrier GR3 'jump-jets' which are employed in the reconnaissance, air-defence, ground-attack, general surveillance and maritime roles as part of the external defence of the independent state of Belize.

No. 1435 Flight

The Malta Night Fighter Unit formed in July 1941 with eight Hurricane Mk IICs and four Hurricane Mk IIBs and was based at Takali for night defence of the island. On 2 December 1941 the Unit was renamed No. 1435 Flight and operations continued throughout the winter until March 1942, when No. 1435 (Night Fighter) Flight was disbanded. In August 1942 it reformed, but this time as No. 1435 Squadron. Thus 1435 Squadron was unique among RAF squadrons in that its designation was not officially approved until after the unit had been operating for some time. It began operations as a squadron on 2 August 1942 based at Luqa equipped with Spitfires and was considerably larger than hitherto. Until the end of 1942 the Squadron was engaged in fighter defence duties but, in January 1943, it became a fighter-bomber unit and flew sweeps over Sicily until the Allied landings. In October 1943 the Squadron moved to Italy where it became part of the Balkan Air Force, carrying out ground-attack missions over Albania and Yugoslavia in addition to air defence duties. In February 1945 the Squadron moved to Falconara to keep in range of the retreating German forces as they evacuated the Balkans. A detachment was based on the Yugoslav island of Vis in the Adriatic from September 1944 until April 1945, when the Squadron was withdrawn from operations and it disbanded on 9 May 1945. No. 1435 Flight was reformed on 1 November 1988 when it replaced No. 23 Squadron in the air-defence role in the Falkland Islands. The Phantom FGR2 aircraft were painted with the Maltese Cross in memory of the Flight's distinguished history and are named 'Faith', 'Hope', 'Charity' and 'Desperation'. The Phantoms were replaced by Tornado F3s in July 1992 and continue the tradition of carrying the Falkland Islands crest together with the Maltese Cross. Individual aircraft names are still carried.

Hercules C1K – No. 1312 Flight
Mount Pleasant – February 1985

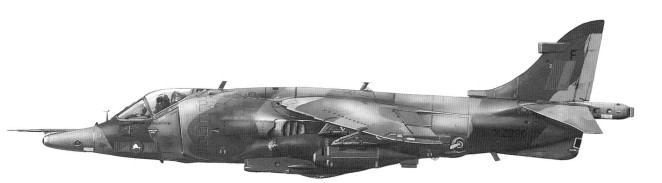

Harrier GR3 – No. 1417 Flight
Belize – April 1992

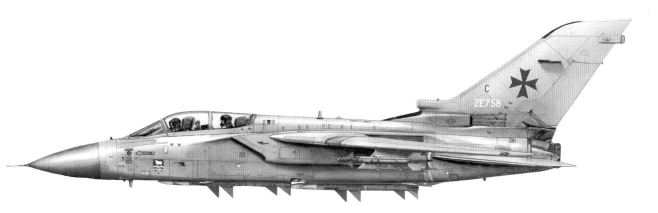

Tornado F3 – No. 1435 Flight
Mount Pleasant – July 1992

No. 1563 Flight

No. 1563 Flight was formed at Benina in Libya on 22 December 1942 as a detachment from No. 1411 Meteorological Flight. Its two Gloster Gladiator aircraft made two climbs per day and passed the weather information gathered to the Mobile Met Unit attached to Bomber Group. In April 1943 the Flight was expanded to five aircraft and in September the Gladiators were exchanged for Hurricanes and, in addition, three Magisters and a Blenheim IV arrived that month but the last Gladiator did not depart until May 1944. In November the unit started making night observations and in July 1945 modified Spitfires fitted with special signalling devices were received. Routine observations continued until May 1946 when the Flight disbanded. No. 1563 Flight reformed at Belize in November 1983 with four Puma HC1 helicopters detached from No. 33 Squadron at Odiham. Its primary role is to provide support for all Army operations in Belize but it is also tasked to provide photo-reconnaissance support, 24-hour medivac/casevac cover and SAR cover for all Harrier operations and the military and civil community. Routine tasks include troop movements and resupply between the main bases and the more remote jungle areas, carriage of underslung loads such as Landrovers and field guns and the carriage of VIPs. In recent years the Flight has been called to the aid of neighbouring countries following natural disasters including Mexico and Columbia in 1985 and Jamaica in 1986.

No. 240 Operational Conversion Unit

No. 240 Operational Conversion Unit was first formed in April 1948 from No. 1382 (Transport) Conversion Unit. Based initially at North Luffenham, it flew Dakota C4s. In 1950 the OCU acquired Valetta C1s and, having moved to Dishforth, flew both types, training crews for the Berlin Airlift. Disbandment followed in 1951 when the unit amalgamated with No. 241 OCU to form No. 242 OCU. Air Training Squadron was later formed at Odiham in July 1967 with specific responsibility for operational helicopter training. The Helicopter Operational Conversion Flight, then equipped with Wessex HC2s, was joined by Pumas in January 1971. Air Training Squadron then became No. 240 Operational Conversion Unit, thus reviving the name. Separate Puma and Wessex Flights operated from Odiham until October 1980 when the Wessex Flight moved to Benson as an independent unit. The Chinook Flight was formed on 31 October 1980 and the first aircraft was officially received on 2 December 1980.

No. 241 Operational Conversion Unit

No. 241 Operational Conversion Unit can trace its origins back to No. 1332 Heavy Conversion Unit which formed at Longtown in September 1944 to train crews for Stirlings, Yorks and Liberators. A few weeks later the unit moved to Northern Ireland and the first training course started at Nutts Corner. In April 1945 the unit moved to Riccall, where the Stirlings were replaced by Skymasters but these aircraft remained for only a short period after which they were returned to the USA and the Liberators transferred to the Far East. A further move to Dishforth was made in 1946 where, in July, No. 1665 HCU with Halifaxes combined with 1332 HCU. The Halifaxes went to Syerston in December 1946 but the Halifax crew training commitment returned on 5 January 1948 and the unit was renamed No. 241 Operational Conversion Unit. Flying Yorks and Halifaxes the Unit was soon engaged in the Berlin Airlift with Hastings replacing the Halifax in September 1948. The York, too, was slowly phased out with the last aircraft leaving in June 1950. On 1 April 1951, No. 241 OCU merged with No. 240 OCU at Dishforth and lost its identity but was reformed at Brize Norton on 1 July 1970 by the merging of the Britannia, Belfast, VC10 and Comet Air Training Squadrons. The Comet element moved to Lyneham on 17 October 1970, the Britannia Flight stopped training on 30 November 1975 and the Belfast operation ceased on 27 August 1976. In October 1976 an Andover Flight was formed but this moved to Benson in 1983. The OCU is currently concerned with the training of flight deck and cabin crew, including air stewards, for VC10 and Tristar aircraft.

Puma HC1 – No. 1563 Flight
Belize – March 1992

Chinook HC1 – No. 240 Operational Conversion Unit
Odiham – May 1981

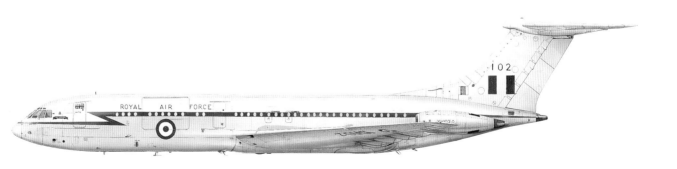

VC10 C1 – No. 241 Operational Conversion Unit
Brize Norton – February 1979

NO. 1 FLYING TRAINING SCHOOL

The first Royal Air Force Flying Training School was formed at Netheravon on 29 July 1919. Originally christened the Netheravon School of Flying, the unit was renamed No. 1 Flying Training School in December 1919. From 1924 Fleet Air Arm pilots were trained by No. 1 FTS until the unit disbanded in 1931. It reformed at Leuchars in April 1935 to train Royal Navy and RAF pilots but soon moved to Netheravon where, at the outbreak of WWII, it was renamed No. 1 Service Flying Training School. In 1942 the school closed but a unit known as No. 1 Service Flying Training School (India) continued training pilots at Ambala until 1945. No. 1 FTS proper was reformed at Spitalgate on 18 June 1947 by the renaming of No. 17 SFTS equipped with Harvard, Magister and Tiger Moth aircraft but disbanded on 25 February 1948. It reformed at Oakington on 1 December 1950 as a refresher unit using Harvard, Prentice and Chipmunk aircraft, moving to Moreton-in-Marsh on 31 October 1951. It disbanded on 20 April 1955 but reformed at Syerston on 1 May where initial flying training for the Fleet Air Arm was provided using Chipmunks, Provosts and Vampires and re-established the connection with the Royal Navy. The School moved to its present location at Linton-on-Ouse on 28 October 1957 and the Chipmunk flight operated from Dishforth between 1962 and 1963. The Navy pilots were joined for advanced training by RAF and overseas officers who had already gained their 'wings' at other RAF Flying Training Schools but this task ceased in January 1966. From mid-1966 to December 1967 the school, now equipped with Jet Provosts as well as Chipmunks, was devoted to the training of FAA pilots, but RAF and pilots from foreign armed forces subsequently joined the school. On 31 July 1969 the last Royal Navy fixed-wing course were presented with their 'wings' and on 15 September, naval helicopter specialist pilot training was transferred to No. 2 FTS at Church Fenton. Basic jet instruction for RAF pilots continued at Linton-on-Ouse and, in mid-1983, FAA student pilots destined for the Sea Harrier were absorbed into the RAF system. The complete reassociation with the Royal Navy took place in April 1984 when initial training of Royal Navy and Royal Marine rotary-wing pilots was established at the school. This unit, the RNEFTS, operated from Topcliffe from August 1985. No. 1 FTS started to replace the Jet Provosts with Tucanos in 1992 and continues to train pilots for both the Royal Air Force and the Royal Navy.

NO. 2 FLYING TRAINING SCHOOL

No. 2 Flying Training School was formed at Duxford in June 1920. The School moved to Digby in 1924 but disbanded in July 1933. No. 2 FTS reformed at Digby in September 1934 with Avro Tutors and later added Audaxes and Furies prior to moving to Brize Norton in August 1937. Oxfords were flown from February 1938 and by the outbreak of WWII the School was equipped with this type and Harvards. One of its Oxfords was shot down by an enemy aircraft on 28 July 1940 but the School lost many of its fleet when Brize Norton suffered a major attack on 16 August 1940 and 46 aircraft were destroyed. On 14 March 1942 the unit was retitled No. 2 (Pilot) Advanced Flying Unit but it disbanded on 14 July 1942. No. 2 FTS did not reform until July 1947 when No. 20 FTS at Church Lawford was renumbered. It flew Harvards and Tiger Moths and relocated to South Cerney in March 1948. The Tiger Moths were later replaced by Prentices but the unit was absorbed into the Central Flying School in May 1952. No. 2 FTS next reformed at Cluntoe in Northern Ireland in February 1953 but moved to Hullavington in May 1954 equipped with Provost T1s for elementary training. It pioneered *ab initio* jet training with Jet Provost T1s and went to Syerston in November 1957 retaining the Provosts until 1958 when the Jet Provost T3s arrived. By 1960 No. 2 FTS had become the first unit in the world to train students exclusively on jet aircraft. The Jet Provost T4s were introduced in 1962 and, together with the T3s, they continued until December 1969 when the School disbanded. It reformed at Church Fenton in January 1970 for the *ab initio* training of naval pilots using Chipmunks but received Bulldogs in 1973. In November 1974 the School was retitled the Royal Navy Elementary Flying Training School (RNEFTS) as part of No. 3 FTS at Leeming. Reformed in its current commission on 1 March 1976 at Ternhill with Whirlwind HAR10 helicopters, No. 2 FTS also had a search and rescue training squadron at Valley. On 1 October 1976 the School moved to Shawbury where it now operates the Gazelle HT2 and 3 on No. 1 (AFT) Squadron and the Wessex HC2 on No. 2 (AFT) Squadron.

NO. 3 FLYING TRAINING SCHOOL

No. 3 Flying Training School formed at Scopwick on 21 April 1920 but was disbanded two years later in April 1922. No. 3 FTS reformed at Grantham on 2 April 1928 and over the next ten years was equipped with a variety of aircraft for pilot training. In August 1937, No. 3 FTS moved to the newly-built airfield at South Cerney where, in June 1938, it was re-equipped with the Oxford for twin-engine pilot training. The unit remained at South Cerney equipped primarily with Oxfords throughout the war, initially as No. 3 Service Flying Training School and, from 14 March 1942, as No. 3 (Pilot) Advanced Flying Unit, responsible for refresher flying and acclimatisation for pilots trained overseas. No. 3 (P) AFU was renamed No. 3 SFTS on 17 December 1945, moving to Feltwell in April 1946 where it regained its original title on 9 April 1947. Here the unit was equipped with Tiger Moth, Harvard and, later, Prentice and Provost aircraft before disbanding on 1 May 1958. On 11 September 1961 No. 3 FTS was again reformed, this time at Leeming where it was responsible for the training of RAF and overseas pilots on the new 'all through' jet training syllabus using the Jet Provost T3, Vampire T11 and, later, Jet Provost T4 and T5. In November 1974, No. 3 FTS assumed responsibility for elementary training of Royal Navy pilots using the Bulldog T1, as well as for refresher training for RAF pilots using the Jet Provost and, briefly, multi-engine advanced pilot training using the Jetstream T1. The school disbanded again on 26 April 1984 but was reformed on 1 February 1989 from the existing flying training school at Cranwell, equipped with the Jet Provost T5A. No. 3 FTS commenced re-equipment with the Tucano T1 in January 1991, the first *ab initio* students commencing flying on the new aircraft in June of that year.

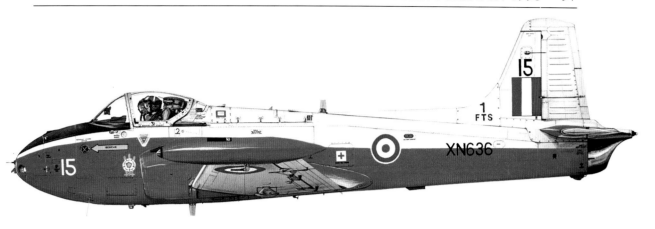

Jet Provost T3A – No. 1 Flying Training School
Linton-on-Ouse – June 1986

Gazelle HT3 – No. 2 Flying Training School
Shawbury – June 1985

Harvard T2 – No. 3 Flying Training School
Feltwell – 1950

No. 4 Flying Training School

No. 4 Flying Training School was formed in April 1921 at Abu Sueir in the Egyptian Canal Zone and equipped with Avro 504K aircraft. In 1936, Hawker Audax and Hawker Hart aircraft were received but, to meet wartime expansion, the School moved to Iraq in 1940. An internal rebellion in that country led to the aircraft being armed and used on operational sorties from April to June 1941. With the end of the troubles 4 FTS disbanded in July 1941. The School reformed on 23 April 1947 at Heany in Southern Rhodesia using Tiger Moths, Chipmunks, Ansons and Harvards until disbanding again in January 1954. On 1 June 1954 the renumbering of No. 205 Advanced Flying School at Middleton St George re-established No. 4 FTS. Now equipped with Vampires, the School moved to Worksop on 9 June 1956 absorbing No. 211 AFS and its Meteors. On 9 June 1958 No. 4 FTS disbanded, its Vampires going to No. 7 FTS at Valley but, on 15 August 1960, it was renumbered No. 4 FTS. Vampires were used for advanced flying training and later equipment included Gnats and Hunters. The British Aerospace Hawk T1 now equips the three squadrons at No. 4 Flying Training School which now includes a tactical weapons course in its programme.

No. 6 Flying Training School

No. 6 Flying Training School formed at Spitalgate in May 1920 as a school for refresher and conversion training. In September 1921 the School moved to Manston disbanding in April 1922. During this period the School was equipped with Avro 504s, Bristol Fighters, Sopwith Snipes and Vickers Vimys. No. 6 FTS reformed at Netheravon in April 1935 as a basic flying training school equipped with Avro Tutors, Hawker Harts and Hawker Furies. In August 1938 it moved to Little Rissington where, in December 1940, it received Airspeed Oxfords and Avro Ansons, but in April 1942 it changed its role and name. Now as No. 6 Pilots Advanced Flying Unit it was tasked to complete the training of pilots who had initially trained in Canada and during the remainder of the war years it saw over 5,000 pilots pass through its hands. After the war No. 6 Service Flying Training School reformed at Little Rissington in December 1945, where it continued in its task of training pilots on piston-engined aircraft. Initially equipped with Tiger Moths and Harvards, it subsequently received Percival Prentices, Boulton-Paul Balliols and Percival Provosts. On 14 May 1947 No. 6 SFTS was renamed No. 6 Flying Training School on its move to Ternhill and it transferred to Acklington on 4 August 1961. This move coincided with a complete change in training and the arrival of the Jet Provost as the RAF's basic trainer. The School disbanded on 30 June 1968 only to reform again at Finningley on 1 May 1970 and operate in a different role. It now controlled the combined Nos. 1 and 2 Air Navigation Schools operating Varsities, Dominies and Jet Provosts. In October 1976 the Air Electronics and Air Engineer School was added and in May 1979, the Multi-Engine Training Squadron formed with Jetstreams. Air loadmaster training started in April 1983. In 1992 new aircraft to serve with 6 FTS include Bulldogs, Tucanos and Hawks alongside the existing Dominies and Jetstreams.

No. 7 Flying Training School

No. 7 Flying Training School formed at Peterborough on 2 December 1935 with Tutor, Hart, Audax and Fury aircraft for pilot training. In May 1939 the School began what was to be a long association with the Royal Navy by taking on the new role of training pilots for the Fleet Air Arm. In August 1940 the unit embarked for Canada as part of the expansion of the Empire Training Scheme but, while en route to its new home, its name was changed to No. 31 (S) Flying Training School. The School reformed again at Peterborough in June 1942 as No. 7 (Pilot) Advanced Flying Unit and was given the role of refreshing and acclimatising pilots trained in overseas schools. The aircraft used at this time were Master, Oxford and Spitfire. In April 1946 the School moved to Kirton-in-Lindsay where, in the following year, it renewed its association with the Royal Navy. The unit regained its original name of No. 7 FTS when it moved to Cottesmore in 1948 where, in 1952, it was made responsible for the training of Royal Air Force students operating in accordance with the 'all through' sequence. Aircraft now used were the Prentice, Harvard and, later, Balliol. The school disbanded in 1954 but reformed from No. 202 Advanced Flying School equipped with Provosts and Vampire T11s in the role of pilot training for the Royal Navy. In June 1958 No. 7 FTS amalgamated with No. 4 FTS and operated under the title of No. 4/7 FTS, but in July 1960 the 7 FTS element was officially disbanded. In April 1962 No. 7 FTS reformed at Church Fenton charged with the basic training of RAF pilots on the new 'all through' jet syllabus using Jet Provost T3 and T4 aircraft. The School disbanded yet again in November 1966, reforming at Church Fenton on 2 April 1979 with Jet Provost T3A and T5A aircraft and was the first FTS to receive the Tucano T1 in 1989. Disbanded again on 1 April 1992, No. 7 FTS was re-established at Chivenor on 1 September 1992 equipped with Hawk T1As where it provides advanced pilot and weapons training for fast-jet students.

Hawk T1 – No. 4 Flying Training School
Valley – June 1991

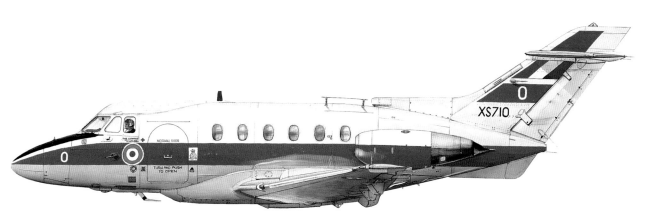

Dominie T1 – No. 6 Flying Training School
Finningley – August 1992

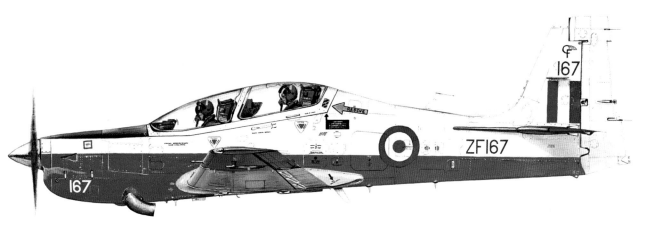

Tucano T1 – No. 7 Flying Training School
Church Fenton – December 1989

TRI-NATIONAL TORNADO TRAINING ESTABLISHMENT

The Tri-National Tornado Training Establishment (TTTE) was formed at Cottesmore in May 1979. It is responsible for the conversion of pilots and navigators of the Royal Air Force, the German Air Force, the German Navy and the Italian Air Force to the Tornado aircraft and is the first unit in the world in which more than two nations have undertaken the joint operational conversion of their front-line aircrews. The TTTE is staffed by instructors from the three nations involved and the aircraft are regularly flown on training sorties by crews of mixed nationalities. The unit is equipped with Tornados from all three nations.

CENTRAL FLYING SCHOOL

The Central Flying School – 'CFS' to all those who have been associated with this famous establishment – was formed in July 1912, at Upavon, and is the oldest flying training school in the world. It was given the task of training the UK's first military pilots, its first Commandant being Captain Godfrey Paine. Initial equipment was brought over from Farnborough in the form of a selection of Avros, Farmans, Be2s and Short biplanes, the first flying course beginning in August. Many of the pilots attending the School in its early days went on to become legendary and influential figures in the Service, and included the 'Father of the Royal Air Force', Marshal of the Royal Air Force, Lord Trenchard. With its reputation for innovation and excellence well established, the expanding CFS moved to Wittering in June 1926. Equipment at that time consisted of 12 Lynx-engine Avro 504s, four Bristol Fighters and five Snipes, with additional aircraft of the same types in reserve. A variety of different aircraft was also received for a valuation and to allow instructing staff to gain wider experience. From 1937, each new aircraft to enter RAF Service was flown by a CFS Examining Officer and 'pilot's notes' produced to help squadrons operate their new aircraft to best effect. In 1942, the work of CFS was largely taken over by a new unit – the Empire Central Flying School (ECFS) – at Hullavington, the first course having students from Australia, Canada, New Zealand, South Africa and the USA, as well as from Britain. The syllabus of the school assisted greatly in improving and upgrading the flying training programme that was so crucial in supporting the air war. The CFS was re-established after the war at Little Rissington, on 17 May 1946. In 1948, types being flown were the Tiger Moth, Harvard, Spitfire, Mosquito, Lancaster and Vampire. All-thorough jet training followed in 1958, using the Jet Provost and Vampire, only to revert to a multi-stream syllabus by 1965. A Helicopter Wing had been established at South Cerney in 1954, later moving to Ternhill. With Little Rissington becoming increasingly inadequate for modern jet operations, it was decided to vacate this hill-top aerodrome in April 1976, the CFS HQ, the Examining Wing and the Jet Provosts relocating to Cranwell, the Bulldogs to Leeming and Hawks to Valley. By 1977, the Cranwell-based elements had been moved to Leeming, with the Hawks remaining at Valley, the helicopters now residing at Shawbury. Today, the CFS HQ is firmly established at Scampton. Its reputation as a centre of excellence in the teaching of the complete range of flying training skills has never been higher, its fame and its unique contribution attracting students from around the world in addition to those of the UK Services.

ROYAL AIR FORCE COLLEGE

The origins of the Royal Air Force College can be traced back to 1915 when the Admiralty acquired some farmland west of Cranwell village in Lincolnshire for the purpose of building a training station for the Royal Naval Air Service. The station was quickly constructed and formally opened on 1 April 1916. Naval officers were trained to fly aircraft, airships and observation balloons but there was also established a 'boys' wing for training naval ratings as mechanics and riggers. The RNAS and RFC were two separate organisations but their amalgamation on 1 April 1918 placed the station, or HMS *Daedalus* as it was known, under a new owner – the Royal Air Force. Now known as RAF Station Cranwell, the base continued on much the same lines as before but with the end of the war later that year a reappraisal of the RAF and its facilities was undertaken, resulting in a memorandum being submitted to Parliament in 1919 with proposals on the Force's future. One proposal was the establishment of a cadet college at Cranwell to provide basic officer and flying training. This was accepted and the first course of flight cadets began on 5 February 1920 – recognised now as 'Founder's Day'. As well as flying training the College continued with the 'boys' wing (now known as the Apprentice School) although this facility moved to Halton in 1927 and, during the years, other elements were added. The main College building, as we know it today, was designed in the late 1920s, but was not completed until September 1933, being formally opened on 11 October 1934 by the Prince of Wales. During WWII the College, as such, closed and was known only as the Royal Air Force College Flying Training School, but the base expanded to cope with other aspects of training both in the air and on the ground. After the war the College formally reopened in 1946 and in the ensuing years there was an expansion of training facilities. The south airfield was extended to accommodate jet aircraft and new buildings were constructed for domestic use and absorption of units from elsewhere in the country. The station now houses the Headquarters of the University Air Squadrons and the College of Air Warfare. The most recent addition, in 1992, was the Directorate of Recruiting and Aircrew Selection. The outward distinguishing mark of aircraft from the RAF College is the pale blue 'Cranwell band' around the rear fuselage. Although the Flying Training School's designation has changed over the years this feature remains today and is carried by the Tucanos of No. 3 FTS.

Tornado GR1 – Tri-National Tornado Training Establishment
Cottesmore – October 1980

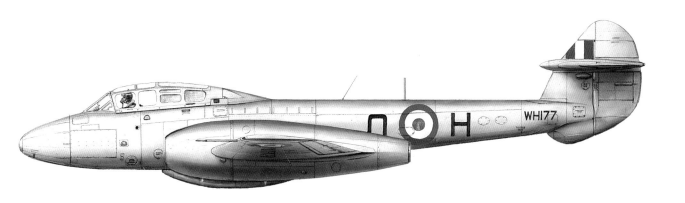

Meteor T7 – Central Flying School
Little Rissington – 1952

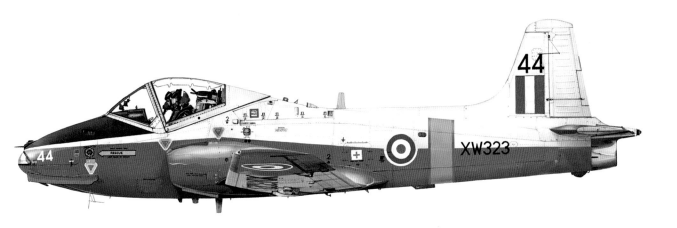

Jet Provost T5A – Flying Training School, RAF Cranwell
Cranwell – December 1984

THE QUEEN'S FLIGHT

Five aircraft and about 180 officers and men of the Royal Air Force make up one of the world's most remarkable flying units – the Queen's Flight. Today the unit consists of three British Aerospace 146 CC2 jet airliners and two Westland Wessex HCC4 helicopters. The role of the Flight is to provide air transport for the Queen, members of the Royal Family, the Prime Minister, certain senior Ministers, visiting Heads of State and the Chiefs of Staff. Its origins can be traced back to 1917 when the Prince of Wales first flew in an RE 8 in France. Later he bought and operated several aircraft privately but it was not until 21 July 1936 that the King's Flight was officially formed at Hendon by Edward VIII. The Flight moved to Benson in September 1939, but in 1942 it was disbanded and formed the nucleus of 161 Squadron, which was engaged on special operations. The King's Flight was reformed on 1 May 1946 with four Vickers Viking aircraft and on 1 August 1952, following the Accession of the Queen, the unit was renamed the Queen's Flight. Between 1955 and 1961 the Vikings were gradually replaced by de Havilland Herons and in 1959, two Westland Whirlwind helicopters were added. Prior to then other helicopters had been used on loan. In 1964 the first of the Andovers arrived and in 1969, the Wessex replaced the Whirlwinds. April 1986 saw the official handover of the first of three BAe 146 aircraft which have replaced the Andovers.

UNIVERSITY AIR SQUADRONS

In 1919 Lord Trenchard conceived the idea of forming Air Squadrons at Cambridge and Oxford Universities with the object of 'encouraging an interest in flying and promoting and maintaining liaison with the universities in technical and research problems affecting aviation'. The idea reached fruition with the formation of both squadrons in 1925 which were essentially civilian in character but had RAF instructors. They were so successful that a third squadron was formed at London in 1935. With the outbreak of war in September 1939, the three units were disbanded but it was soon discovered that the Army was now attracting the pick of the graduate recruits. In 1940 the three units were resurrected and 20 additional squadrons were formed with their main function being to provide Service pre-entry ground training. After the war the squadrons all received Tiger Moth aircraft to conduct *ab initio* training. They were entirely devoted to the uncommitted RAFVR member and, as a result, came close to disbandment on several occasions as their numbers fluctuated. The establishment of the Graduate Entry Scheme in the late 1960s saved the squadrons and they now number 16 with another non-flying squadron at RMCS Shrivenham. The University Air Squadrons (UASs) came under the command and control of AOC No. 22 Group and his staff until December 1971 when the Group disbanded. They are now under the control of the AOC and Commandant, RAF College Cranwell where HQ UAS is located. All squadrons are now equipped with Bulldog T1s having previously flown Chipmunk T10s.

ELEMENTARY FLYING TRAINING SQUADRON

The forerunner of the Elementary Flying Training Squadron (EFTS), the Flying Selection Squadron (FSS), began operating at Swinderby in July 1979 as a detachment of the Flying Training School at Cranwell. Equipped with the reliable single piston-engined Chipmunk T10, the six-week course of 14 flying hours was set to evaluate and grade trainees before they started their otherwise all-jet flying training sequence. A reassessment of the role of FSS was carried out in January 1985 following which EFTS was established on 1 June 1987. The course, now 16 weeks long, totals 54 hours of flying (14 of which are solo), and is the first stage in the RAF pilot training scheme for students with less than 30 hours previous flying experience. It is structured as a mini-version of the Basic Flying Training School (BFTS) course with the exception of night flying. Students then proceed to the next stage at BFTS on the Tucano. The Chipmunk, designed by the de Havilland Aircraft Company of Canada, first entered service with the RAF in 1950 and over 700 examples were delivered for use in University Air Squadrons, Reserve Flying Schools and other basic training establishments., Of the 70 aircraft remaining in service 14 are flown by EFTS and many of the others equip Air Experience Flights. WB550'F' was the second Chipmunk T10 to be built for the RAF and is now flying with the Elementary Flying Training Squadron.

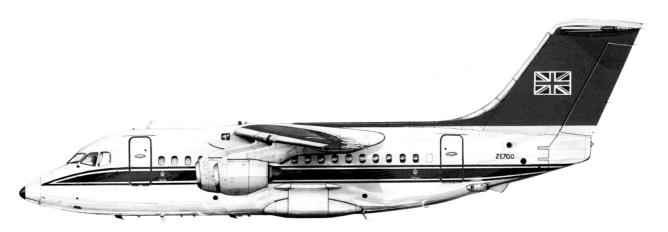

BAe 146 CC2 – The Queen's Flight
Benson – April 1988

Bulldog T1 – Universities of Glasgow & Strathclyde Air Squadron
Glasgow Airport, Abbotsinch – February 1985

Chipmunk T10 – Elementary Flying Training Squadron
Swinderby – April 1990

THE BATTLE OF BRITAIN MEMORIAL FLIGHT

The Battle of Britain Memorial Flight can trace its origins back to June 1957 when the three remaining Spitfire PR XIXs of the Meteorological Flight at Woodvale were flown to Duxford for storage. The following month they went to Biggin Hill to join the lone Hurricane IIC, LF363, and formed the Historic Aircraft Flight. One of the Spitfires, PS915, was withdrawn for ground-display duty although it rejoined the Flight in 1984. Later in 1957, two Spitfire LF16s were added but early in 1958 Biggin Hill was closed for flying operations and the aircraft moved to North Weald. That airfield, too, was soon closed and the Flight moved to Martlesham Heath. A second Spitfire PR XIX, PS853, had left the Flight while at North Weald but it too rejoined in April 1964. In September 1959, during the annual London flypast, one of the Spitfire LF16s suffered engine failure and had to force land on a cricket pitch at Bromley in Kent. It never flew again and the other LF16 was retired. In November 1961 the Flight's two remaining aircraft moved to Horsham St Faith in Norfolk and were struggling for survival but it was soon realised that such historic aircraft should be collected and preserved. With the closure of Horsham St Faith in April 1963 the Flight moved to Coltishall and during the next few years more aircraft were added. The first acquisition was a Spitfire VB, AB910, in 1965 and the Spitfire IIA, P7350, arrived in 1968 after appearing in the film *The Battle of Britain*. This aircraft actually took part in the battle. In 1972 a second Hurricane IIC, PZ865, was presented by Hawker Aircraft and the Lancaster B I, PA474, joined in 1973. In 1976 a move to the present home at Coningsby in Lincolnshire was made and this has allowed a visitor centre to be created alongside the Flight's hangar. In addition to the display aircraft the Flight also operates a Chipmunk T10 for continuation piston-engine training and a Devon C2, VP981, for multi-engine and communications duties. The pilots are drawn from the Coningsby-based Tornado squadrons. The Flight is justifiably proud of its position as keepers of the RAF's heritage.

Hawk T1A – The Royal Air Force Aerobatic Team – The Red Arrows
Scampton – January 1992

THE RED ARROWS

The Royal Air Force aerobatic teams were originally formed by front-line fighter squadrons, a tradition which went back to the 1920s, but, in 1964, it was decided to provide two aerobatic teams from RAF Flying Training Command. The Central Flying School formed the 'Red Pelicans' with Jet Provosts and No. 4 Flying Training School formed the 'Yellowjacks' with five Gnats. The following year the RAF formed a full-time aerobatic team with Gnats which was officially named 'The Red Arrows'. Under the command of the Central Flying School, the Team was initially based at Fairford but moved to Kemble in 1966, where it established a permanent home. For 15 years the nine scarlet Gnats were a familiar sight at air shows throughout the United Kingdom and also in many countries overseas. In 1980, the Gnat was replaced by the RAF's new advanced trainer, the British Aerospace Hawk T1, and this aircraft brought a new dimension to formation aerobatics. The Team's official badge was approved in 1982 and is carried on the port side of the aircraft with the CFS badge appearing on the other side. In the spring of 1983 the Red Arrows moved to their present base at Scampton in Lincolnshire, which has a long and distinguished history, operating such types as Lancasters, Canberras and, latterly, Vulcans. The Red Arrows have performed over 2,700 public displays in 45 different countries and have visited the USA on two occasions. They have also hosted teams from other countries including the 'Russian Knights' from Moscow.

Spitfire IIA, Battle of Britain Memorial Flight (41 Squadron)
Coningsby – April 1985

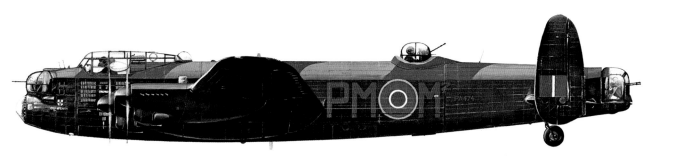

Lancaster B I, Battle of Britain Memorial Flight (103 Squadron)
Coningsby – May 1988

Hurricane IIC, Battle of Britain Memorial Flight (111 Squadron)
Coningsby – March 1979

AIR EXPERIENCE FLIGHTS

Air Experience Flights were formed in 1958 when 50 Chipmunk aircraft became available after the closure of the RAFVR flying schools. The object of the flights is to provide at least 25 minutes per annum flying experience for all air cadets who have passed their first-class cadet examination. Members of other youth organisations with an air affiliation are also flown on an opportunity basis. There are presently 13 flights based at Manston, Hurn (Bournemouth), Colerne, Exeter, Teversham (Cambridge), Benson, Newton, Shawbury, Finningley, Woodvale, Leeming, Turnhouse (Edinburgh) and Sydenham (Belfast). The pilots are mainly ex-servicemen who hold commissions in the RAFVR(T) and follow a variety of careers. They are also assisted by ATC officers. There are about four pilots per aircraft and they attend annual training and summer camps. The number of aircraft per flight varies with the largest, No. 6 AEF at Benson, having seven Chipmunks and No. 13 AEF at Sydenham operating a single Bulldog. Some aircraft carry unit markings while others apply aircraft identification letters or numbers.

AIR CADET CENTRAL GLIDING SCHOOL

In 1939 the Air Defence Cadet Corps started basic glider training at Dunstable Downs and by 1943 gliding was part of the official cadet training programme with 84 Schools in being by December 1945. On 30 May 1946 the responsibility for the Air Training Corps (ATC) was vested in the newly-reformed Reserve Command at Alexandra House in London. By then there were 87 gliding schools equipped with a variety of types. In October 1946 the Command Headquarters moved to White Waltham aerodrome and two months later plans were made for the formation of a Central Gliding School. This became reality on 1 July 1949 with the birth of the Home Command Gliding Instructors School at Detling. Its title changed to the Home Command Gliding Centre (HCGC) in 1955 and in September it moved to Hawkinge. By this time the main equipment was Sedbergh and Cadet Mk 3 gliders serving 27 gliding schools. Flying Training Command took over the responsibility of all cadet training on 23 March 1959 and the HCGC was reorganised to form No. 1 Gliding Centre at Hawkinge to serve the southern Group and No. 2 Gliding Centre formed at Newton to serve the north. No. 2 GC moved to Kirton-on-Lindsey in early 1960 and, with the closure of Hawkinge, No. 1 GC moved to Swanton Morley in December 1961. No. 2 GC transferred to Spitalgate in 1965 and HQ Air Cadets moved from White Waltham to Brampton in October 1968 attached to the newly-formed HQ Training Command (combining Flying Training and Technical Training Commands). This led to the formation of the Central Gliding School (CGS) in January 1972 with headquarters at Spitalgate and two years later the present title of Air Cadet Central Gliding School (ACCGS) was adopted. In 1975 HQ ACCGS moved to Syerston with the detachment at Swanton Morley remaining until 1977 when the two units amalgamated. Twelve schools re-equipped with Venture self-launching gliders from 1977 and in September 1983 three new types of glider were bought for evaluation. This resulted in the acquisition of 100 Grob 103 Vikings in 1984. In March 1990 the first of 53 Grob 109B Vigilant self-launching gliders was accepted as replacement for the Ventures.

Chipmunk T10 – No. 12 Air Experience Flight
Turnhouse – July 1989

Viking T1 – No. 662 Volunteer Gliding School
Arbroath – July 1990

Vigilant T1 – No. 663 Volunteer Gliding School
Kinloss – May 1991

From our library of paintings we include illustrations of other aircraft and, although these are no longer in service, they each played an important part in the RAF's history. During WWII, people from Commonwealth, European and many other countries assisted Britain in its fight against the enemy. Some served in established units while, in other cases, new, dedicated squadrons were formed reflecting the make-up of their members.

Catalina IB – No. 333 (Norwegian) Squadron
Based at Woodhaven in Fife, No. 333 Squadron
was part of Coastal Command flying the Catalina
flying boat until the end of the war

Halifax BIII – No. 158 Squadron
The Halifax made a significant contribution
to Bomber Command's offensive in the war.
No. 158 Squadron received the Mk III version in
January 1944 at its Yorkshire base at Lissett

Hurricane 1 – No. 43 (Fighter) Squadron
The Hurricane equipped more squadrons in the
Battle of Britain than the Spitfire and accounted
for a higher number of victories. No. 43 Squadron
flew this type from Tangmere during the conflict

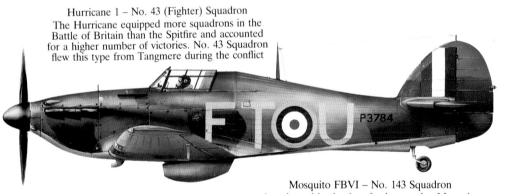

Mosquito FBVI – No. 143 Squadron
A truly multi-role aircraft, the wooden Mosquito
served in the fighter, bomber, pathfinder and
coastal fields with great distinction. No. 143
Squadron was part of the Banff Strike Wing
dedicated to attacking shipping off the Norwegian
coast towards the end of the war

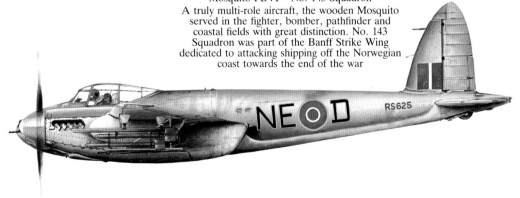

Lancaster BX – No. 405 Squadron,
Royal Canadian Air Force
The Lancaster BX was a Canadian-built version
of Avro's celebrated 'heavy'. No. 405 Squadron
was based at Linton-on-Ouse and had previously
flown the Wellington and Halifax before
re-equipping with the Lancaster

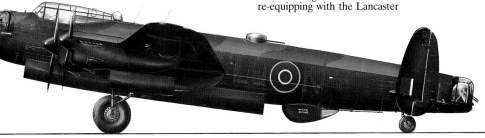

Lancaster BIII – No. 61 Squadron
Typical of the 'standard' Lancaster, this
illustration features the aircraft in which
Flight Lieutenant Bill Reid won his VC on
3 November 1943

Shackleton AEW2 – No. 8 Squadron
Although designed as a maritime-patrol aircraft,
the Shackleton served longer in its modified
airborne early warning role and was the RAF's
last front-line piston-engined aircraft

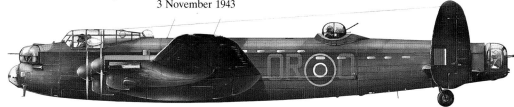

Spitfire VB – No. 310 (Czechoslovak) Squadron
This Spitfire is preserved by the Shuttleworth
Trust at Old Warden and depicts the aircraft
when flown by 310 Squadron in August 1942
when based at Exeter. It now displays the code
letters 'NN-A' it carried in 1942

Spitfire IXE – No. 43 (Fighter) Squadron
The Squadron flew the Mk IX from August 1943
until May 1947 but is shown here when based
at Zeltweg in 1946. Over 5,600 examples of this
model were built

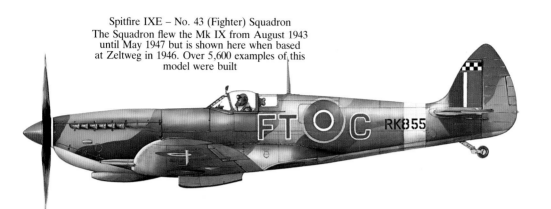

Spitfire LF16E – No. 604
(County of Middlesex) Squadron
Based at Hendon, No. 604 Squadron was part of
the Auxiliary Air Force which had reformed in
1946. Over 1,000 of these Merlin-engined fighters
were built

Spitfire F22 – No. 602 (City of Glasgow) Squadron
The last major Spitfire derivative was the
Griffon-engined Mk 22 which equipped twelve
squadrons in the Auxiliary Air Force. No. 602
Squadron flew this type from Abbotsinch and
Renfrew between 1948 and 1951

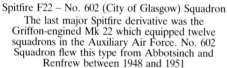

Tiger Moth T2 – No. 11 Reserve Flying School
Many of the RAF's wartime pilots learned to fly
in the Tiger Moth which equipped flying schools
in the UK and overseas. They continued to be
used by many units until replaced by Chipmunks
in the early 1950s. No. 11 RFS (previously
No. 11 EFTS) was based at Scone

Vampire FB5 – No. 603
(City of Edinburgh) Squadron
The Vampire was the RAF's second jet-fighter
but did not see active service during the war.
It subsequently equipped many front-line and
auxiliary units

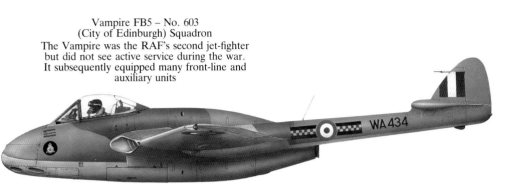

Wellington IV – No. 300 (Polish) Squadron
This model of the Wellington was fitted with
Pratt and Whitney engines. No. 300 was the first
Polish-manned squadron in the RAF

Tornado GR1 – Bahrain
The JP233 airfield denial weapon was used to
good effect in the Gulf War in 1991

Tornado GR1 – Tabuk, Saudi Arabia
Only two prototypes of the GEC-Ferranti thermal
imaging and laser designator (TIALD) were
available in the Gulf War but they were put
to good use

From time-to-time aircraft have been specially painted to commemorate anniversaries or other significant events. A selection of some of these are shown below.

Phantom FG1 – No. 111 (Fighter) Squadron
Painted to commemorate the heyday of the Squadron's 'Black Arrows' Hunter aerobatic team and the last year of Phantom operations, 'Black Mike' was one of the last FG1s to fly

Tornado GR1 – No. XV Squadron
Painted to celebrate the Squadron's 75th anniversary in 1990

Tornado F3 – No. 65 Squadron
The 1990 Tornado F3 display aircraft carried these marks in 65 Squadron colours to highlight the 50th anniversary of the Battle of Britain

Phantom FGR2 – No. 19 (Fighter) Squadron
Painted to mark the Squadron's 75th anniversary and the end of Phantom operations in Germany

Tornado F3 – No. 29 (Fighter) Squadron
Painted to mark the Squadron's 75th anniversary in 1990

Hercules C1P – Lyneham Wing
Specially painted to celebrate the 25th anniversary of Hercules operations in the RAF

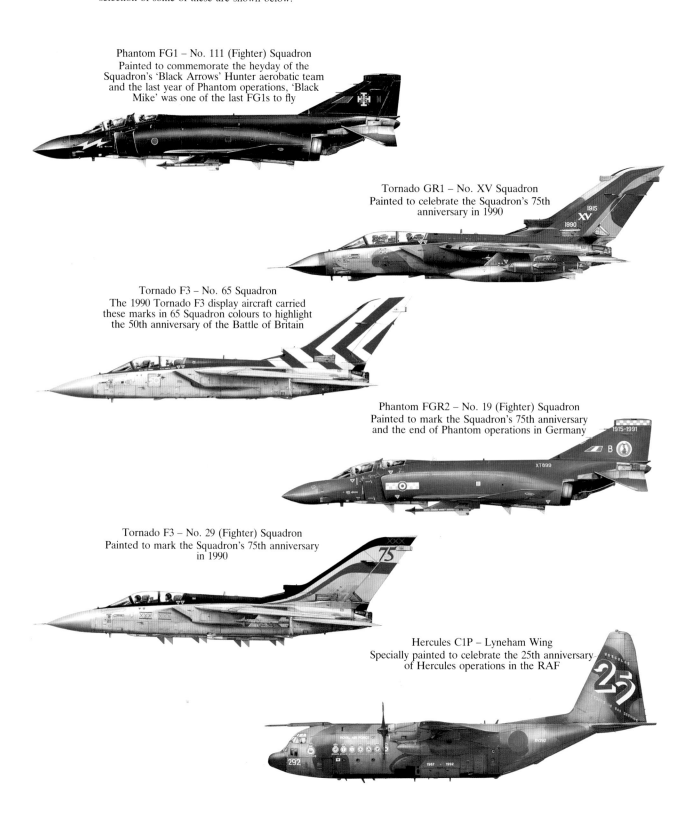

The Far East Air Force in the 1960s

SQUADRON LEADER DAVID BINNIE AFC RAF (Retd)

In 1960 the RAF and Commonwealth Squadrons in the Far East formed part of a Commonwealth Strategic Reserve. Developed during the 1950s, to broaden the base on which the defence of South East Asia was built, the first stage had been completed in 1955 when the South East Asia collective defence Treaty Organisation (SEATO) came into force.

Although no forces were permanently assigned to SEATO, all eight members deployed substantial resources in the area and Britain signed a mutual defence and assistance treaty with Malaya in 1957. Rapid reinforcement from the United Kingdom was becoming much simpler with the formation of Transport Command's new long-range squadrons, and the development of Gan as a major staging post. No. 38 Group had been established as a tactical support force and in-flight refuelling was allowing modern fighters to reach the Far East without the need to use staging posts not under RAF control.

Consequently, in the event of an emergency in SE Asia, the Far East Air Force (FEAF) was in a strong position with well-trained forces already in-theatre and reinforcements within reach. FEAF was, of course, a textbook tactical air force and, therefore, had many roles to play including transport, maritime, attack, reconnaissance, helicopter support and air defence. This latter role was carried out by No. 60 Squadron, later augmented in 1965 by No. 64 Squadron, equipped with the Gloster Javelin.

The Javelin was the last of a long series of fighters designed by the Gloster Aircraft Company Ltd, by this time, a division of the vast Hawker Siddeley Aviation (HSA) organisation. The prototype first flew on 26 November 1951 and the F(AW)1 on 22 July 1954. Weighing some 44,000 lbs, this was the heaviest fighter to be used by the RAF until this time, and the first to be classified as 'all-weather' due to its blind-firing capability. It was primarily a bomber destroyer rather than a close-combat fighter, although it could hold its own with contemporary fighters at high level in manoeuvre and rate of climb. The delta planform gave a good load-carrying capability and reduced supersonic drag, but its poor stall characteristics could lead to 'deep stalling' (from which the only recovery was to spin!) and its low aspect ratio wing gave high induced drag in turns, leading to rapid speed loss. The airbrakes were an outstanding feature of the Javelin and it was possible to be at 40,000 feet on the runway centre line at 14 nautical miles and still break comfortably into the circuit at 1,000 ft. This, however, was not to be recommended if the circuit was at all busy, as the cockpit was totally misted up for the ensuing 20 minutes!

Night Patrol – Javelin FAW9 of No. 60 Squadron, Tengah, Singapore, October 1966

No. 60 Squadron Javelins at dispersal, Tengah, Singapore, 1967

The basic armament consisted of four 30 mm wing-mounted Aden cannons and four Firestreaks carried on under-wing pylons. It carried 915 gallons of fuel in the wing tanks and 250 gallons in each of two ventral tanks giving a total of 10,895 lbs fuel, sufficient for around one hour sortie duration. The aircraft was limited to 535 knots/.9 mach up to 20,000 ft and 1.08 above 35,000 ft. The normal 'G' limit was 5 G with the ventrals empty, 3 G otherwise.

Four Mk9Rs of No. 25 Squadron, accompanied by Valiant tankers, were the first Javelins to visit Singapore in November and December 1960 for a theatre-reinforcement exercise. On 26 June 1961 the main deployment of Javelins to Singapore commenced when five Javelins supported by two Hastings took off from Waterbeach on the first leg to Orange in France. Inevitably, a number of minor technical problems had to be overcome. The Javelins also temporarily lost their Hastings support to other tasks when Kuwait, which had been granted full independence on 19 June, was threatened with invasion six days later by Iraq. The Javelins arrived at RAF Tengah on 13 July, 17 days after leaving the UK, having covered 8,007 nautical miles, used 15 scheduled staging airfields and flown 17 hrs, 40 mins apiece.

Of the next wave of six aircraft, only four were to arrive safely. XH840, flown by Flight Lieutenant Botwright was destroyed following a starter fire at Luqa. A much more serious accident occurred on 5 August when, on the climb out of Dum Dum, one engine exploded on XH791 flown by Flight Lieutenant Owens and Master Navigator Melton. Control was lost and ejection initiated. Although Melton was found safely in the jungle after three days, Owens sadly was found dead in his seat after it malfunctioned. The full 16-aircraft unit was duly complete in Singapore on 27 November 1961.

The aircraft had to be painted in the squadron colours and it was decided that the lightning-flash marking was not suitable for painting on the broad fin of the Javelin, so alternate black and silver stripes were applied, in line with and just below the tailplane. The Kabuli Markhor head in silver, with a blue outline for A Flight, red outline for B Flight and, in due course, green outline for C Flight was painted on the tail below the stripes.

And so the squadron settled down to operations in the Far East. A series of performance trials were carried out during Practice Interception (PI) flights. Inevitably, the take-off runs were slightly longer and the initial climb-rate suffered in the heat, but above approximately 20,000 ft the cold upper air gave an improvement in performance up to the tropopause. Thus reheat ('overdrive') could be selected at 15,000 ft rather than the 20,000 of temperate climates.

The squadron operated by flights, one on day flying and the other on nights. Times varied but latterly day flying commenced with the first pair at 0630 hrs followed by the second pair at 0700 hrs. Day flying normally ceased around lunch-time. The first sortie of the day was a marvellous time to fly. Walking out to the aircraft it would still be dark with the faintest hint of pink to the east. After the normal pre-flight (pilot walk round, navigator upper surface) checks you climbed into the cockpit, strapped in, put on your flying helmet and started the left to right cockpit checks. At this time in the morning it was cool and comfortable. A quick check with your wing man and you gave the wind-up signal with one finger.

You confirmed with the ground crew that you were clear to start, lifted the flap and pressed the button to start the left engine. The silence of the night was shattered by the explosion of the cartridge-initiated AVPIN followed by the familiar boom of the Sapphire at idle. You taxied out and ran up your engines on runway 36 at Tengah with the Officers' Mess just on the left, secure in the knowledge that, if you could not sleep at this hour of the morning, well then, neither could anybody else. Dawn came swiftly, and by the time you were airborne it was day. You headed west. Mist was lying in the valleys, the air was as smooth as cream and the Malacca Straits looked like a mirror. You were able to fly your aircraft extremely accurately, the altimeter and Air Speed Indicator (ASI) needles appeared welded in position and you reflected again on what a superb time of day it was to fly.

Air-to-air-firing became a routine part of training. The banner was towed by Meteors of the Seletar Target Towing Flight (TTF) and firing normally took place in MS8 in the South China Sea, although firing was also mounted out of RAAF Butterworth. Before being allowed to fire live ammunition, several cine sorties had to be flown and the film used to assess the pilot's technique and safety. It was a good handling exercise and also great fun. The idea was to lock the radar on to the banner spreader bar and the gun sight would then work out the correct deflection. Occasional tug locks in error were readily identifiable. It was important to commence the attack from an accurate 'perch' position; too far forward and the attack was uncomfortably tight, too far aft and a very shallow tailchase ensued. This led to very narrow angles on the flag and sometimes the flag *and* the tug would appear on the same frame – a feat guaranteed not to impress the squadron Pilot Attack Instructor (PAI). There was also an understandable lack of enthusiasm amongst the Meteor tug pilots when 30 mm ammunition started to whistle past their cockpits!

The early 60s was still the time of nuclear tests in the Pacific and in December 1961 the squadron was asked to check for nuclear particles in the atmosphere. Measurement equipment was fitted to a Javelin and readings were taken by Flight Lieutenants Gooding and Meredith. Gooding had been a member of the RAF team on Christmas Island when British bombs were exploded there.

The squadron had enjoyed an enviable safety record since arriving in-theatre – a testimony to the quality of the air and ground crews involved. The climate played havoc with some electrical systems and predictable supply problems occurred because of the distance from the UK. However, serious engine problems began to arise by the end of 1962. The T3 had been on strength since November 1961 and, after a brief appearance in January 1962, disappeared back into the hangar with engine defects. By May, five 100 series engines had failed and on 18 September Squadron Leader Francis of the Fighter Command IRS team was carrying out a flight check on Flight Lieutenant Gordon Allin when both engines failed in cloud. This led to almost total loss of the hydraulic controls. Despite this, Gordon Allin carried out a text-book forced landing at Tengah – a masterly performance considering it was 'for real' and, that it was a procedure which was never ever practised. On 29 October the aircraft of Flight Lieutenant Tyler and Flying Officer Simpson suffered a single engine failure and on 3 December Wing Commander Smith, the Squadron Commander, and Squadron Leader Joliffe were forced to eject following double engine failure.

Having suffered one-and-a-half compressor blade failures per month for some time, the situation had clearly become unacceptable and the Javelins were duly grounded. After initial investigation, a limited clearance was given to operate below the freezing level, but a ban on flying in cloud remained in place for some time – a considerable handicap for an all-weather squadron! The problem was diagnosed as 'centre line closure'. Flying in or near heavy CB cloud caused cooling of the compressor casing by ice crystals. The resultant radial shrinkage eventually brought the casing into contact with the high speed compressor blades with catastrophic results. The solution was to apply abrasive pads to the inside of the casing to 'file' away the blade tips if and when they came into contact. This 'fix' was treated with understandable hilarity by the aircrew, but, in fairness, it worked, though other compressor blade problems were to crop up a few years later.

All was not gloom, however, and amusing incidents were frequent. One such occurred during a station dining-in night at Tengah. Whilst the meal was in progress (before the main course, as one seems to recall) a Javelin could be heard passing overhead. The noise died in the distance, followed immediately by three distinct explosions, which sounded for all the world like an aircraft crashing. One's heart sank and the Station Commander, Group Captain Phil Lagesen, shot from the dining-room. It transpired that one of the squadron's trusty pilots had decided to practise a total electrics failure and attract the attention of Air Traffic by banging in the reheat at low level. He was done on three counts: ruining the Station Commander's main course, using reheat to raise Air Traffic and not knowing that one of the services lost with a total electrics failure was . . . the reheat!

In the meantime, political tensions in the area were rising. In December 1962 a revolt against the Sultan of Brunei, led by the leader of the People's Party, A.M. Azahani, was put down by British, Gurkha and Brunei troops. Air power was also present in the form of Hunters and Canberras of Nos. 20 and 45 Squadrons respectively. The defeated Azahani retreated over the border in Indonesia to lick his wounds and to continue plotting, with President Sukarno, the subjugation of all North Borneo territories by Indonesia.

In 1963, to combat the increased threat, No. 60 Squadron was put on alert at Tengah and Butterworth in February and March respectively. Between May and September modified engines were installed in time for the north-east monsoon, which affected the Malaysian Archipelago from October each year, and cloud flying was resumed with no further problems. In mid-1963 a new Ground Control Intercept (GCI) was introduced on nearby Bukit Gombak. This gave closer liaison between controllers and the fighter crews, increased coverage and a much-improved capability overall. In May 1963 Wing Commander Peter Smith handed over to Wing Commander 'Jock' Fraser who, in the event, was to preside over the growth of No. 60 Squadron into the largest squadron in the Royal Air Force.

This was brought about by the increasingly belligerent stance of President Sukarno which led to the period of tension known as the 'Indonesian Confrontation'. Indonesia claimed Sarawak and Sabah (formerly British North Borneo) and chose to 'confront' the Malaysian states until its wishes were met. British and Malaysian embassies in Djakarta, along with consulates elsewhere, were attacked and burnt by mobs. Border incursions increased in frequency and depth of penetration. Alert states were raised both in Tengah and Butterworth and the first interception of an

Lightning F6 of No. 74 (F) Squadron landing over No. 60 Squadron Javelins at Tengah, 1968

Echelon Starboard – Javelin FAW9s of No. 60 Squadron, 1967

Late finals – Beverley C1, XL150 of No. 34 Squadron, Seletar landing at Hong Kong, 1967

'enemy' Badger in Malaysian airspace took place on 17 October 1963.

With so many crews and aircraft tied up with the operational requirements, reinforcements were needed. A detachment of four No. 64 Squadron aircraft, with Mk9Rs, arrived in November 1963. The Mk9R, with two underwing 230-gallon tanks, provided a useful addition in both range and duration. More aircraft were detached, until, by March 1964, No. 60 Squadron had 24 Javelin FAW9/9Rs, two T3s and 77 crew members, in addition to the Mk9Rs on loan from No. 64 Squadron and the crews attached on rotation. No less than 347 people were on the posted strength of No. 60 Squadron by 1 April 1964. Incursions by the Indonesian Air Force continued and four Hunters of No. 20 Squadron were deployed to each of Labuan and Kuching, followed four days later by Javelins to provide the Night All-Weather (NAW) role. Conditions were rudimentary. Both airfields had a CADF, Eureka and NDB whilst Kuching also boasted a 787 Approach Control Radar (ACR). Terrain screening was a major factor and the pylon tanks on the 9Rs adversely affected the Distance Measuring Equipment (DME) and Automatic Direction Finding (ADF). Furthermore, tropical rainstorms could take out an airfield at very short notice.

Although the runways had been lengthened to 2,000 yds, it was still marginal for a fully-laden aircraft at the prevailing temperature of 30°C or more. Happily, no engine failures occurred on take-off. The difficulties caused by the high terrain were exacerbated by a lack of suitably detailed maps, despite years of photo survey, latterly by the Canberra PR7s of No. 81 Squadron. Crews began to fill in the gaps with features and approximate spot heights as a result of their increasing familiarity with the terrain.

The political situation continued to deteriorate and on 4 July 1964 it was announced that six more crews and 36 groundcrew were to be posted in, and the four No. 64 Squadron aircraft would be retained. The West Malaysian ADZ was established in September 1964 and low level Combat Air Patrols (CAPs) were introduced. The weather could play havoc with normal operations and so it proved at RAAF Butterworth on the night of 6 September. Flight Lieutenant David and Sergeant Kirk had returned from a west coast patrol to find that the airfield was out in a storm. After a number of missed approaches they finally saw the airfield and landed, but were unable to prevent the aircraft aquaplaning off the left-hand side of the flooded runway. Coincidentally, Flight Lieutenant Reekie and Flying Officer Woodward came back from an east coast patrol to meet with the same situation. They too were able to land safely but once again could not stop the aircraft going off the left-hand side of the runway. However, there was no real risk of collision as they had landed in opposite directions!

In January 1965 it was decided that No. 64 Squadron should be permanently moved to FEAF. However, the Valiant tankers had been grounded the previous year and the replacement Victor tankers were not yet available. Route staging was impossible for political reasons. The aircraft were therefore flown down to Lee-on-Solent whence they were shipped out as deck cargo to Singapore. No. 64 Squadron was to suffer the loss of several aircraft in their first few months in operation, often involving crew with close ties to No. 60 Squadron. On 22 June, Flight Lieutenants Hart and Dell suffered a catastrophic compressor failure whilst intercepting a Malaysian DC-3 and ejected safely. On 8 November Flight Lieutenants

Fitchew and Evans were unable to lower their undercarriage at night and were ordered to eject in the pre-planned ejection area to the east of Changi. Flight Lieutenants Poppe and Unsted were ordered to search the area and, finding their Violet Picture unserviceable, elected to carry out a visual search, in the course of which they flew into the sea. Poppe died in the crash but Unsted, miraculously, not only survived the impact but was able to escape from the aircraft on its way to the sea bed.

On 27 March 1965 No. 60 Squadron took part in Exercise Showpiece which was a firepower demonstration for some 150 VIPs including Tunku Abdul Rahman, the Malaysian Prime Minister. Four carriers, HMS *Eagle*, HMS *Bulwark*, HMS *Albion* and HMAS *Melbourne* were steaming in line astern off the east coast of Singapore. The demonstration consisted of a 'balbo' of 27 Javelins, 16 Canberras, 12 Sabres and six Hunters all led by a Victor Bomber. The Canberras, Sabres and Hunters then carried out attacks on splash targets, and the exercise culminated in a salvo of 35 1,000-lb bombs dropped from a Victor. This last item was rather more impressive and certainly more memorable for the spectators than planned. The bombs in question were rather old and on the way down two of them met the shock-waves of the preceding bombs on the way up, resulting in their premature detonation, thus showering the VIPs in high-speed shrapnel!

In November 1965 Wing Commander Jock Fraser was replaced by Wing Commander Miller who would guide No. 60 Squadron through its final years in Singapore. Wing Commander 'Dusty' Miller, of 47 Cranwell entry, was an aggressive and spirited pilot in the air. He was equally passionate on the ground for his squadron. His enthusiasm also extended to motor sport where he enjoyed some success.

Indonesia found itself increasingly isolated and in May 1966 agreed to negotiate a cease-fire. The Bangkok Accord between Indonesia and Malaysia was formally signed on 11 August 1966. Alert states were cancelled, detachments withdrawn and the squadron reverted to a peace-time footing. Squadron establishments were reduced to 12 aircraft and 16 crew. Despite this, the variety of flying was undiminished. The arrival of 'first tourists' for the first time in many years meant that written Standard Operating Procedure (SOP) had to be produced! Air-to-air firing continued and, as it was thought at the time that a number of crews might go on to the Phantom, air-to-ground strafe was also introduced. This was carried out at Song Song, a remote island off the Malaysia/Thailand border. Although the Javelin was never designed with this role in mind, highly creditable results were achieved. The squadron was required to provide a Range Safety Officer (RSO) who normally spent a full week on duty. Very basic, but clean and comfortable, accommodation was provided on a nearby island where it was actually possible to watch a film in the evening (*Casablanca* was the favourite). To do so, via a rickety, flickering black-and-white projector, and to wake in the morning to a steaming plate of scrambled turtle's eggs was truly to know the meaning of life!

It was decided to re-equip the Night All-Weather Fighter (NAWF) squadrons with Lightnings and the first aircraft of No. 74 Squadron arrived in the Far East on 11 June 1967, to replace No. 64 Squadron. The latter duly disbanded on 17 June 1967 and No. 60 Squadron inherited their Mk9Rs. No sooner had the aircraft been repainted in their new squadron markings than a new detachment was ordered. Communist activity in China had generated civil unrest in Hong Kong and a fighter presence was deemed necessary. The aircraft were staged up through Labuan and Clark Field in the Philippines. Flying in Hong Kong mainly consisted of PIs under the control of Taimo Shan radar or reconnaissance flights over the New Territories at low level to 'wave the flag'.

Before being allowed to fly over the colony it was first necessary to carry out a border familiarisation flight with the resident Army Air Corps unit. The authorities were understandably edgy about border violations after a Hunter pilot on a previous detachment became engrossed in carrying out cine quarters on a train and found himself, if not right in the centre of China, at least comfortably on the wrong side of the border! Three such detachments were mounted in 1967.

Plans to re-equip No. 60 Squadron with the Lightning were shelved with the impending withdrawal from east of Suez, and the date for the disbandment of the squadron was set for 30 April 1968. The Ceremonial Parade was held at 1830 hrs, and at the first General Salute to mark the arrival of the Reviewing Officer, Air Marshal Sir Rochford Hughes, a diamond nine of Javelins flew overhead. Darkness fell, and at the second General Salute, a box four of Javelins in reheat appeared. All nine aircraft taxied in and formed up before the Reviewing Officer. Engines and lights were extinguished together, and a spotlight played on the Ensign as it was lowered to *The Last Post*. The squadron standard was marched off in slow time to conclude a unique and fitting, but sad, disbandment ceremony to mark the completion of 52 years almost unbroken service, mainly in India and the Far East.

On 2 May 1968 six of the aircraft flew from Tengah to Seletar for the last time to be handed over to the Singapore Air Force for technical training. And so the Javelin was laid to rest. Although few would claim it was one of the world's great aircraft, it was certainly a very fine aircraft which did an outstanding job in extremely arduous and testing conditions. All who had the pleasure of being involved in Javelin operations in Singapore, both air and ground crew, will look back on its life and times with fond memories.

SEE INSIDE BACK COVER PHOTOGRAPHS OF ABOVE PARADE

Black Buck – XM597 was one of the Vulcan B2s used on the operations from Wideawake airfield in Ascension Island. Squadron Leader Neil McDougall and his crew flew three such long-range missions against the airfield at Port Stanley

Operation Corporate –
the Falklands Campaign

AIR VICE-MARSHAL PETER SQUIRE DFC AFC RAF

At the outset of Operation Corporate it was difficult to see how the RAF could play a major role because of the vast distances involved and the lack of suitable mounting bases. Before the Argentinian invasion took place the RAF's capability would have amounted to no more than flying C130 Hercules Transport aircraft in to Port Stanley's short and reportedly unsuitable runway, with but a few lightly-armed troops. There was little off-runway parking space and insufficient fuel available to recover the aircraft, even if they had been sent. The nearest base to which access was available was Wideawake Airfield on Ascension Island, some 3,900 miles away across open ocean, and approximately only halfway between the Falklands and the UK.

Hence the task of recovering the Islands was at first perceived as being largely a Royal Navy/Royal Marine operation. Indeed, it was initially hoped that the presence of the Task Force would be sufficient in itself to cause the Argentinians to withdraw. However, this changed as the pattern of events unfolded until eventually the UK became involved in a full-scale joint operation which included amphibious landings and an extensive land campaign – with all the demands for air support, that they entailed. However, when considering the campaign it is necessary to bear in mind that initial perception of the situation.

Nevertheless, in the time which it took to assemble the Task Force and then for it to travel south to the combat zone, the RAF acquired, or in some cases re-acquired, the ability to project effective air power over these enormous distances. Many of the aircraft which subsequently became involved required modification and the time available on this occasion was put to good use; ingenuity and an outstanding response from British industry plus some timely assistance from allies, notably the US, provided the capabilities which in the end enabled the RAF to make an important contribution to the success of the operation. Some of these modifications and capabilities had, of course, been recognised as desirable beforehand, but, as they were not so immediately relevant to our NATO and European-orientated defence policy, they had been given a low priority in the RAF's budgetary considerations.

At the start of the crisis, the first requirement was to build up an airhead on Ascension, a small volcanic island, with some 1,700 residents, whose airfield normally handled just two or three aircraft per week. It lacked fuel, water and aircraft parking areas. There were no hangars and, while the climate is equable and the weather generally excellent, it is just a volcanic cone with hazards of volcanic ash and dust which prevent aircraft or helicopter movements anywhere but on concrete or tarmac surfaces, and these were sadly lacking. But had Ascension Island not been available, the job of repossessing the Falkland Islands and South Georgia would undoubtedly have been very much more difficult. Indeed, it might well have proved militarily impossible.

From the outset VC10 and Hercules transport aircraft delivered a constant stream of men and freight for trans-shipping by helicopter to the vessels of the Task Force, which had been assembled and sailed in haste, often with loading incomplete, because not all of the equipment required was immediately available. This trans-shipping was carried out by RAF Chinooks and Sea Kings as well as by Royal Navy Wessex helicopters. RAF helicopters alone trans-shipped 2,500 tons of freight and over 1,000 men. Recognising the vital importance of Ascension Island to the operation, steps were taken to defend it. At first, RAF Harriers armed with air-to-air missiles, and supported by a mobile air defence radar, provided the air defence cover. Subsequently, the Harriers were replaced by more capable F4 Phantoms. The Navy, despite a shortage of ships, provided a guardship offshore, and Nimrods mounted a continuous anti-shipping patrol around the island. Elements of the RAF Regiment were also deployed to defend the airfield against a possible attack by Argentinian Special Forces.

Once the Task Force had sailed south from Ascension and the supply lines stretched to 8,000 miles, vital equipment, spares and, of course, the equally important mail were carried south and air dropped from Hercules aircraft, sorties which often took more than 24 hours. The Task Force knew that, provided it was air portable, a spare part could be with them off the Falklands sometimes within as little as 48 hours. Thus the Air Transport Force provided a vital link in the logistics chain, a role that was to continue for many months after the conflict was over, a contribution which is often taken for granted.

The distance of the Falklands from the UK, and more particularly from Ascension Island, dictated the use of in-flight refuelling for practically all air operations mounted into the South Atlantic. To enable even the RAF's fairly long-range aircraft to operate in-theatre, it was necessary to equip them for receiving fuel in-flight. The equipment on the Vulcan, for example, had not been used for over ten years because of the aircraft's purely European role, for which it had adequate range; this had to be reactivated and the crews trained. The Nimrod in-flight refuelling installation was designed, installed, tested and cleared for use in a mere three weeks and permitted the mounting of long-range surveillance operations right down the Argentinian coast to the Falkland Islands themselves. As a result, the RAF's two squadrons of Victor tankers were very heavily committed in support of these operations.

Each Vulcan raid alone needed the support of half of all available tankers and this placed considerable constraints upon other operations. Tankers with larger fuel capacity were clearly needed, but these were not available until some two years after the operation. At the height of the campaign, therefore, a sizeable part of the Victor force was deployed to Ascension Island. At the same time, those Victors remaining in the UK were busy providing training for the Vulcan, Nimrod and Hercules crews, who rapidly had to learn the skills involved in air-to-air refuelling.

The most dramatic and highly-publicised of all the long-range operations were undoubtedly the Vulcan bombing attacks on Port Stanley airfield. However, the Vulcans' part in offensive counter-air operations against Port Stanley airfield is not always understood, and it is important to put these operations into perspective. There were three main reasons why the Task Force Commander adopted the Vulcan option. An early appreciation showed that the major threat to the Task Force must be from the air, and with only two carriers, and a limited number of Sea Harriers, it was possible to deploy only one quarter of the combat aircraft strength possessed by the Argentinians. At the same time, their aircraft were older, less sophisticated and, although operating only 350 to 400 miles from their bases, were short on combat endurance over the Falklands. This handicap would be remedied, however, if the Argentinians could use Port Stanley airfield as a forward operating base for refuelling and re-arming their Mirages and A4s.

The Argentinians had to be denied, therefore, the use of Port Stanley for the operation of fighter and fighter-bomber aircraft and, since the limited number of Sea Harriers had to be preserved for the air defence of the Task Force, the Vulcan offered the only option with any reasonable statistical chance of penetrating and cutting the runway with the weapons available. This it did on the very first raid and, although the Argentinians were able to maintain a limited airlift with transport aircraft, no high-performance aircraft ever used the Port Stanley runway and, since that was the foremost aim, the Vulcan and subsequent Harrier counter air effort can be seen to have been highly successful. Furthermore, there is little doubt that the initial raid against Port Stanley airfield on 1 May, which heralded the opening of active hostilities in the campaign, had a most salutary effect upon the enemy. Not only must it have dented the morale of the Argentinians on the Islands but, more importantly, it showed the Junta that the UK had the capability to attack any targets, not only in the Falklands but possibly on the Argentinian mainland itself.

The Vulcan bombing attacks were remarkable achievements of long-range navigation, planning and aircrew performance; each mission required up to 18 Victor tanker sorties to support a round trip of over 16 hours. At that time, these raids were the longest-range operational bombing missions in the history of air warfare. In all, three bombing attacks were made, the last being at dawn before the final assault on Port Stanley and designed to prevent any remaining Argentinian Pucara aircraft from joining in the battle. The Vulcans were also assigned to attack the Argentinian early-warning radars, using Shrike Anti-Radiation Missiles (ARM). These radars were being used not only to detect friendly aircraft but also to provide position reports on the carriers for use in Exocet attacks by the Super Entendard aircraft of the Argentinian Navy. The first of these Shrike attacks was also successful; for apart from the physical damage which it caused, the Argentinians thereafter closed down their radars whenever they detected Task Force aircraft approaching. For those pilots flying over the islands regularly that was a considerable help.

Nimrod Maritime Patrol aircraft were the first combat aircraft to become involved in Corporate; they began operating from Ascension just five days after the Argentinian invasion. Effective surface and sub-surface surveillance of Argentinian naval forces was of great importance to the Task Force. This was a formidable task which seemed impossible at the outset, given the distances involved and the great expanse of ocean to be covered. By the end of April, however, the hastily-fitted air-to-air refuelling capability enabled them to provide direct support to the Task Force as far south as the Falklands, and to monitor shipping in the inshore areas off the South Argentinian ports. Many maritime patrol flights exceeded 18 hours – double the aircraft's normal un-refuelled endurance. The Nimrod's offensive capability was also rapidly enhanced by the early clearance into service of the Stingray torpedo and the acquisition of the US Harpoon air-to-surface missile. Nimrod was also cleared to carry 1,000-lb and cluster bombs and even Sidewinder air-to-air missiles. The latter were fitted to give the aircraft an offensive capability against the Argentinian long-range reconnaissance aircraft, which were used to shadow the Task Force.

A warning order issued on 8 April 1982, directed No. 1(F) Squadron to prepare for operations from a carrier as attrition replacements for Sea Harrier battle losses. The Squadron had not operated at sea for some years and so modification of the aircraft was the first major task. A number of navalisation modifications were required and these included the fitting of shackles for lashing-down, anti-corrosion treatment, and the fitting of specialist transponder equipment to assist recoveries to the carrier in bad weather. The RAF Harrier – at that time the GR3 – was bought as an attack aircraft with only integral guns for self-defence. Thus, if it was to be used to replace the Sea Harrier, a better air defence capability would be required. Within a few days of receiving the initial warning order, both industry and the Service were working round the clock in order to give the aircraft an air-to-air missile fit. Thanks to a great deal of effort and ingenuity, the initial batch of aircraft were equipped, and the system proved and tested within two-and-a-half weeks. Further modifications, which were later incorporated to increase the aircraft's capability, included the installation of a flare and chaff dispenser and an active I-band jammer, for self-protection, and the ability to carry and fire the Shrike ARM. While the modification programme was being carried out, nominated pilots went through an intensive work-up programme. This included air-combat training against French Air Force Mirage aircraft, air-to-air missile firing, operational weapon delivery profiles, ultra low flying and initiation into the Ski-Jump Club.

At the same time, work began to find a means of getting the reinforcement aircraft, which were due to include not only Harrier GR3s but also additional Sea Harriers and helicopters, south to the Total Exclusion Zone (TEZ). After a detailed inspection, it was decided that the container ship, *Atlantic Conveyor,* would provide the ideal platform. Following some modification work to permit VTOL operations, the ship was ready to sail, its five car decks having been loaded with enormous quantities of stores, weapons, food and clothing. The helicopters were loaded in the UK but the GR3s and Sea Harriers were flown to Ascension using in-flight refuelling. Once at Ascension, the aircraft were flown onto the *Atlantic Conveyor* and tightly parked in an 'aircraft hide', which had been built between the walls of containers. The aircraft were also bagged to give added protection against salt water.

Having left Ascension on the evening of 7 May, the *Atlantic Conveyor* in company with other ships of the Amphibious Group made a rendezvous with the Task Force on 18 May and the Harriers were transferred to the two carriers, ten to *Hermes* and four to *Invincible.* All the GR3s went to Hermes and after just one day of work-up training the Squadron flew its first operations sortie on 20 May. In the period between the arrival of the Task Force in the TEZ and the arrival of No. 1(F)

Harrier and Wessex aircraft on board the *Atlantic Conveyor* on the way to the South Atlantic. The airframes were wrapped in bags to protect them against the elements

Harrier GR3 vertical take-off from the deck of the *Atlantic Conveyor*. The aircraft was being transferred to HMS *Hermes*

Runway and dispersal at Ascension Island. Aircraft on the pan include Victors, C-130s and a C-5 Galaxy

Squadron, no Sea Harriers had been lost in air combat and so, instead of being replacements, the GR3s were used as reinforcements and dedicated to the attack role. In this capacity the full gamut of offensive support missions was carried out, ranging from offensive counter-air to close-air support and armed reconnaissance.

The aims of the offensive counter-air missions were twofold: firstly to deny the use of Stanley airfield and the various outlying strips, and secondly to destroy aircraft in the open. Low-level laydown deliveries were flown against a number of the airstrips such as Goose Green while against the runway at Stanley a great variety of profiles were used. Laydown attacks were successful in hitting the runway but, in the process, the aircraft were particularly vulnerable to the Argentinian air defences, and the resulting damage to the runway was not very extensive. On the other hand, while high-angle and loft deliveries kept aircraft out of range from ground defences, the accuracy of weapon delivery was poor. As already stated, the runway remained open to Hercules and Pucara type aircraft, but the Argentinians were not able to use the airfield as a forward operating base for fighter-bomber aircraft and that was the Task Force's main concern.

For its attack tasks, the GR3 carried and delivered a variety of weapons, including cluster bombs, RN two-inch rockets, 1,000-lb bombs and, subsequently, the laser-guided bomb (LGB). Regrettably, the full potential of the LGB could not be realised until just one day before the cease-fire. It was not until then that the laser target markers were correctly deployed. However, four bombs delivered from loft profiles that day achieved two direct hits on pinpoint targets and served notice on the Argentinians that the Task Force now had a weapon of extreme accuracy; this may well have been one of the factors that swayed the decision to surrender so quickly. The GR3 was also capable of carrying a reconnaissance pod and, using this capability and the organic processing facilities on board *Hermes,* it was possible to locate concentrations of enemy defensive positions and other lucrative targets. On one occasion photographs revealed a sizeable but well-camouflaged headquarters bunker just west of Stanley, while on another occasion a line of more than 20 soft-skinned vehicles was identified; both targets were subsequently attacked.

Shortly after the landings in San Carlos Water, a Harrier forward operating base (FOB) was built close to the settlement at Port San Carlos. Refuelling facilities were available and up to four aircraft could be parked on the strip at any one time. Once available for use, it was normal for two GR3s to be detached on a daily basis to provide quick reaction support for ground forces, while the Sea Harriers used it extensively in order to lengthen significantly their time on combat air patrol.

It would, however, be quite wrong to suggest that the Harrier detachment had it all its own way. Indeed the loss of an aircraft on the second day of operations was a swift reminder that the Squadron was unlikely to survive unscathed. Experience quickly showed that the greatest threat was from ground-to-air weapons, which varied from surface-to-air missiles (SAM) to small-arms fire. The two major SAM systems were Roland and Tiger Cat. With an accurate knowledge of where these were located, pilots planned to fly outside or below their respective engagement zones and although substantial numbers of both types of missile were launched at the Harriers, none was successful. The remaining SAM threat came from the shoulder-launched missiles, which were in plentiful supply. Photo reconnaissance confirmed the presence of both Blowpipe and the Russian SAM 7 but, again, the tactics employed of flying very low and fast seemed to negate this threat, although it is likely that the first of the aircraft to be shot down was engaged by Blowpipe.

The Argentinians were also equipped with a large quantity of AAA guns ranging from 20 mm to 35 mm, some of which were linked to Fire Control Radars. Although these tended to be sited in known areas, they posed a high threat to the Squadron, and a second aircraft was lost during the attack on Goose Green. However, the largest number of hits by far was the result of small-arms fire and in the latter stages of the campaign, when almost every mission took the aircraft close to Stanley, aircraft were frequently hit. Apart from one aircraft which had a massive fuel leak and just failed to make it back to the carrier, all the others returned safely, thus dispelling the concern that the aircraft might be somewhat fragile to battle damage. Not only did this prove to be incorrect, but once back on board the engineers were able to effect some ingenious repairs and no aircraft spent longer than 48 hours in the hangar before it was flying again. However, as a result of losses, which by 8 June had totalled four – the fourth being a crash landing at the FOB – replacements were flown direct from Ascension to the Task Force using in-flight refuelling, long and apprehensive flights indeed for pilots who, without diversions *en route*, had eight-and-a-half hours to prepare for their first ever deck landing.

Following the ceasefire, a full site was built ashore at Stanley airfield and on 4 July 1982 the GR3 detachment, now armed with Sidewinders and in the air defence role, went ashore and, despite atrocious conditions early on, maintained a detachment at RAF Stanley until May 1985, when the airfield at Mount Pleasant was opened for operations.

Returning to the conflict itself, no mention of the Falklands Campaign would be complete without discussion of support helicopter operations. The Royal Navy provided the vast majority – mainly Sea Kings and Wessex – of the fleet of some 160 helicopters, which were in-theatre at the height of the land battle. The Army Air Corps provided Scout and Gazelle light helicopters and, after losing three Chinooks which went down with the *Atlantic Conveyor*, the RAF contribution was but a solitary Chinook. That one aircraft, ZA718 'Bravo-November', was fortunately airborne on task in the vicinity of Port San Carlos at the time that the *Atlantic Conveyor* was hit.

After the San Carlos landing, it quickly became apparent that many of the wheeled vehicles could not be used in the advance on Port Stanley and, with the prevailing ground conditions and lack of roads, support helicopters became the primary means of movement and resupply. In fact the scale of helicopter support operations was unprecedented in the experience of British Forces; it put great strains on the refuelling organisation, which had not been planned to match the required rate of operations, and, in any case, it had lost much of its vital equipment with the *Atlantic Conveyor*. Moreover, that one Chinook was the only means of moving some of the larger items of refuelling equipment, as well as a host of other important items. Over the next four weeks two crews and a handful of ground crew and support unit personnel, with a few borrowed tools and considerable ingenuity, kept the Chinook flying. That one aircraft carried over 2,000 troops, 600 tons of equipment and 650

Nimrod MR2P with under-wing Sidewinder
missiles

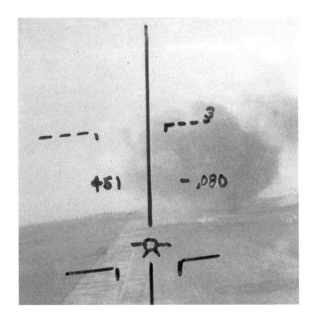

Harrier GR3 attack on Stanley airfield as seen through the
Head-Up Display (HUD). The lines and numbers were
added to the original photograph to emphasise the HUD
markings

Vulcan B2 at Ascension Island carrying a Shrike ARM

Stanley airfield showing the results of the Vulcan raids. Two
rows of craters can be seen running across the top left corner
and centre of the runway. The three aircraft circled were
originally identified as Etendards but, when subsequently
attacked, turned out to be Aermacchi light attack aircraft

POWs – significantly more than a whole squadron of naval Sea Kings during the same period. However, they had some tense moments and on one occasion, using night vision goggles on a covert tactical night sortie, in and out of snowstorms, they flew into the water after a radio altimeter failure. Nevertheless, they lived to tell the tale – the only loss being the crewman's helmet and one of the side doors – and the aircraft kept on flying.

During the urgent build up of forces at Fitzroy and Bluff Cove, that Chinook carried 75 fully-armed troops in one lift and on a subsequent sortie 81 troops were lifted in. It should be noted that our Chinook's normal peacetime load is 38 fully-armed troops, yet these much greater loads were still within the increased maximum all-up weight clearance: one of the many measures adopted quickly as this great workhorse hurried off to war so early in its career in the RAF.

Throughout the campaign, the air defence of the Task Force remained the primary task of the Sea Harriers, and the associated ship-borne weapons systems. Sea Harriers flew over 1,100 air defence sorties and, while scoring 27 claimed kills, suffered no losses in air-to-air combat. The pattern of air supremacy was clearly set early in the conflict. On 1 May four engagements resulted in three kills and two possibles being claimed by the Sea Harriers. As a result it was not until 21 May, when their fighter bombers attacked the Task Force in San Carlos Water, that Argentinian aircraft reappeared.

The Argentinian tactical employment of their aircraft leaves many questions unanswered: for instance, they made no attempt to challenge the Sea Harriers and no close-air combat occurred. Admittedly they were operating near the extreme edge of their range but they had, and were using, their C130 AAR capability and it is surprising that they did not fly a few missile-armed Mirage IIIs as escorts to their fighter bombers.

The success of the Sea Harrier/Sidewinder combination was remarkable, but the Argentinians appear to have made little attempt to defeat the infra-red missile by manoeuvring; nor do they appear to have fitted their aircraft with effective flare and chaff dispensers – a relatively simple, cheap and quick modification, which we had installed. The RAF made a small but significant contribution to this Sea Harrier effort. One in four of the pilots to fly with those two high-scoring naval squadrons came from the RAF and, indeed, the first Argentinian aircraft shot down were destroyed by RAF pilots flying RN Sea Harriers.

It is not possible to do justice to all aspects of RAF support of the Task Force in a comparatively short essay. In the final analysis, the RAF made a significant contribution to a notable victory, but it would be unwise to ignore some of the lessons which the experience in the Falklands taught or, in many cases, retaught the Service. On the other hand the unique circumstances surrounding this campaign must be remembered and care taken not to draw conclusions which would prove irrelevant in a NATO or other out-of-area context. As in the Gulf War some nine years later, the Service got the most out of its equipment and for that a great deal is owed to the outstanding support received from the UK's aircraft industry. Indeed, the ingenuity of men and women, service and civilian, allowed the crews to get much more out of their equipment than many people would have considered possible.

The importance of strategic reach was once again seen to be a key to victory and the first indications of the supremacy to be gained from technology became evident – both major factors in the air war in the Gulf. The need to retain a breadth of role capabilities was again proven and this remains so, despite the changed world situation and the drive to reduce defence expenditure. Moreover, the emergence of a less stable world and a revised strategy within NATO, based on the provision of Reaction Forces to manage and contain crises, make it all the more so. But at the end of the day, it was the quality of the men and women in the armed services as a whole who secured the victory in the South Atlantic. This commitment at sea, on the ground and in the air, together with a background of first-class training, won the day.

Chinook (BN) refuelling from the deck of HMS *Dumbarton Castle* off East Falkland

Enter Pavespike – On 7 February 1991 four Tornado GR1s and two Buccaneer S2Bs were tasked with the destruction of the Ar Ramadi rail bridge west of Baghdad. The Buccaneers were used to designate the Laser Guided Bombs carried by the Tornados. The leading pair of Tornados, ZA455 'EJ' and ZA469 'I' were accompanied by Buccaneer, XW547 'R', crewed by Flt Lt Glen Mason and Sqn Ldr Norman Browne who subsequently received the DFC

Enter Pavespike – Buccaneering in the Gulf

SQUADRON LEADER NORMAN BROWNE
DFC RAF

On 21 January 1991 I was in Ulster attending my mother-in-law's funeral. Naturally the many friends and relations present were anxious to know if my squadron would be involved in the Gulf Conflict that had recently commenced. I truthfully reassured everybody that there were no plans to involve the Maritime Buccaneer Wing and reinforced my declaration by admitting that two Buccaneer squadrons were actually on detachment at that time. When I returned to work two days later I discovered that my reassurances had been ill-founded and that within three days, I and personnel from all the Buccaneer units at RAF Lossiemouth would be deployed to Bahrain and very much involved in Operation Desert Storm.

The rapid recall, preparation and deployment of the Buccaneer Wing was extremely successful and undoubtedly laid the foundation for the invaluable contribution the Buccaneer was to make to the Allied bombing campaign. Within three days of the recall the first two Buccaneers had deployed wearing a new colour scheme and embodying a number of significant modifications – notably a Havequick radio and Mk XII IFF. By 30 January, 184 personnel, 275,000 lbs of freight and six aircraft were in Bahrain and ready for operations.

Combined tactics with Tornado aircraft were quickly evolved and training missions were flown over Saudi Arabia to acquaint crews with high-level designation techniques. The Pavespike laser-designation system used by the Buccaneers is a manual system and visual acquisition of targets from high altitude was considered to be the greatest problem facing the crews. After two training sorties, discussions with the mission planners at Headquarters in Riyadh, and awaiting a slot in the preplanned raid programme, the first operational sortie was successfully flown on 2 February – only ten days after the initial recall signal to RAF Lossiemouth.

The crews to fly on this first mission were Flight Lieutenant Glenn Mason, the author, Wing Commander Bill Cope (the Buccaneer Detachment Commander) and Flight Lieutenant Carl Wilson. With Squadron Leader Pablo Mason and his formation of four Tornados, they were to attack a road/rail bridge two miles north of the town of As Samawah in southern Iraq and hopefully destroy it with 12 laser-guided Paveway bombs. Poor weather en route was forecast but a clearance was expected at the time on target. This was essential if the target was to be visually acquired. After a comprehensive brief for formation *Belfast 31*, we had our first nervous 'walk' to our aircraft with everybody wishing us a 'good one'. I must confess that I was somewhat relieved to be airborne and away from the faces of our support staff and groundcrew who tried, but could not hide, their looks of concern for us. A long transit followed during which we tanked with VC10 Polaris 31, checked in with USAF AWACS and listened eagerly to hear our fighter escort of four USAF F-15s. For some two hours we flew through abysmal weather with the pilots struggling to hold formation as we entered Iraqi airspace and we climbed to bombing altitude. Thankfully, our escorting F15s had pushed ahead of us and were able to assure us that the target area was clear. At 1100 hrs, six hours after starting the mission brief, I heard Glenn say 'I've got the target'. Now it was head down for me and, as I acquired the bridge on my tiny television screen, I transmitted 'happy' to the Tornados thus clearing them to release their bombs when they reached their dropping range. For what seemed an eternity I tracked the target until, at last, the bombs reached my aiming spot and the bridge was enveloped in an enormous explosion. Delight at achieving our objective was short lived as Glenn and I concentrated on rushing homewards, continually dropping chaff to confuse the numerous Iraqi SAM radars looking at us. It was especially pleasing to hear Carl call 'splash' indicating his element had also successfully attacked the bridge. Back at base it was wonderful to replay the video tape to everybody involved in the mission showing the destruction of the bridge. I will always remember the enormous cheer which accompanied that first viewing. Not a cheer which celebrated hitting Iraqi lorries and killing civilians, but a cheer of relief that a new tactic had worked. It meant that we could reduce the risks to our Tornado crews while still making a significant contribution to the air campaign. The boss's celebratory bottle of champagne that first evening was the most expensive he had ever purchased but he had promised it if we were successful and it was thoroughly enjoyed by all.

Life now became a routine of planning, flying, debriefing and discussing ways of improving tactics. Although the task of the Buccaneer crews remained the same – to mark the aiming point with a laser spot – the targets varied in number, size and type with each mission, requiring careful study of co-ordination, heights, timings and aiming points. Squadron Leader Terry Yarrow, on loan from the Central Trials and Tactics Organisation at Boscombe Down, spent many long hours studying our videos and then persuaded both Headquarters and aircrews that even better results could be achieved. Thanks to his efforts, and his contribution of numerous bitten-off pipe stems, the Buccaneers progressed to self-designating their own LGBs. These were delivered from 40-degree dive attacks – an option which would give a significant degree of flexibility to the Buccaneer crews, as the land war became more imminent.

By 10 February six more aircraft and crews had been deployed and our groundcrew were working tirelessly to ensure a mission was never lost. The combined efforts of Squadron Leader George Baber and Squadron Leader Dave Tasker, ably supported by two experienced Flight Sergeants, John Menzies and 'Chalky' White and their men, meant that over the full period of the war 109 operational missions were flown with the outstanding serviceability rate of 89.9 per cent. Not bad for a 32-year-old aircraft deployed at short notice to a hostile environment – to work in a regime it was not designed for – and had never been in before.

Fortunately the Pavespike designation system incorporates its own internal video recorder so the world was able to see at first hand the success achieved by the Buccaneer detachment. The clinical designation of a bridge for Tornado-delivered bombs or the erratic high speed tracking of an enemy aircraft whilst in a 40-degree dive was all visual evidence of a job successfully completed. No aircrew or aircraft were lost during operations but many suffered near misses and frights from SAMs and anti-aircraft shells. Only one Tornado aircraft was lost during combined Tornado/Buccaneer operations.

Statistically (and therefore in reality) it was from beginning to end a very successful operation and one that generated a great deal of pride amongst all who were involved. Planning to locate a target by flying around it for several minutes while, inside the cockpit, keeping your head and staring at a small television screen which shows people shooting at you does not seem a desirable way to go to war. I must confess it did not appeal to me when the idea was first conceived nor did it improve in action. However, when confronted with a job that must be done, fear is replaced by determination and I know that all my colleagues gave 100 per cent concentration to marking their targets regardless of events outside the cockpits. Hard, realistic training in a highly-disciplined force produced groundcrew and aircrew capable of adapting to a new scenario and of producing excellent results. The Buccaneer was more than ready to accept all that was asked of it – as my friends and relations obviously knew before I did!

The Port of Al Jubayl – it could have been purpose-built for
the Gulf Conflict, as it was exactly what was needed

The Tornado detachment in Bahrain

Many troops were moved huge distances across the desert by
air. This is a typical scene at a desert airstrip

The effects of a PGM on a hardened shelter on a Kuwaiti
airfield

Three Tornados flying from Bahrain on a fly-past of the USS
Nimitz after the end of hostilities on 25 April 1991

Flight Lieutenant Mike Wood at work on a Buccaneer. Photo
taken during the conflict on 17 February 1991

Words to Saddam Hussein on a 1000lb LGB on a Tornado –
17 February 1991

Nimrods did vital work in helping to enforce the UN
embargo on Iraq. This picture was taken on patrol in the
Arabian Gulf. Note the BOZ chaff dispensing pod under the
wing

The Gulf Conflict – Some Personal Reflections

AIR VICE-MARSHAL IAN MACFADYEN
CB OBE FRAeS RAF

I was at my desk in the Ministry of Defence one morning in November 1990, contemplating a new posting to another area in the department, when I first heard of a possible change of plan – a move to Riyadh! A new post was needed in the expanding British Headquarters, but it had yet to be decided if the job, Chief of Staff in General Sir Peter de la Billiere's newly-formed Headquarters British Force Middle East (BFME), was to go to the Army or the Royal Air Force. It is now a part of history that the job came to the RAF, and 10 days later I was on my way to the Gulf.

I arrived in Riyadh on an RAF Tristar on a regular flight of mixed freight and passengers. The first week was a hectic round of visits, touring that vast sub-continent, to find out what British forces were doing and something of the problems it would be my job to try and help solve. I paid brief visits to the RAF at Dhahran, the Army at the port of Al Jubail and the HQ of the 7th Armoured Brigade, the Royal Navy at Jebel Ali in the UAE, and then the RAF again on Bahrain Island and over in the extreme west of Saudi Arabia at Tabuk. All in all, from the extent of the work that was going on, by all the nations involved, it was clear that a huge operation was underway.

Back in Riyadh, I was faced with trying to get to grips with a wide range of problems. First, there was the urgent need for some new accommodation to cope with a huge influx of new people into HQBFME; this offered the opportunity to make the Headquarters rather more joint-service. Although it was never to prove possible to bring all the RAF into HQBFME because of the need for joint air planning at the highest level, the Royal Navy was to become fully integrated alongside the Army and some RAF when we moved to a new HQ. But first, the hunt was on to find a building to house us all (eventually around 700 people). We soon found an ideal site in the former British Aerospace headquarters about half a mile from our existing HQ. Negotiations then began with our Saudi hosts to lease the building from the owner – an essential step since it was Saudi generosity which was paying the bill. This was, however, to take time and it was not until 31 December that we finally had the nod to go ahead. A few days later a huge party of contractors as well as the Royal Engineers and Royal Signals all moved in. Within three weeks a remarkable transformation had taken place: the building was completely 'gutted' with substantial internal changes, re-wired and carpeted throughout, and fitted with a new and highly-complex telephone exchange with provision for secure speech both around Riyadh and back to the UK via our own satellite terminals. However, I am moving a little too far ahead . . .

Back in early December HQBFME was feverishly busy over plans for such things as logistics plans, casualty evacuation, the need for a Prisoner of War guard force and POW camp for several thousand people, and the setting up of hospitals – besides the move of the 1st (British) Division into the Kingdom. The Royal Navy and RAF too were gradually growing in size. There were numerous meetings and telephone calls on all this with our UK 'masters' – the Joint Headquarters at RAF High Wycombe. Increasingly I had to attend meetings around Riyadh, chiefly in the Saudi Ministry of Defence and Aviation, but also the headquarters of the Royal Saudi Air Force where the RAF had set up an element HQ alongside a large mobile USAF air headquarters.

As the size of the British forces grew towards its maximum of 45,000 so did the complexity of the work. We needed, for instance, to invite help from outside the UK to expand our hospital capacity for our own possible casualties, and for injured Iraqis taken as POWs who would clearly need the same treatment. Eventually nine nations were to become involved in this humanitarian operation which thankfully, in the event, was to be little used.

Something that was to occupy much of my time up to early January was the organisation and hosting of our many visitors. That they were carefully controlled in number was essential if we were not to lose sight of the main aim – to prepare for war. However, it was important to brief and explain to visitors (who included the Prime Minister and HRH the Prince of Wales) the complexities of an operation the scale of which most of us had never seen.

The port of Al Jubail was to become one of the largest military logistic centres in history with, at a peak, 40 miles of traffic leaving every day. Distance, too, is not easy to comprehend. The trip from the British Army's forward logistic centre was the equivalent of a journey from London to Edinburgh – and that was merely halfway to the eventual destination of our troops. The build-up by air was equally impressive; besides the massive build-up of offensive air power, the American Civil Reserve Air Fleet (CRAF) was activated for the first time. The CRAF consists of many US civil air carriers whose aircraft are especially adapted for emergency use. At one stage, on average one Boeing 747 equivalent was arriving in-theatre every 11 minutes!

As the United Nations deadline for Iraqi withdrawal by mid-January loomed, it seemed increasingly likely that war was unavoidable. Coalition flying rates were gathering in intensity with major exercises to test elements of the planned air campaign. In the last week before 17 January, a gradual build-up of air defence aircraft activity took place, along with the four AWACs permanently up on patrol that was to be the norm during the air campaign. It was not, however, until some 36 hours beforehand that I first heard of the decision to attack. It was quite a moment as I reflected that thousands of combat aircrew were about to be committed to combat for the first time. It is now clear that the air build-up was part of an elaborate deception plan; in the last hour or so before the first raids into Iraq, bombers were substituted for some of the fighters that had been on patrol for a number of days. Surprise was complete. I can recall lying in bed that first night listening to KC-135 after KC-135 taking off from their airbase in Riyadh. Few people even then realised what was about to happen, and most in HQBFME were surprised to see me in the operations room at 2.45 a.m. – just 15 minutes before the first raids on Baghdad. It was only then that I was able to tell those on duty what was about to happen. CNN had been installed the previous evening. It was fascinating to watch events unfolding in those early hours. A dramatic moment was the sudden ending of a live report from Baghdad, as a 2,000-lb laser-guided bomb from an F-117A took out the top of the Baghdad communications tower, the equivalent of the GPO tower in London. The world could only wonder when two days later the video tapes were released of the remarkable work being done by these stealth aircraft. For the RAF, the opening days of the conflict were not always easy, because of our Tornado losses. Late-night telephone calls to the house which Air Vice-Marshal Bill Wratten, the Air Commander, and myself shared were never welcome. Happily, the early losses were only occasionally repeated as the conflict went on.

By any standards the planning and execution of the air campaign was brilliant. For this the USAF has my greatest admiration; they were the architects not only of the campaign but they put together the most complex detailed daily tasking of aircraft in the history of air warfare. It was known as the Air Task Order (ATO), and was sent out to all air units, both in-theatre and around the world (a few USAF bombers were even flying from the USA to Saudi Arabia) daily. It was anything up to 1,000 pages of A4 in length, and gave all the detail anyone ever wanted with which to execute the plan – aircraft numbers, weapon load, routes, frequencies, tanker tow lines etc. The success of the air campaign owes much to the ATO, but also to the skill and professionalism of those aircrew who flew their allotted tasks to the second.

During the air campaign the routine in the headquarters changed. Briefings took place twice a day in the HQ, timed not to coincide with Coalition conferences or with the briefings at High Wycombe. Indeed the output from our briefings in-theatre was passed on to High Wycombe and then on up to the Ministry of Defence in London. Besides these briefings, which lasted up to an hour at a time, I was the British representative at the daily Coalition Commanders' conference in the Saudi Ministry of Defence and aviation. This briefing was very useful to get a wider perspective on the progress of the campaign, and allowed me to get up-to-date with many of the other activities going on. There was also a daily meeting in HQBFME, chaired by General de la Billiere, to brief him in detail on British activities and to allow him to direct affairs accordingly. He otherwise spent much of his time in the US War Room alongside General Schwarzkopf. Inevitably, I had to spend several hours every day on one of the secure telephones to High Wycombe and more meetings often followed. After such an absorbing day there was no problem in falling asleep at night!

From the start of the conflict, we were worried about the threat from Scud missiles. We did not have long to wait. On the second night the air-raid sirens began sounding in Riyadh. This was to be a regular feature of the night for the first few weeks, although the number of missiles involved was to drop quickly to one or two at a time, due to the relentless air patrols that were to be set up to counter this threat, backed up by Special Forces operations. There was an elaborate warning system, including air-raid sirens, which gave us time to warn the people of Riyadh to take shelter. Few besides the military had any gas masks of their own. As time went by, and people became more used to the raids, many civilians would happily go outside and watch the spectacular sight of Scuds being intercepted by Patriot missiles.

While the air campaign was underway, another elaborate deception plan was being executed. This concerned the move of US, French and UK forces well out to the west of Kuwait ready for the 'long left hook' as it was to become known. I was privileged to visit HQ 1 (British) Division just 48 hours before they launched their attack. It was very clear that the training was over, and everyone was ready, even eager, to get the job done. The brilliant success of the ground campaign is well-known and I will not repeat it here. We were all amazed by so few casualties, and stunned by the tragic accidental loss of life in what has become known as 'the friendly fire' incident. It brought home the fact that war is a complex and risky business.

Almost as suddenly as they had begun, hostilities were over. We then had to set about the task of repatriating 45,000 men and women as quickly as was safely possible, whilst reassuring our Coalition partners of the UK's support. I was privileged to subsequently take over command of this operation from General de la Billiere; but that is another story.

Tornado GR1 (EE) over the causeway linking Bahrain Island with Saudi Arabia

Tornado GR1 (EG) running in to the break to land over Bahrain Island

A flight of three Tornados over the Arabian Gulf

A typical dispersal scene in Bahrain. Note the concrete Splinter Protection Units (SPUs) especially made to protect aircraft from the effects of blast

Kuwait CAP – Tornado F3s of No. 43 (F) Squadron flying over the burning oil wells in Kuwait, March 1991

A low approach in West Nepal during Operation Khana Cascade, 1973 *(Courtesy RAF Lyneham)*

Aircraft refuelling in Addis Ababa during Operation Bushel, 1984–85 *(Courtesy RAF Lyneham)*

Unloading grain stock at a remote airstrip in Ethiopia, Operation Bushel, 1984 *(Courtesy RAF Lyneham)*

Humanitarian Aspects of the Service

1. HELP FROM THE HERCULES

SQUADRON LEADER GEORGE C. MARTIN RAF

Although formed as a fighting force, the RAF has, over the years, become involved in many non-military and humanitarian tasks. In recent years many of these exploits have been widely publicised in the press and on television bringing home to us the relief work carried out by the Service. These have mostly covered famine, flood or hurricane relief but the repatriation of hostages has also been well covered in the news and pictures of hostages returning to RAF Lyneham have become familiar. This station, with its large fleet of Lockheed C130H Hercules transport aircraft, operates 24 hours a day, 365 days a year and provides a worldwide support capability for British Forces, their families and civilians alike. On any day of the year, RAF Hercules aircraft are found operating in a diverse range of roles; from straightforward route flying to air-to-air refuelling (AAR) and tactical support. The Hercules, too, has also been in the limelight having celebrated its 25th year in RAF service in 1992.

As well as the many operational tasks it is called upon to undertake, the Hercules fleet has been involved in medical evacuations and humanitarian relief missions in many of the world's stricken regions. While the aircraft serves as the guardian angel, Lyneham remains the hub and nerve centre throughout. The station has supported Nos. 24, 30, 47 and 70 Squadrons and the Hercules OCU No. 57 (Reserve) Squadron (previously No. 242 OCU) in their global tasks that have included the evacuation of Aden and Cyprus and the reinforcement of Northern Ireland, Belize, the New Hebrides, Zimbabwe, Cambodia, the West Indies and Bangkok. It is, however, the relief operations that tend to catch the public eye and the station has become renowned for its humanitarian efforts: earthquake relief in Nicaragua, Turkey, Italy, Mexico and the Philippines; hurricane relief in Australia and Belize; flood relief in India and Holland; and, most notable of all, famine relief in Nepal, Sudan, Ethiopia, Iraq and, most recently, Bosnia. Some of these are covered in greater detail below.

In 1973 and 1980, Operation Khana Cascade supported a detachment of 220 men operating 14 aircraft in the remote areas of West Nepal, with ten aircraft bringing in some four million pounds of grain and four aircraft taking part in the dropping exercise. The nature of the flying in the high mountains of the Himalayas provided the most severe test so far of the versatility of the Hercules and the skills of the crews that handled them. Flying through narrow mountain valleys in an area with six of the highest mountains in the world, all over 26,000 ft high, with drop zones at altitudes over 9,000 ft was not easy. Some 4,000,000 lbs of food were dropped to famine victims in a total of 187 sorties in ten isolated centres. The task was completed in 29 days, some three weeks ahead of schedule, which was of the utmost importance due to the onset of the monsoon season in which flying would have been impossible. The operation had to be repeated in 1980.

In 1984–85, two Hercules aircraft flying from Addis Ababa in Ethiopia in Operation Bushel used the aircraft's short takeoff and landing capabilities for airlifting supplies to famine victims. On 4 November 1984 the RAF was the first foreign military detachment to get its relief airlift underway. Despite the capabilities of both aircraft and crews being limited by the heat and altitude of the Ethiopian plateau (Addis Ababa itself being 8,000 ft above sea level), 35,556,000 lbs of food and equipment were delivered into the makeshift airstrips of Makelle and Axum in the affected area. From the advanced landing grounds, trucks from various charities were used to ferry supplies to the emergency feeding centres. However, some areas were almost totally inaccessible by road and, starting on 26 January 1985, a further 28,760,000 lbs of food were air-dropped in 954 sorties. A typical aircraft load consisted of eight pallets to be dropped from 50 ft at 140 mph. Each pallet held 20 50-kg sacks of grain attached by cord designed to break on impact with the ground. By this technique, developed in Nepal some years earlier, about 80 per cent of the sacks remained intact.

Following the Argentinian invasion of the Falkland Islands and the British response of sending a Task Force, the armed forces were presented with huge problems in terms of logistics support. Within 24 hours of the invasion the first Hercules was en route for Ascension Island and, as the Task Force deployed, the flying rate increased to the despatch of one aircraft every four hours. In the first three weeks of the operation some 3,250,000 lbs had been flown to the island. It soon became apparent that with the distance from Ascension Island to the Falklands and the inability of aircraft to refuel in South America, some form of in-flight refuelling would be essential. On 15 April 1982 Marshall of Cambridge (now Marshall Aerospace) received a request to design, manufacture and install such equipment. By 5 May the first aircraft was ready to fly to the Falklands and a further five were completed in the next month allowing fuel to be received from Victor tankers. With this facility, Hercules aircraft could support the 3,100 mile airbridge to the South Atlantic – the longest continuous journey completed with AAR lasted 28 hrs 4 mins. The installation was so successful that the design has now embraced the entire RAF Hercules fleet. By June the aircraft had flown 10,000 hrs, or the equivalent of 3,000,000 miles and following the Argentinian surrender, the first Hercules landed at Port Stanley on 24 June bringing with it a small air movement unit for handling subsequent aircraft.

On 30 April 1982 Marshall of Cambridge were given a second challenge when asked to provide four Hercules with in-flight tanker capacity. This involved fitting the Mk17B Hose Drum Unit (HDU) on the aircrafts' rear ramp floor together with other modifications and after trials the first installation was delivered after 76 days from the order being placed. The other three aircraft were delivered within the next week and a further two were similarly modified in early 1983. This additional facility has allowed Hercules tankers to be based in the Falkland Islands and support the other RAF aircraft in the area.

In response to the Iraqi invasion of Kuwait some 25 Hercules aircraft were

The joy of freedom *(Courtesy RAF Lyneham)*

Terry Waite's arrival in the UK at Lyneham *(Courtesy RAF Lyneham)*

Preparation of aircraft prior to departure for Operation Bushel, 1984 *(Courtesy RAF Lyneham)*

Hercules C1K refuelling a Hercules C1P over the South Atlantic, 1982 *(Courtesy Marshall Aerospace)*

committed within three days to the task of resupplying the forces in the Middle East. During the first seven months of Operation Granby some 40,000 hrs were flown – almost three times the normal rate. Within the same period 24,000,000 gallons of aviation fuel were consumed in the moving of over 50,000 tonnes of freight over a total of 12,000,000 miles. On 28 February 1991 an RAF Hercules was the first coalition fixed-wing aircraft to land at Kuwait International Airport.

Operation Provide Comfort began in April 1991 in support of the Kurdish population of Northern Iraq. Three aircraft dropped thousands of pounds of emergency supplies to the starving and persecuted tribesfolk. Later in the month No. 3 Royal Marine Commando was deployed to this area to establish places of safety for the Kurds within their own country. Operation Safe Haven required the Hercules to carry out an average of 12 sorties per day into Iraq over a 21-day period. By the end of the operation on 16 June 1991 the aircraft had amassed over 50,000 flying hours.

Operation Cheshire began on 2 July 1992: a Hercules carrying a load of 30,000 lbs of food left Lyneham for Zagreb to await the opening, under United Nations control, of the airport at Sarajevo on 3 July. In the following week one aircraft operating between Zagreb and the beleaguered city two or three times each day delivered aid consisting of family packs (water, food and toiletries), Meals Ready to Eat (MRE or American Compo), medicines and general foodstuffs. In the first nine days this one aircraft carried over 817,000 lbs of relief supplies and on 12 July was replaced by another Hercules to continue the ongoing task. By 3 September when aid flights were suspended, 123 RAF sorties had been flown and over 3,000,000 lbs of freight delivered to Sarajevo.

In the wake of Hurricane Andrew three Hercules relief sorties were flown in support of Operation Halland into Eleuthen in the Bahamas during the last week of August 1992.

Besides the worldwide humanitarian operations the RAF, and Lyneham in particular, was in the public eye when, in the second half of 1991, it was used for the arrival and reception of the last three British hostages released from Beirut. On 8 August the news of an imminent arrival broke and the station set into action a contingency plan for dealing with both the requirements of the freed hostage and the considerable demands of the world's press. At 10.30 that night John McCarthy arrived at the Wiltshire base in the full glare of the media circus. After a brief welcoming ceremony he was taken to the relative security and serenity of the Officers' Mess where he remained for eight days. At that time there was much hope, not to mention a little trepidation, that the whole process was soon to be repeated. On 25 September, following two-and-a-half years in captivity, we saw the arrival of Jackie Mann who was welcomed by a victory roll from an overflying Spitfire. The media arrived again on 19 November 1991 for the third and last British hostage to be released. Terry Waite arrived on a blustery autumn day walking down the 18 steps from the VC10 onto British soil after 1,763 days in captivity. After his arrival and welcome by the Station Commander, the Foreign Secretary and Lord Runcie, Terry Waite gave a powerful and memorable speech that was broadcast worldwide. The last and best-known British hostage had come home.

In addition to the sterling work done by the Hercules fleet, Tristars, VC10s and other aircraft have also been involved in relief and humanitarian missions.

Humanitarian Aspects of the Service

2. ROYAL AIR FORCE SEARCH AND RESCUE
FLIGHT LIEUTENANT CHRIS HAWARD RAF

When the RAF was formed in 1918 search and rescue, as we know it today, was an almost unknown concept. Land-based aeroplanes of the time did not carry survival equipment and there was no service organisation dedicated to co-ordinating search and rescue activities. Aircrew flying over the sea who got into difficulties relied on passing shipping or the lifeboats of the RNLI. Early shipborne aviators were issued with flotation jackets and their aircraft had rudimentary flotation equipment to keep them afloat after ditching.

A number of marine craft were in service by the mid 1930s, mainly short-range boats that operated close to their parent station or serviced coastal bombing and gunnery ranges. In August 1936 the first purpose-built safety boat – High Speed Launch No. 100 – entered service at RAF Manston capable of going to sea with up to four stretchers in all but the roughest seas. The success of this launch led to further boats being ordered. These high speed launches were primarily established for use with their parent units; however, they could also be called to the assistance of other aircraft in distress.

The need for improved rescue facilities grew along with the increased capabilities of the more modern aircraft that were carrying out ever longer sorties over the sea. By 1938 most aircraft, other than fighters, were equipped with dinghies containing red smoke flares, emergency rations for each crew member and a first aid kit. The equipment was provided to allow aircrew to survive after a ditching for what was hoped to be only a short period before rescue.

By the end of 1938, Bomber Command envisaged the main part of its force would be operating across the North Sea. It was therefore essential that the training of bomber crews should include extensive over-water flying but such training flights were restricted because of a general lack of rescue arrangements other than the high speed launches of Coastal Command that were often only available after some delay. Clearly there was a need to provide some organisation co-ordinating both marine craft and aircraft engaged in rescue. In February 1939, it was decided that rescue launches would be placed under the operational control of Coastal Command. More would be ordered with the aim of providing a chain of launches based from Wick in Scotland clockwise round the coast to the Isle of Man.

With the outbreak of war, rescue arrangements continued much as they had in peacetime when ditched aircraft were searched for by other aircraft from their own stations. If the search was successful, arrangements were then made for any available surface vessel to carry out a rescue. HM Coastguard were called in during the search phase and they, in turn, could alert the lifeboats of the RNLI.

A key factor throughout the Battle of Britain was the availability of pilots. During the early phases of the Battle many pilots were killed or reported missing over the sea and it was thought likely that some who successfully baled out may have perished through exposure. As a result, a number of Lysander aircraft were borrowed from Army Co-operation Command which, together with light naval craft and RAF high speed launches, were formed into a rescue service. In August 1940 it was decided to place these resources under the control of Fighter Command. The Lysanders were deployed at various fighter stations with a responsibility for searching up to 20 miles from the coast with operational aircraft searching beyond that.

While these first steps were being taken to establish an air/sea rescue (ASR) service other efforts were being made to improve the survival chances of downed aircrew. Fighter aircraft did not carry dinghies so an idea developed by many RAF stations was to produce survival kits that could be dropped from search aircraft to survivors awaiting pick-up by surface craft. (Using items of equipment already available, these kits were continually improved and one of them known as Lindholme Gear is still in use today.) Urgent efforts were made to produce a single-seat dinghy and orders were placed for some 12,000 K-type dinghies which, by late summer 1941, had been provided for all single-seat aircraft.

In January 1941 a Directorate of Air/Sea Rescue was formed at Headquarters Coastal Command with officers established at Group Headquarters tasked with co-ordinating air and sea searches. The Directorate was responsible for developing and introducing all safety and survival equipment for aircraft and the training of aircrew in ditching and survival drills.

As the war continued, more resources were made available for ASR. The number and variety of dedicated aircraft and maritime craft gradually grew such that by the end of 1941, there were four composite ASR Squadrons operating Lysanders and Walrus amphibians. Hudson aircraft fitted with long-range radar were added to the role in 1941. Survival equipment was continually developed and the introduction of dinghy radios and effective pyrotechnic signals increased the chances of survivors being located. Dropable motorised lifeboats were also developed and used successfully on many occasions.

ASR resources were used rescuing aircrew who came down in the sea. However, many others came to grief over land in mountains and other remote areas where little or no help was available. In 1942 individual RAF stations near mountainous areas formed unofficial teams of volunteers to search for and rescue any survivors from aircraft crashes. These teams were eventually incorporated in the Air/Sea Rescue Organisation.

By the end of hostilities in 1945, more than 13,000 lives (including some 8,000 aircrew) had been saved by the organisation. At peak strength eight-and-a-half squadrons with 169 aircraft were established operating from the United Kingdom – overseas theatres also had their own resources of dedicated aircraft and marine craft. Types of aircraft used for ASR towards the end of the war included the Hudson, Walrus, Warwick, Anson and Spitfire; among other aircraft often called on to help were Liberators, Catalinas and Sunderlands.

The first recorded helicopter rescue mission took place in 1944 when a USAAF

A Wessex HC2 gives a helping hand *(Courtesy MOD)*

A Sea King HAR3 carries out a rescue from a rocky coastline *(Courtesy MOD)*

Sikorsky R4 carried out a hazardous journey of some 600 miles over inhospitable mountainous jungle from its base in India to a point in Japanese-held Burma where the crew of a spotter plane had made a forced landing following engine failure. The tiny helicopter had only a limited range and payload and this successful mission involved many stages over several days. Other life-saving flights soon followed but it was in November 1945 that two men were rescued from a barge that was foundering near Long Island. In gale force winds they were winched one at a time into a helicopter and flown to safety – the first time this technique had been used during wartime.

The modern helicopters used in search and rescue owe much to the efforts of Igor Sikorsky who carried out considerable pioneering development work in the late 1930s. This led to the first practical single-rotor helicopter known as the R4 which first flew in June 1942. Although it was only able to carry a very limited payload it was the first machine to enter production and was used extensively to carry out trials in many different roles.

RAF involvement with rotary wing aviation had begun in the 1930s with autogiros used for communication and calibration duties. From the autogiro pilots came the first RAF pilots to fly the R4 and orders were placed for a number of these machines known in Britain as the Hoverfly. The next model produced by Sikorsky was the R5 with a greater lifting capability. With some changes it evolved into the S51, later known as the Dragonfly when it appeared in British form. While Sikorsky continued to develop helicopters in America, many British firms were actively producing several experimental helicopters from which emerged the Skeeter, Sycamore and Belvedere.

It was the Malayan emergency that really started the search and rescue (SAR) activities of RAF helicopters. In 1950, three Dragonfly helicopters and three pilots formed the Far East Casualty Evacuation Flight which demonstrated the ability to evacuate quickly wounded personnel from otherwise inaccessible locations for medical attention. The value of helicopters in such situations was very soon apparent and they were employed in ever-increasing numbers. However, payload and performance were very limited in the Dragonfly and often only one casualty could be carried over short stages. It was not until the early 1960s when the gas-turbine powered Whirlwind 10 entered service that there was a significant increase in carrying capacity.

Since the end of the war, ASR had relied on fixed-wing aircraft for search and surface craft for rescue of ditched aircrew. The rescue potential of helicopters was well proven but before they could be deployed in sufficient numbers to provide a full rescue service crews had to be trained, equipment (such as hoists) had to be developed and rescue techniques had to be invented. In 1953, No. 275 Squadron was formed with its headquarters at Linton-on-Ouse as the first home-based helicopter Search and Rescue Unit equipped with the Sycamore (ASR had by then been renamed SAR). This squadron was subsequently renumbered, eventually becoming No. 202 Squadron in 1965. A second squadron, No. 22, formed in 1955 with Whirlwind Mk2s with its headquarters at St Mawgan.

As with the earlier wartime rescue units, these squadrons were established for the prime purpose of rescuing aircrew forced to abandon or ditch their aircraft.

Flights from these squadrons were established at coastal bases close to areas used by other service aircraft and soon links were built up with local Coastguard and the RNLI. History shows that as soon as an SAR flight was set up there was also a sizeable civilian rescue task which led to the flights becoming 'integrated' with local rescue services.

Rescue Co-ordination Centres (RCCs) were set up near Edinburgh (Pitreavie Castle) and at Plymouth (Mountbatten) in 1969 and assumed responsibility for the operational control of the SAR helicopters. The RCCs work closely with HM Coastguard and receive information about incidents from many sources such as Air Traffic Control Units, maritime radio stations, police and other emergency services. In addition to the RAF SAR helicopters, the RCCs can call on many resources including RAF Mountain Rescue Teams, long-range maritime Nimrods and, in liaison with the Coastguard, can call upon civilian rescue agencies.

At the time of writing No. 22 Squadron is equipped with the Wessex HC2 with detached flights at Leuchars (near Dundee), Coltishall (Norwich), Chivenor (North Devon) and Valley (Anglesey). The Wessex was built by Westland Helicopters and is based on the Sikorsky S58. It is powered by two Rolls-Royce Gnome gas turbines and has an endurance of up to two-and-three-quarter hours giving an effective radius of action of approximately 90 nautical miles in still air. Operated in the SAR role by a crew of three (pilot, navigator/winch operator and winchman), the Wessex is fitted with a 300 ft winch capable of lifting up to 600 lbs and it can carry up to 14 survivors depending on fuel state. Although originally introduced in 1964, it is still a very capable aircraft in the rescue role.

In 1978, No. 202 Squadron started to replace its single-engined Whirlwind HAR10s with Sea King HAR3s. This much larger helicopter was also built by Westland and is based on the Sikorsky S61. Also powered by two Rolls-Royce Gnomes, the single rotor Sea King has a radius of action of some 280 nautical miles or an endurance of up to seven hours depending on the amount of fuel carried. The hydraulic winch has a 245 ft cable and a lifting capacity of 600 lbs. External loads of up to 6,000 lbs can be carried from the underslung cargo hook and the cabin can accommodate a maximum of 17 seated survivors. (It should be remembered that the payload of a helicopter has to be split between crew, fuel, cargo and passengers – a light load can be carried a long way with maximum fuel whereas a heavy load means that less fuel can be carried thus reducing the range.) RAF Sea Kings have a comprehensive navigation fit which includes VOR/ILS, DME, ADF, DECCA and Radar. A flight control system (similar to a fixed-wing aircraft's autopilot) can automatically transition the aircraft to and from the hover, allowing a 24-hour capability for SAR operations in conditions where a normal visual hover may not be possible. The crew normally consists of two pilots, a radar operator and winchman. The radar operator controls the winch when at the scene of a rescue and, at the same time, gives guidance to the pilots to enable them to position the aircraft as required for the situation. When needed, the crew can be supplemented by extra lookouts or a doctor. No. 202 Squadron has five flights located at Lossiemouth (North Scotland), Boulmer (Northumberland), Leconfield (Humberside), Manston (Kent) and Brawdy (South Wales).

Other areas of the country are covered by Royal Navy helicopters and commercial helicopters chartered by the Department of Trade and Industry. Overseas the RAF provides SAR-capable helicopters in Hong Kong (Wessex of No. 28 Squadron), Cyprus (Wessex of No. 84 Squadron) and the Falkland Islands (Sea Kings of No. 78 Squadron) where SAR is combined with other troop-support roles.

In the 40 or so years since the RAF has used helicopters for SAR many thousands of people in distress have been helped. Many call-outs may be to people who are only slightly injured, many others are to major disasters such as the Piper Alpha oil platform explosion. In 1991, the RCCs called out helicopters to 1,806 incidents and some 1,382 people were helped, the Sea Kings at RAF Lossiemouth being the busiest with 222 call-outs. At each flight there is always an aircraft and crew on standby ready to be airborne within 15 minutes (at night the reaction time is up to one hour). Fortunately, these days, there are few calls to assist military aircrew – the original reason for setting up the organisation.

SELECTED BIBLIOGRAPHY

Ashworth, Chris, *Encyclopaedia of Modern Royal Air Force Squadrons*
    (Patrick Stephens Ltd)
Congdon, Philip, *Per Ardua ad Astra* (Airlife)
Department of Public Relations (RAF), *Royal Air Force Briefing Book* (MOD)
Halley, James J., *The Squadrons of the Royal Air Force* (Air Britain)
Jackson, Paul, *Royal Air Force* (Ian Allen)
Moyes, Philip, *Bomber Squadrons of the RAF and their Aircraft*
    (Macdonald and Jane's)
Rawlings, John, *Fighter Squadrons of the RAF and their Aircraft*
    (Macdonald and Jane's)
Rawlings, John, *Coastal, Support and Special Squadrons of the RAF
    and their Aircraft* (Jane's)

RAF
ORDER OF BATTLE
1 April 1993

STRIKE COMMAND
HQ RAF High Wycombe, Bucks

NO. 1 GROUP
HQ RAF Upavon

1 Squadron	Harrier GR7	RAF Wittering, Cambs
20 (Res) Squadron	Harrier GR7, T4A	RAF Wittering, Cambs
6 Squadron	Jaguar GR1A	RAF Coltishall, Norfolk
41 Squadron	Jaguar GR1A	RAF Coltishall, Norfolk
54 Squadron	Jaguar GR1A	RAF Coltishall, Norfolk
16 (Res) Squadron	Jaguar GR1A, T2A	RAF Lossiemouth, Moray
2 Squadron	Tornado GR1A	RAF Marham, Norfolk
13 Squadron	Tornado GR1A	RAF Honington, Suffolk
27 Squadron	Tornado GR1	RAF Marham, Norfolk
617 Squadron	Tornado GR1	RAF Marham, Norfolk
15 (Res) Squadron	Tornado GR1	RAF Honington, Suffolk
TTTE	Tornado GR1	RAF Cottesmore, Leics.
33 Squadron	Puma HC1	RAF Odiham, Hants
230 Squadron	Puma HC1	RAF Aldergrove, Ulster
7 Squadron	Chinook HC1	RAF Odiham, Hants
240 OCU	Chinook HC1/Puma HC1	RAF Odiham, Hants
60 Squadron	Wessex HC2	RAF Benson, Oxon
72 Squadron	Wessex HC2	RAF Aldergrove, Ulster
2 Squadron RAF Regt	Field Squadron (Para)	RAF Catterick, North Yorks HONINTON
2620 Squadron RAF Regt	RAuxAF Field Squadron	RAF Marham, Norfolk
2623 Squadron RAF Regt	RAuxAF Field Squadron	RAF Honington, Suffolk

NO. 2 GROUP
HQ RAF Rheindahlen, Germany

3 Squadron	Harrier GR7	RAF Laarbruch, Germany
4 Squadron	Harrier GR7	RAF Laarbruch, Germany
9 Squadron	Tornado GR1	RAF Brüggen, Germany
14 Squadron	Tornado GR1	RAF Brüggen, Germany
17 Squadron	Tornado GR1	RAF Brüggen, Germany
31 Squadron	Tornado GR1	RAF Brüggen, Germany
18 Squadron	Chinook HC1/Puma HC1	RAF Laarbruch, Germany
1 Squadron RAF Regt	Field Squadron	RAF Laarbruch, Germany
26 Squadron RAF Regt	Rapier Squadron	RAF Laarbruch, Germany
37 Squadron RAF Regt	Rapier Squadron	RAF Brüggen, Germany

NO. 11 GROUP
HQ RAF Bentley Priory

8 Squadron	Sentry AEW1	RAF Waddington, Lincs
5 Squadron	Tornado F3	RAF Coningsby, Lincs
11 Squadron	Tornado F3	RAF Leeming, North Yorks
23 Squadron	Tornado F3	RAF Leeming, North Yorks
25 Squadron	Tornado F3	RAF Leeming, North Yorks

29 Squadron	Tornado F3	RAF Coningsby, Lincs
43 Squadron	Tornado F3	RAF Leuchars, Fife
56 (Res) Squadron	Tornado F3	RAF Coningsby, Lincs
111 Squadron	Tornado F3	RAF Leuchars, Fife
15 Squadron RAF Regt	Rapier Squadron	RAF Leeming, North Yorks
16(R) Squadron RAF Regt	Rapier Training Unit	RAF West Raynham, Norfolk
27 Squadron RAF Regt	Rapier Squadron	RAF ~~Leuchars, Fife~~ HONINGTON · 7·2·95
48 Squadron RAF Regt	Rapier Squadron	RAF Lossiemouth, Moray
2503 Squadron RAF Regt	RAuxAF Field Squadron	RAF Waddington, Lincs
2729 Squadron RAF Regt	RAuxAF Oerlikon Gun Sqn	RAF Waddington, Lincs
2890 Squadron RAF Regt	RAuxAF Oerlikon Gun Sqn	RAF Waddington, Lincs

NO. 18 GROUP
HQ RAF Northwood

12 Squadron	Buccaneer S2B	RAF Lossiemouth, Moray
208 Squadron	Buccaneer S2B	RAF Lossiemouth, Moray
22 Squadron HQ	Wessex HC2	RAF St Mawgan, Cornwall
'A' Flight		RAF Chivenor, Devon
'B' Flight		RAF Leuchars, Fife
'C' Flight		RAF Valley, Gwynedd
'E' Flight		RAF Coltishall, Norfolk
SARTU	Wessex HC2	RAF Valley, Gwynedd
51 Squadron	Nimrod R1P	RAF Wyton, Cambs
360 Squadron	Canberra T17	RAF Wyton, Cambs
39 (1 PRU) Squadron	Canberra PR7/PR9/T4	RAF Wyton, Cambs
100 Squadron	Hawk T1A	RAF Wyton, Cambs
EWAU	Andover	RAF Wyton, Cambs
42 (Res) Squadron	Nimrod MR2P	RAF Kinloss, Moray
120 Squadron	Nimrod MR2P	RAF Kinloss, Moray
201 Squadron	Nimrod MR2P	RAF Kinloss, Moray
206 Squadron	Nimrod MR2P	RAF Kinloss, Moray
202 Squadron HQ	Sea King HAR3	RAF Boulmer, Northumberland
'A' Flight		RAF Boulmer, Northumberland
'B' Flight		RAF Brawdy, Dyfed
'C' Flight		RAF Manston, Kent
'D' Flight		RAF Lossiemouth, Moray
'E' Flight		RAF Leconfield, S Yorks
SKTU	Sea King HAR3	RNAS Culdrose, Cornwall
2622 Squadron RAF Regt	RAuxAF Field Squadron	RAF Lossiemouth, Moray
2625 Squadron RAF Regt	RAuxAF Field Squadron	RAF St Mawgan, Cornwall

NO. 38 GROUP
HQ RAF High Wycombe

10 Squadron	VC10 C1/C1K	RAF Brize Norton, Oxon
101 Squadron	VC10 K2/K3	RAF Brize Norton, Oxon
216 Squadron	Tristar K1/KC1/C2	RAF Brize Norton, Oxon
241 OCU	VC10	RAF Brize Norton, Oxon
24 Squadron	Hercules C1P/C3P	RAF Lyneham, Wilts
30 Squadron	Hercules C1P/C3P	RAF Lyneham, Wilts
47 Squadron	Hercules C1P/C3P	RAF Lyneham, Wilts
57 (Res) Squadron	Hercules C1P/C3P	RAF Lyneham, Wilts
70 Squadron	Hercules C1P/C3P	RAF Lyneham, Wilts
55 Squadron	Victor K2	RAF Marham, Norfolk
32 Squadron	BAe 125, Gazelle, Andover	RAF Northolt, Middlesex
115 Squadron	Andover E3	RAF Benson, Oxon
The Queen's Flight	BAe 146 CC2, Wessex HCC4	RAF Benson, Oxon
2624 Squadron RAF Regt	RAuxAF Field Squadron	RAF Brize Norton, Oxon

RAF CYPRUS

84 Squadron	Wessex HC5C	RAF Akrotiri, Cyprus
34 Squadron RAF Regt	Field Squadron	RAF Akrotiri, Cyprus

RAF HONG KONG

28 Squadron	Wessex HC2	RAF Sek Kong

RAF BELIZE

1417 Flight	Harrier GR3	Belize International Airport
1563 Flight	Puma HC1	Belize International Airport

RAF FALKLAND ISLANDS

78 Squadron	Chinook HC1, Sea King HAR3	RAF Mount Pleasant
1312 Flight	Hercules C1K	RAF Mount Pleasant
1435 Flight	Tornado F3	RAF Mount Pleasant

OTHER UNITS

Tornado F3 Operational Evaluation Unit	Tornado F3	RAF Coningsby, Lincs
Strike/Attack Operational Evaluation Unit	Tornado GR1, Harrier GR7, Jaguar T2A	Boscombe Down, Wilts
Battle of Britain Memorial Flight	Hurricane IIC, Spitfire IIA/VB/XIX, Lancaster BI	RAF Coningsby, Lincs
Institute of Aviation Medicine	Hunter T7, Jaguar T2	Farnborough, Hants
3 Squadron RAF Regt	Field Squadron	RAF Aldergrove, Ulster

SUPPORT COMMAND
HQ RAF Brampton, Cambs

Central Flying School	Bulldog T1, Tucano T1, Hawk T1, Jet Provost T5A	RAF Scampton, Lincs
No. 1 Flying Training School	Bulldog, Tucano, Jet Provost	RAF Linton-on-Ouse, Yorks
No. 2 Flying Training School	Gazelle HT3, Wessex HC2	RAF Shawbury, Salop
No. 3 Flying Training School	Tucano T1	RAF Cranwell, Lincs
No. 4 Flying Training School 74 (Res) Squadron 234 (Res) Squadron	Hawk T1/T1A	RAF Valley, Gwynedd
No. 6 Flying Training School School of Navigation 45 (Res) Squadron	Bulldog, Tucano, Hawk Dominie, Jet Provost Jetstream T1	RAF Finningley, Yorks
No. 7 Flying Training School 19 (Res) Squadron 92 (Res) Squadron	Hawk T1/T1A	RAF Chivenor, Devon

DISPLAY TEAM

The Red Arrows	Hawk T1A	RAF Scampton, Lincs
63(QCS) Squadron RAF Regt	Ceremonial Unit	RAF Uxbridge, Middlesex

UNIVERSITY AIR SQUADRONS

UNIVERSITY AIR SQUADRONS	Bulldog T1	HQ RAF Cranwell, Lincs
Aberdeen, Dundee & St Andrews Universities Air Squadron		RAF Leuchars, Fife
University of Birmingham Air Squadron		RAF Cosford, Salop
Bristol University Air Squadron		Colerne, Wilts
Cambridge University Air Squadron		Teversham, Cambridge

East Lowlands Universities Air Squadron   RAF Turnhouse, Lothian
East Midlands Universities Air Squadron   RAF Newton, Notts
Universities of Glasgow & Strathclyde Air Squadron   Glasgow A/p, Strathclyde
Liverpool University Air Squadron   RAF Woodvale, Merseyside
University of London Air Squadron   RAF Benson, Oxon
Manchester & Salford Universities Air Squadron   RAF Woodvale, Merseyside
Northumbrian Universities Air Squadron   RAF Leeming, N Yorks
Oxford University Air Squadron   RAF Benson, Oxon
Queens University Air Squadron   Belfast, Ulster
Southampton University Air Squadron   RNAS Lee-on-Solent, Hants
University of Wales Air Squadron   RAF St Athan, S Glam
Yorkshire Universities Air Squadron   RAF Finningley, Yorks

AIR EXPERIENCE FLIGHTS

		HQ RAF Newton
No. 1 AEF	Chipmunk T10	RAF Manston, Kent
No. 2 AEF	Chipmunk T10	Hurn, Bournemouth, Dorset
No. 3 AEF	Chipmunk T10	Colerne, Wilts
No. 4 AEF	Chipmunk T10	Exeter Airport, Devon
No. 5 AEF	Chipmunk T10	Teversham, Cambridge
No. 6 AEF	Chipmunk T10	RAF Benson, Oxon
No. 7 AEF	Chipmunk T10	RAF Newton, Notts
No. 8 AEF	Chipmunk T10	RAF Shawbury, Salop
No. 9 AEF	Chipmunk T10	RAF Finningley, Yorks
No. 10 AEF	Chipmunk T10	RAF Woodvale, Merseyside
No. 11 AEF	Chipmunk T10	RAF Leeming, N Yorks
No. 12 AEF	Chipmunk T10	RAF Turnhouse, Lothian
No. 13 AEF	Bulldog T1	Belfast, Ulster

CENTRAL GLIDING SCHOOL Viking T1, Vigilant T1, Valiant T1, RAF Syerston, Notts
           Janus C

VOLUNTEER GLIDING SCHOOLS

No. 611 VGS	Viking T1	Swanton Morley, Norfolk
No. 612 VGS	Vigilant T1	RAF Halton, Bucks
No. 613 VGS	Vigilant T1	RAF Halton, Bucks
No. 614 VGS	Viking T1	Wethersfield, Essex
No. 615 VGS	Viking T1	Kenley, Kent
No. 616 VGS	Vigilant T1	Henlow, Beds
No. 617 VGS	Viking T1	RAF Manston, Kent
No. 618 VGS	Viking T1	West Malling, Kent
No. 621 VGS	Viking T1	RAF Kemble, Glos
No. 622 VGS	Viking T1	RAF Upavon, Wilts
No. 624 VGS	Vigilant T1	RAF Chivenor, Devon
No. 625 VGS	Viking T1	RAF Kemble, Glos
No. 626 VGS	Viking T1	Predannack, Cornwall
No. 631 VGS	Viking T1	RAF Sealand, Clwyd
No. 632 VGS	Vigilant T1	RAF Ternhill, Salop
No. 633 VGS	Vigilant T1	RAF Cosford, Salop
No. 634 VGS	Viking T1	RAF St Athan, S Glam
No. 635 VGS	Vigilant T1	Samlesbury, Lancs
No. 636 VGS	Viking T1	Swansea, W Glam
No. 637 VGS	Vigilant T1	Little Rissington, Glos
No. 642 VGS	Vigilant T1	RAF Linton-on-Ouse, Yorks
No. 643 VGS	Vigilant T1	RAF Syerston, Notts
No. 644 VGS	Vigilant T1	RAF Syerston, Notts

No. 645 VGS	Viking T1	RAF Catterick, N Yorks
No. 661 VGS	Viking T1	RAF Kirknewton, Lothian
No. 662 VGS	Viking T1	RM Condor, Arbroath, Tays
No. 663 VGS	Vigilant T1	RAF Kinloss, Moray

SCHOOLS OF TECHNICAL TRAINING
RAF HOSPITALS
MAINTENANCE UNITS
COMMAND AND STAFF TRAINING

Extended caption for In the Beginning, *the Montrose painting on page 14 by Ian G. McIntosh of the Montrose Aerodrome Museum Trust*

Prototypes of the BE 2 were designed, built and tested at the Royal Aircraft Factory at Farnborough. Once the design was proved to be successful, series production of the BE 2 was contracted out to private manufacturers. One of these was the British and Colonial Aeroplane Company Limited, whose works at Filton, Bristol, produced machines which soon became renowned for their excellent quality and workmanship.

One of these Bristol-built machines, No. 218, was flown from Farnborough to Montrose, in stages, by Lieutenant C.A.H. Longcroft, arriving at Upper Dysart field on 26 February 1913. Here it formed part of the initial equipment of No. 2 Squadron, Royal Flying Corps, along with its companions on the journey north, these being BE 2 No. 217, also Bristol-built, and three Maurice Farman S 7s. It was noted that No. 218 had behaved 'impeccably' during its long journey, thus it became the usual 'mount' of Captain Longcroft, as he now was generally recognised to be No. 2's 'star' pilot.

As the Squadron 'worked up', reliability of airframes and engines increased to the extent that it was felt some mark of significance should be attempted as an indication of how far military aviation had progressed at this northern outpost. To this end, First Class Air Mechanic, No. 116 H.C.S. Bullock, designed, built and then fitted into No. 218 a long-range petrol tank capable of holding 54 imperial gallons (246 litres) of fuel, enough for eight hours' flying. To allow this tank to be placed inside the fuselage, the front passenger seat was removed and the opening faired over, so that the machine could be flown as a single-seater by Captain Longcroft.

By now the well-travelled staging route between Farnborough and Montrose had a number of weather reporting points, in touch by telephone, so that it was possible to receive current information regarding flying conditions *en route* as a simple form of flight planning. The weather reports being favourable, at 0855 hrs on 22 November 1913, No. 218 took off from Montrose, heavy with fuel, bound for Farnborough, on the first non-stop flight between these two points. After an uneventful trip, Farnborough was reached with so much fuel to spare that Captain Longcroft made for Portsmouth, where he circled the navy base before making for his goal, landing at 1610 hrs still with petrol in the tank.

This flight was judged to be the most outstanding in Britain that year so Captain Longcroft became the first recipient of the handsome Britannia Trophy, newly put up for such events by aviation enthusiast, Horatio Barber. The Trophy is currently on display within the premises of the Royal Aero Club in London – although No. 218 was wrecked on 2 May 1914 during service with No. 6 Squadron, RFC.

No. 205 was the reconstruction of a Howard Wright biplane to BE 2 configuration, following the practice of the Royal Aircraft Factory in its early years, and as such was one of the small batch of prototypes of this design produced there. First flown in June 1912, No. 205 was progressively re-engined and modified to keep it at the forefront of the then state of the art. Once up to operational standard, the machine was flown north, in stages, from Farnborough to Montrose by the Commanding Officer of No. 2 Squadron, Major C.J. Burke, Royal Irish Regiment. Arriving in mid-May, the machine was taken on charge by No. 2 Squadron to increase its establishment of BE 2 aircraft.

A few weeks after its arrival, on 27 May 1913, No. 205 took off from Upper Dysart on a morning's flying exercise, piloted by Lieutenant Desmond Arthur, a newcomer to the Squadron, with no passenger. At an estimated 2,500 ft (762 metres), watchers saw the machine pitch over, as the right wing collapsed, at which Lieutenant Arthur was thrown out, his seat-belt having failed. Both pilot and plane fell to the ground east of Lunan Bay railway station, and it was commonly held that if Lieutenant Arthur had not fallen out, he would have probably survived the incident as the aeroplane had not been badly wrecked in the crash.

Examination of the machine revealed previously unsuspected damage to the top right wing tip, which had been crudely repaired, although the fabric covering had been carefully replaced to hide this. It was this repair which had failed in flight, so starting off the collapse of the starboard wings which led to the death of the unfortunate pilot. Despite intense investigation, it was found impossible to attribute the fatal repair to anyone or any place. The outcome was a system of inspection and recording of repairs so that the work done on any aeroplane was noted in writing and reference could be made in the event of any future incidents.

The death of Lieutenant Arthur later gave rise to the legend of the 'Montrose Ghost' which, reputedly, still haunts the Air Station, whilst his grave can be seen in Sleepyhillock Cemetery to the north-west of the town.

No. 2 Squadron, Royal Flying Corps, transferred from Farnborough to Montrose on 26 February 1913 to liaise with the fleet at Rosyth and Cromarty and develop the concept of operational military aviation. Less than a year later it moved to the Old Military Camping Ground at Broomfield, north of Montrose, as Upper Dysart proved to be unsuitable. Montrose had become the UK's first truly operational military airfield.

Battle of Britain Squadrons.
63 LAA SQD.

SEE PAGE 121.

SEE PAGE 121.

■ *Final flight . . . A pilot walks away from a Chipmunk after a training session. The aircraft is now due to be sold off by the Ministry of Defence.*

P&J 28-3-97

Chipmunk trainer flies off into the sunset

THE Chipmunk training aircraft, in which the Prince of Wales and the Duke of Edinburgh learned how to fly, was finally retired after 50 years at a graduation ceremony for trainee pilots yesterday.

The de Havilland-built plane — a favourite of Army and RAF pilots — first flew in Canada in 1946.

It replaced the Tiger Moth as the training aircraft for young pilots.

But yesterday's ceremony at Middle Wallop, Hampshire, was the final farewell for the much-loved aircraft.

A Ministry of Defence spokesman said: "They will be sadly missed. People have built up a lot of respect for them."

Pilots always found the Chipmunk "very gentle and friendly to use".

Last year the RAF decided to replace the two-seater with the Bulldog, which is newer and cheaper to maintain.

The Army has now decided to follow suit and 17 Chipmunks will be auctioned along with the only remaining flying Comet 4C, by Phillips of New Bond Street.

A spokeswoman for the auctioneers said the Chipmunks, which have a top speed of 125mph, "will probably cost between £10,000 and £15,000".